Satisfaction

10 ALBUMS
THAT CHANGED
MY LIFE

MARTIN POPOFF

Foreword By

NANCY WILSON
OF HEART

ROCK'S BIGGEST STARS REVEAL THEIR TOP INFLUENCES

Published by

Krause Publications, a division of Penguin Random House LLC
www.penguinrandomhouse.com

ISBN-13: 9781440249082
ISBN-10: 1440249083

Designed by Rebecca Vogel
Edited by Paul Kennedy

Printed in the United States of America
10 9 8 7 6 5 4 3 2 1

Some of the content included in this book previously appeared in *Goldmine* magazine.

CONTENTS

FOREWORD BY
NANCY WILSON

From The Beatles to Bob Dylan, Nancy Wilson's music influences led to her stardom with Heart and induction into the Rock and Roll Hall of Fame.

PHOTO BY KEVIN MAZUR/GETTY IMAGES

Our family moved to Seattle the year of the Seattle World's Fair during the time the Space Needle was still under construction.

Everything was just so wonderfully "Space Agey" in the early '60s. It was all about the fabulous and futuristic machines and gadgets coming to modernize us and to change our lives for the better forever. Exciting stuff!

Flying cars, automatic no-cook/no-clean kitchens and friendly push button robots, who could auto-immaculate your house with absolutely no fuss, no muss and no mood swings!

There were programmable ovens that could dispense a gourmet family dinner by just selecting a meal and miraculously, it would arrive in mere moments.

And then there were other mysterious contraptions. By simply talking into a microphone on the beverage dispenser you could instantly enjoy your favorite icy cold or hot beverage in the blink of an electric eye.

Just add water and stir the freeze-dried Tang powder and enjoy the odd orange taste. We had all seen our hero astronauts drinking Tang in space, images of which were beamed down into the new color TV!

The World's Fair in Seattle was all about Futurama. We were little kids watching the Jetsons while living in the Boeing Jet City way before Microsoft.

Pre-Seattle, my family was stationed in the California desert at Camp Pendleton Marine Corp base for many years. Those days predated any kind of standardized air conditioning and there were heat waves that would shut down the schools for days: The opposite of Snow Days.

So, when we were to be stationed in Seattle for a year, we piled in and drove the station wagon north, climbing out of the punishing heat of the desert, with a cooler filled with ice, Cokes and washcloths to fight off the sweltering sun.

SEATTLE WORLD'S FAIR PREVIEW
APRIL 21 • OCTOBER 21 • 1962

As we got farther and farther north there were majestic cathedrals of fir trees and pines and then the snow-crowned godly mountains appeared beyond.

Then, whoosh, the rains and sparkling lush greens of The Great Pacific Northwest ... such a revelation! It felt like the soul quenching blue green cool baptism of forgiveness.

I wrote "The Rain Song" as a love letter to the rain when I was 12.

My sister Ann and I were already fledgling songwriters in a number of baby bands we'd started with friends, mainly girls from school. We played with school friends and family around beach fires, fireplaces and all kinds of rooms – especially echoing bathrooms and stairwells that made us sound cooler. We sang in backyards, churches, schools, parks, inside cars and on top of cars, in the flatbeds of pickup trucks and once even at a drive-in theater before the movie!

Our set list then was a lot of Simon and Garfunkel songs (harmonies!), some Dylan and a wide variety of genres plus Top 40 radio pop. And we loved the many novelty hits we learned off the radio: "Ahab the Arab," "They're Coming To Take Me Away" and "Tie Me Kangaroo Down, Sport."

We also learned more songs, the deep cuts, from our increasing collection of vinyl albums. You could switch the turntable to half speed for easier slower absorption in the same key.

We were Beatles fanatics although playing the Beatles' songs seemed almost sacrilegious to us because changing the gender around for any song lyrics (her to him or she to he) was simply WRONG.

And I Love Him? Never.

We only played Beatles songs privately at home, never at a gig.

So we played any kind of gigs we could get and doggedly aimed our sights on becoming singer-songwriters. We were unstoppable Marine Corp brats complete with swagger and we were never going to take no for an answer. I guess that sort of worked out.

Seattle. What a great town. Seattle has always been a deeply rooted music town like so many great seaport towns. Ray Charles, The Wailers, The Sonics, Hendrix, Paul Revere and the Raiders, Marilee and the Turnabouts were some of the many other Pacific Northwest hit makers.

Another huge wave of hit makers washed ashore when Nirvana, Pearl Jam, Alice In Chains and Soundgarden – among other great local bands – forged a whole new formidable rock force like no other.

There was this other unusual band from Seattle fronted and led by two sisters. And I'm lucky enough to be one of them.

The rainy weather of the northwest winter encourages you to go inward, to light the fireplace and stare introspectively into the flames. To read the tea leaves of the embers. To write a confessional song. To put on headphones and take a magical ride through your favorite albums...

FLIRT WITH THE MUSE.

Nancy Wilson

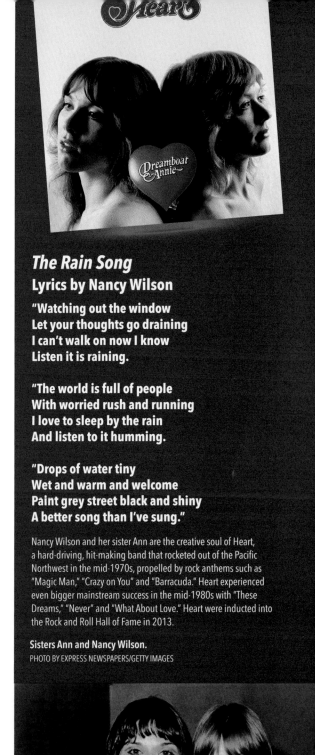

The Rain Song
Lyrics by Nancy Wilson

"Watching out the window
Let your thoughts go draining
I can't walk on now I know
Listen it is raining.

"The world is full of people
With worried rush and running
I love to sleep by the rain
And listen to it humming.

"Drops of water tiny
Wet and warm and welcome
Paint grey street black and shiny
A better song than I've sung."

Nancy Wilson and her sister Ann are the creative soul of Heart, a hard-driving, hit-making band that rocketed out of the Pacific Northwest in the mid-1970s, propelled by rock anthems such as "Magic Man," "Crazy on You" and "Barracuda." Heart experienced even bigger mainstream success in the mid-1980s with "These Dreams," "Never" and "What About Love." Heart were inducted into the Rock and Roll Hall of Fame in 2013.

Sisters Ann and Nancy Wilson.
PHOTO BY EXPRESS NEWSPAPERS/GETTY IMAGES

INTRODUCTION

THIS IS A BOOK BASED ON A SIMPLE QUESTION:
WHAT MUSIC INFLUENCED SOME OF THE BIGGEST STARS OF CLASSIC ROCK?

The answers to that question, we discovered, are far more complex and revealing than a list of albums. That makes sense. Music is, after all, nothing if not personal. What we hear and when we hear it matters. That's as true for you and me as it is for Stewart Copeland of the Police or Ian Anderson of Jethro Tull, and so many other artists who are featured here. Music doesn't happen in a vacuum. It enters life when we are full of wonder and full of hormones. It touches us in some primal way that is often difficult to explain. And yet, these artists – 18 of whom are in the Rock and Roll Hall of Fame – pull back the curtain, drop the façade, and share what music shaped them along their musical journey – and why.

This has been a most pleasurable book to write and compile: Some of these stories first appeared in *Goldmine* magazine, where the idea originated. In the process of reading these stories and seeing how these folks skip and jump their way through a list of ten records, barely containing themselves in many cases, I realized how profound and essential music is to us all.

Through the process of picking two fistfuls of albums, poignant trips down memory lane are shared: stories of first records heard, and first records made; tales of being on the spot when history happens; stories of the records their mothers played, and of a home filled with music; accounts of audio lightning bolts exploding, inspiring a kid to pick up drumsticks for the first time … It all comes pouring out.

Invariably, these stories had me scurrying over to my record racks, the CD racks, and Spotify or YouTube for listens that were languid or indeed pointed, looking for the comparison explained or the nick of a riff admitted to or other clear forms of imitation and instruction from one generation to the next. I hope reading these responses has the same effect on you. Because indeed, in the aggregate, this book adds up to a pretty swell history of classic rock 'n' roll from a pretty wide range of years, but with one thing in common – these records have been around long enough to have stood the test of time.

This is a big, bold celebration of classic rock, which is called that for a reason. Broadly speaking then (but only broadly), what falls out of the exercise as somewhat of a trend is the idea of artists from the '70s and '80s teaching us about artists and albums from the '60s and '70s, and also, in some instances, from the '50s or older – thank you, Art Garfunkel! You will also see more than a few references to classical music. Influences, it seems, come from many places and many genres. You'll also notice a few artists were brief, providing only three influential albums. No matter, when artists talk about the records that inspired them to do what they do they often examine their formative years.

Anybody who jumps at a chance to do a list like this loves music. The only thing that they might love more than the songs themselves is telling other people about them. I'm sure you'll agree. It's easy to get swept up and sold by the enthusiasm on display here. No matter what your age and experience consuming music, you will be checking these records out to find out what the fuss is all about.

All told, I hope you learn as much reading these stories as I did and are filled with the same rich sense of nostalgia. I have discovered quite a few new records to enjoy deeply, ones I otherwise had not paid enough attention to or treated with the amount of respect that they deserved. That is the ultimate benefit I've gained from this exercise and I hope that by journey's end, you get to that place as well.

MARTIN POPOFF

ART ALEXAKIS
EVERCLEAR

Everclear in 1997: Drummer Greg Eklund, Art Alexakis and bass guitarist Craig Montoya. PHOTO BY KEVIN WINTER/GETTY IMAGES

Everclear was formed in 1991 by lead songwriter, vocalist and guitarist Art Alexakis in Portland, Oregon, during the height of the grunge movement. Everclear never became as big of a household name as Nirvana or Alice in Chains, but the band did outlast those grunge icons (for obvious reasons), and have evolved through shifting musical trends (and band lineups). Everclear is best known for their 1997 release *So Much for the Afterglow*. The album went double platinum on the strength of "Everything to Everyone," "I Will Buy You a New Life" and "Father of Mine." As a result, Everclear was hailed as "Modern Rock Artist of the Year" by *Billboard* in 1998. Alexakis announced in 2019 that he had been diagnosed several years ago with multiple sclerosis. The condition has not slowed Alexakis who continues to tour as a solo act as well as with Everclear.

PHOTO BY KEVIN WINTER/GETTY IMAGES

The Beatles, *The Beatles*

I love how raw and vulnerable The Beatles sound on the white album, even now, in hindsight, as an adult. I know they were in the middle of falling apart, yet the dysfunction brought out the uniqueness of all four people (who sometimes refused to be in the same room together) and created a different kind of chemistry together. That resulted in a flawed but incredibly beautiful and powerful masterpiece.

Public Enemy, *It Takes a Nation of Millions to Hold Us Back*

This album change the way I (and many other people) think of music and what it can and could be. Using noise, rhythm, funk, intelligent yet angry militant lyrics, I feel this record raised the bar for not just hip-hop, but all cutting-edge popular music. It became my new punk rock. Chuck D's voice and the Bomb Squads' beats and production created a whole new vision, taking the emphasis away from old school, sucker MC-type East Coast rap tunes, creating songs that combined lyrical ideas and musical hooks that both ignited emotions and inspired action. I would walk to my office job every morning in a suit, with my little ponytail and wire-rimmed glasses, with my headphones blaring, shouting the words at the top of my voice, freaking out all the nice business people in downtown San Francisco.

Pixies, *Doolittle*

I was working in San Francisco at the time when this came out (spring of 1989). I remember buying it on cassette on my lunch break and popping it into my Sony Walkman. I was instantly hooked. In fact, I called out of work the rest of the day and just sat on the city bus listening to the record over and over and over. I was so inspired that I went home that night and told my first wife (who didn't want me to play music anymore) that I was starting a band. I guess it's pretty obvious how that turned out.

Neil Young, *Harvest*

I grew up listening to Neil Young on my brother's and sister's albums, so early on I saw that what one person was capable of, not just writing and singing and playing your own songs, but having the vision to define your own unique sound. This record undoubtedly helped shape me, not just as a singer/songwriter, but as a musician and producer. This album helped show me the type of artist I wanted to be.

Bruce Springsteen, *Nebraska*

I originally became a Bruce Springsteen fan from his 1980 **The River** album, but I really connected with **Nebraska** two years later. It was a darker record. The stories in the songs (all stark acoustic guitars and raw vocals, recorded on four-track cassette!) tell stories of an America that goes from grainy black and white to technicolor, sometimes in the same song. This was one of the records that I learned when I was teaching myself how to play and sing at the same time, and it helped inspire me to write my own songs… my way.

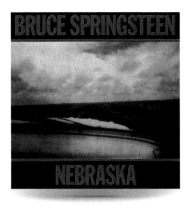

X, *Los Angeles*

This 1980 debut album is a classic American punk rock album. It helped to define the West Coast punk scene, and it resonated with me, because along with the buzz saw sound of the guitars and drums, it has elements of pop, country and blues, tied together with the dissonant vocals and poetic songs of John Doe and Exene Cervenka, who I idolized at the time. I remember buying this record at the Tower Records on Sunset Boulevard and almost getting into a fistfight with some knucklehead with a Mohawk because he was pissed-off that a kid with long hair was buying it!

X, *Wild Gift*

Just one year after **Los Angeles**, this record took X to a whole new level. It was rawer, grittier and opened their sound up to even more elements of Americana. This record was on every rock critic's Top 10 Albums of the Year lists. I played it so much that I'm pretty sure that it was one of the reasons my heavy metal girlfriend broke up with me!

Aerosmith, *Rocks*

I saw Aerosmith open for Mott the Hoople when I was 13, and sold all my pot to my friend so I could buy **Toys in the Attic**, their third record, the next day. And it started an obsession with this band that I will have for the rest of my life. Everything they did up to 1976 was great, but when **Rocks** came out, it rewrote the book on how a rock 'n' roll record is supposed to sound. From the songs (not a weak one in the bunch!) to the Jack Douglas production, it never lets up! One of my favorite albums to crank up backstage before we play.

Joni Mitchell, *Blue*

My sister used to play this record constantly and even though I liked it, it didn't really connect or resonate with me until my first heartbreak. This is one of the records that helped me get through my 20s. I love listening to this album in the dark, appreciating both the complex emotions and the simplicity of the songs. I will always feel deeply connected to this record. It is a must-have that I always have in my collection. Throughout the years, I have probably bought this album at least five times.

Led Zeppelin, *Physical Graffiti*

Physical Graffiti is a huge, twisted, crumbling thing of wonder comprised of mostly unreleased tracks and outtakes from three previous albums. It opened my eyes to the possibilities of how an album could be made to create a vibe. The album is huge with big sounds and ideas that go to so many places. I was inspired to produce my own records because of the brilliance and vision of Jimmy Page.

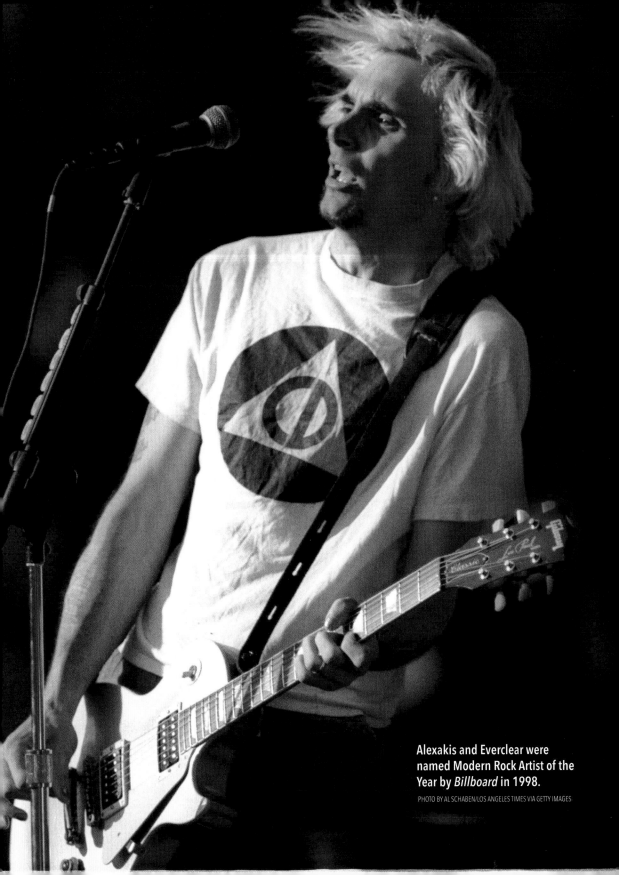

Alexakis and Everclear were named Modern Rock Artist of the Year by *Billboard* in 1998.

CARLOS ALOMAR
DAVID BOWIE

Carlos Alomar (far right), David Bowie (center) and Carmine Rojasto perform in 1983. PHOTO BY PAUL NATKIN/GETTY IMAGES

After 32 International gold and platinum records, Carlos Alomar's place in music history is secure. The legendary guitarist burst upon the rock scene with David Bowie in the mid-1970s, when he, Bowie, and John Lennon co-wrote the hit song "Fame." Over the course of the next 30 years, Alomar would record and tour the world as Bowie's music director. Alomar grew up mostly in the Bronx and Upper Manhattan, hearing R&B and religious music in his father's church. He began playing guitar in church at 10, but was soon sneaking out to play in rock bands with his friends. At 17, he became the youngest guitarist in the history of the Apollo Theater. His ability to play R&B, Philly soul, hard rock and ambient music meant that he was always in demand – and able to keep up with Bowie's quicksilver changes of musical persona. He also co-wrote Mick Jagger's first solo effort, "She's The Boss," Iggy Pop's comeback hit "Sister Midnight," and played guitar for a Who's Who of pop/rock royalty, including Paul McCartney, John Lennon, Simple Minds, Yoko Ono, Bruce Springsteen, Alicia Keys, Graham Parker and Duran Duran.

Carlos Alomar in New York in 2013
MIKE COPPOLA/WIREIMAGE FOR NARAS

The Beatles, *Revolver*

It's very difficult to speak about the Beatles because to me they were "it," for ten years from the '60s to maybe the '70s. So basically all of the Beatles albums rank as one influence, but **Revolver** was by far the one that made me leave that nice, nice area they were in, going into the more psychedelic, with Harrison stepping out more as a guitarist and writing. That album for me was a landmark.

The Jimi Hendrix Experience, *Are You Experienced*

A friend of mine introduced me to this, and as a guitarist I went crazy. First of all, it was coupled with the advent of the stereophonic, hi-fi system. Remember, even with some of the Beatles, we had kind of the pseudo-mono. It hadn't really evolved the way it should have. So Jimi Hendrix came out and he was so influential as a guitarist. During that same '60s period, with not only the Beatles but you had Herman's Hermits, and all these other bands that were playing at that time. But the guitarist wasn't the main force. He was interesting as some component, and every once in a while a guitarist would step out to play a little lead. But the issue of a power trio was unheard of. And when Hendrix stepped in front with a Marshall and a Strat, I couldn't believe it. First of all I had to listen to the record a few times when I first heard it with this friend, and he's saying "What's wrong with you?!" And then I bought the record and that was it–it got scratched up immediately because I had to learn every note. And I did–I learned that whole album!

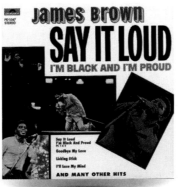

Cold Blood, *Cold Blood*

This is a San Francisco Bay area band I was into in the late '60s. We're going from the psychedelic thing, now into a kind of R&B, rock and blues and jazz thing. They had this amazing horn section and a singer, Lydia Pense, who was like Janis Joplin, rough and hard, singing the blues and singing hardcore. The horn section rivalled Blood Sweat & Tears and Chicago. They were like ridiculously awesome, but were a group fronted by a horn section.

James Brown, *Say It Loud – I'm Black and I'm Proud*

Now that was influential to me in a different way. Obviously because of the funk factor, but for me if was mostly influential on a different esoteric level. They did not teach Latin American history at that time. It was late '60s, I was 18 and the whole issue of pride came up at that point. And so not understanding my own history, I finally find out that the Puerto Rican is actually a combination of the Taino Indian, the African slaves and the Spaniards. So the consciousness of that song, "Say It Loud – I'm Black and I'm Proud" really created a moment in my life where black music was a little bit harder felt for me. That music influenced me as a character, as a personality, as a person.

Santana, *Abraxas*

Now Santana, being a Latino, once again we're going toward that influence. Now, I see for the first time, a Latin guitar player being fronted by any singer he wanted. And from that album you have "Black Magic Woman." Oh my God, that album was crazy; that album was amazing. "Black Magic Woman," "Oye Como Va," "Incident at Neshabur"… all these songs were really heavy duty.

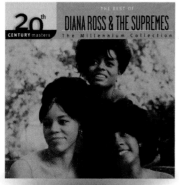

The Supremes, *The Best of Diana Ross and the Supremes*

I used to listen to this with my wife Robin. It had "Baby Love," "Where Did Your Love Go," "Stoned Love" and "Reflections." As you can see, none of the albums I listed are girl trios or girl singers in particular. But there was something about that music. When I was very, very young I heard "Baby Love" through a rolled-down car window. And that influenced me so much. I was a minister's son and so I was only allowed to play church music. So for me to hear R&B music—The Supremes, The Temptations–I was like "Oh my God, what are those chords? Oh my God, what are those progressions? Oh my God, how amazing!" They had a bridge—I never knew what a bridge was. A bridge by definition is a totally different song that you just take and put inside of a song. But the reason is, when you think of a song, usually the highlight of a song is the chorus. Now when you think the song can not get any higher, when you think it can't get any better than it is, you take it to the bridge and that other song kicks in there for about two seconds. Your brain just explodes and then you go into super-overdrive!

Kraftwerk, *Trans-Europe Express*

One of the influences that Bowie introduced me to was Kraftwerk, this German instrumental band, and this album, which was influential in that it introduced me to this, for lack of a better term, new age music. Not psychedelic, but that trance-like melodic theme you get also in disco music, soundscapes. Yes, it is instrumental music, but it isn't instrumental music like for movies. It had a type of beat to it and it had the pounding kick drum and, of course, songs that go on for like eight minutes. Kraftwerk was a major, major influence to me, taking my mindset away from R&B and from rock 'n' roll and kind of couple it with classical music. It allowed me to understand the development of a song. Because usually in pop music and in different cultures we have to get to it right away—verse, chorus, verse, chorus, bridge, out. And yet in classical music, you introduce the scene with anything; there's a prologue to everything.

Sly and the Family Stone, *Dance to the Music*

Sly and the Family Stone were the first interracial band to perform at the Apollo Theater. And this was I guess '68. Myself, my wife and my best friend Luther Vandross were at a small workshop in the basement of the Apollo Theater. We were part of a workshop called Listen My Brother. We rehearsed, rehearsed, and rehearsed and our big thing was that we were going to be the opening act for Sly and the Family Stone, in the Apollo Theater.

When we entered into that world, Sly and the Family Stone changed us very quickly. Remember, we were going from classic R&B rhythm session/band, where you're sitting down. You don't stand up; only the lead singer gets in front of the microphone. Suddenly, Sly and the Family Stone comes to the Apollo Theater and the back line gets Fender amplifiers from the floor over three or four stories high to the top of the curtain. From the stage, all you saw was the gray material of the amplifiers.

They destroyed that theater so bad it was never the same! And they destroyed me as well! When we went backstage and then to the hotel with them, that was it. I had just finished coming from the chitlin circuit of R&B music where the managers would have to get their guns ready while everybody waited by the bus when they had to go in to get their money. The bus would stop somewhere in the woods and there would be this speakeasy or whatever it would be called. So I'm coming now from that into the light of rock 'n' roll. Come on. I was like, "Oh my God, I want to do this." And a few years later when I had the chance to meet Bowie, that was it. I left R&B and never looked back.

The Main Ingredient, *Afrodisiac*

I joined The Main Ingredient and that was the first album that I performed on, and that was because I was a session artist for RCA. So it was the place where I finally got the chance to show the world what I had. In particular, there is a song on that album called "You Call Me Rover" which, if you listen to it, you'll hear little bits of what would later become David Bowie's "Fame." So that one has to be noted because my whole R&B history at that point kind of came to an end. Not to an end, but there was a period where that stopped and I joined Bowie and obviously slipped into the rock 'n' roll epoch of my life.

Iggy Pop, *Lust for Life*

Another influential album for me—although I played on it, I have to acknowledge it. In 1977 I was introduced to Iggy Pop by David Bowie. And the difference in that influence was that it changed my sensibility in my performance, to revisit punk music as a driving force of what made me feel good and what I needed in order to be a guitarist. Pop culture in the '60s and rock 'n' roll culture in the '70s created this nuance that gave me a more sophisticated, not only technique, but my own feeling of comfort. The minute I joined Iggy Pop on his albums, and then later on touring, that whole sensibility took a big change. As there is no back line in punk music, everybody is in the front line with the singer. I wasn't looking at myself as a rhythm guitar player anymore. Now I was a lead guitar player that will kick you in your face if I felt like it! So Iggy gave me a force that I would take into my later life.

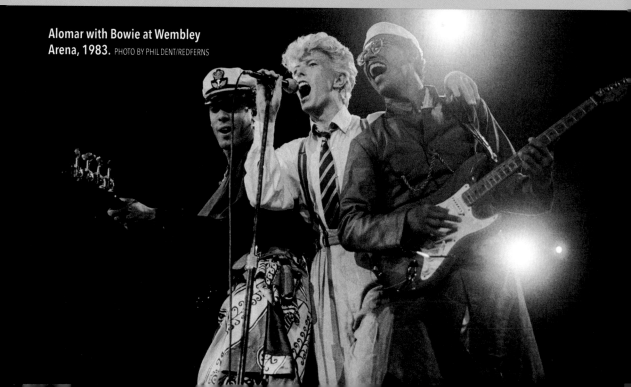

Alomar with Bowie at Wembley Arena, 1983. PHOTO BY PHIL DENT/REDFERNS

IAN ANDERSON
JETHRO TULL

Jethro Tull in 1972 (from left): John Evan, Ian Anderson, Barrie Barlow, Martin Barre and Jeffrey Hammond. PHOTO BY PHOTO BY GIJSBERT HANEKROOT/REDFERNS

There may be progressive rock bands as impactful and venerable as Jethro Tull, but in terms of personality being focused in one band member, mad flautist on one leg, Ian Anderson is as iconic as they get. As the band's only continuous member since the beginning in 1967, as its lead singer and overwhelmingly as Tull's main songwriter, Anderson has created UK rock royalty with his visionary mix of folk, hard rock, mathematical rhythm and... flute! The flute came about after Anderson realized he would never play the guitar as well as Eric Clapton and picked up the one thing that would make him unique. A bold move indeed, but once Anderson mastered his blues-rock style his playing helped to create the trademark sound for Jethro Tull, who *Rolling Stone* described as "one of the most commercially successful and eccentric progressive rock bands." Albums such as *Aqualung*, *Thick as a Brick* and *Songs from the Wood* helped the band sell more than 60 million records worldwide.

PHOTO BY FRANK HOENSCH/REDFERNS

Captain Beefheart,
Trout Mask Replica

Back around 1967, Captain Beefheart became known to British radio listeners because there was a radio program by a BBC disc jockey by the name of John Peel, who had a show. And I think usually on some days he would play Captain Beefheart. He more or less singlehandedly popularized Captain Beefheart in the UK and perhaps even into Europe too. So I think I heard Captain Beefheart in his very early days prior to **Trout Mask Replica**, but by the time that album was released and that particular edition of the band was out there and following it up, we all kind of knew who he was.

That album was a work of very abstracted, kind of crazy, almost deliberately childlike musical composition, if that's the word, because of course it turned out that Beefheart actually didn't really write anything. He would sit there at a beaten-up old piano in a house he and his musicians lived in, and would basically just bang away at the piano which he couldn't play at all. I mean actually the only thing that he played that he had any idea about was a bit of harmonica, but he couldn't play soprano saxophone, which he made a lot of squealing and crazy noises on, but actually couldn't play it.

So he just banged away at random kind of stuff and then would turn to Zoot Horn Rollo, who was the guitar player and say, "Learn that." And so Bill Harkleroad, a.k.a. Zoot Horn Rollo would sit down and write the whole thing out, methodically teach it to the members of the band and then Beefheart would come in and half-sing, half-talk his way through the very abstracted poetry that passed for lyrics. But then the end result was remarkable in that it had a huge impact on the underground music scene. And shortly after that, with a couple of albums later, Captain Beefheart toured with Jethro Tull in the USA in 1972 at a time when, I think he'd got to hear the fact that I liked his music and introduced himself by phone to me somewhere (laughs) and said, "Hey, can we come on tour?" Which he did. And so we kind of got to know him and his band in 1972.

The Graham Bond Organization,
The Sound of '65

This had its roots in jazz and blues, with the three musicians apart from Graham Bond who played alto saxophone and then Hammond organ. The other three were Dick Heckstall-Smith on tenor saxophone and Jack Bruce on bass and vocals and Ginger Baker on drums. So, you know, you had two-thirds of Cream in there as they became a couple of years later.

But Graham Bond was a bandleader, rather like Frank Zappa. I mean he was someone who perhaps wasn't necessarily the sharpest musician of the band, but he had the skills to get people together and organize things in such a way as they could do gigs and make a few records. And **The Sound of '65**, despite the very uninspiring title, actually contained quite a lot of innovative music. It was a precursor of what became progressive rock a few years later.

The album had a few songs and a few instrumentals, which were amongst the first pieces of music that we, in the band that I was in at school, then called The Blades or then the John Evan Band, were able to play. So it was part of our musical identity in those early days. And we got to see Graham Bond play a few times back in 1966, '67 and I met him a couple of times in the early days of Jethro Tull.

Blind Faith, *Blind Faith*

I was living in Kentish Town, London when I heard this, just at the time when Tull was getting started. They gave me the courage to develop improvisation and extended song development.

J.B. Lenoir, *Alabama Blues*

Re-released these days as **Passionate Blues**. This taught me the difference between white man's blues and black man's blues. Lenoir sang about race riots, lynchings, beatings and the plight of black Americans in the early '60s.

Led Zeppelin, *I*

Led Zeppelin's first album showed us that you could be a huge success in the USA without singles, hype and showbiz clout. The music stood and still stands up for itself. Zeppelin was a few months ahead of us on the road in the USA. I mean they too began technically in 1968, like Jethro Tull; they started up at the end of '68 as The New Yardbirds, with Jimmy Page kind of inheriting the name. But then with the promise of an American tour, they changed their name to Led Zeppelin and the first album came out and pretty much out of the box was a big hit. We were their opening act in the summer of 1969, by which time they'd become a headliner and we were fresh off the airplane from the U.K.. So we had some of our introductory moments in front of American audiences with Led Zeppelin. The music from that album was very much in my ears from being around backstage and hearing it, but also of course hearing it played on American radio.

John Mayall, *Blues Breakers with Eric Clapton*

It was the John Mayall album that had a picture on the front with the new member of the band, Eric Clapton, reading the Beano comic paper, a sort of popular boys' comic paper of the '50s and '60s. And so it's often referred to as The Beano Album amongst John Mayall aficionados. But when I heard Eric Clapton on that album, I realized that he was just so far ahead of the game in terms of being a very competent, very fluid blues guitarist that it really seemed rather pointless for me to try and follow in the footsteps of someone already so advanced. It would have taken me another couple of years to play guitar as well as that. And I didn't have that time. I really wanted to crack on. So I thought I'll switch to finding something else to play. And the flute just presented itself without any real thought or intention and it just sort of became part of my life. And thank goodness that it did because I wasn't ever going to be a great guitar player.

The Jimi Hendrix Experience, *Are You Experienced*

I first heard Jimi Hendrix when I was living in a bed sitter [small apartment] in north London. It was the summer of 1968 and of course we'd heard Jimi Hendrix on the radio playing "Hey Joe" and "Purple Haze." So I bought the album. I mean, for me buying an album back then was a big deal because I had no money. I must've gone hungry for two or three days to pay for the album. It was either listening to Jimi Hendrix or eat. So I had the album and it was an example of how someone could take one form of music and then be much more inventive and innovative in what he did.

So I suppose in a way it gave me a bit of a direction that I could maybe try and be as creative and find some new things to do with my own music rather than just stick with something that was very much established, like the blues. Jimi Hendrix took the blues and turned it into something completely different. And that was a very admirable thing. So it wasn't that I was musically inspired by the actual songs on it. I was just musically inspired by the idea of being creative and being able to balance songwriting with musical instrumental expertise. But Jimi, when he first appeared in London, he was unknown, really, in America, and unknown in the U.K., but he appeared in clubs in London and wowed the likes of Jeff Beck and Eric Clapton and Jimmy Page and Richie Blackmore. And all these people went to see Jimi Hendrix and went, "Wow." So it sharpened everybody's game, that's for sure.

Roy Harper, *Come Out Fighting Ghengis Smith*

Roy had a girlfriend that had just given birth to a baby. I suppose being present at the birth, Roy came up with this title, **Come Out Fighting Ghengis Smith**, Smith being the common sort of nondescript man's name. It was like Ghengis anybody or Ghengis everybody, depending on your point of view. But I rather liked the title. It was an album that I played in the summer of 1968 when it came out after I'd met Roy and we'd done a few shows. There was a quite famous, very first Hyde Park concert [in London] in 1968 which feature Jethro Tull, Roy Harper and Pink Floyd. That was quite a concert to be at, if you were wandering through Hyde Park in the summer of 1968. Especially for Pink Floyd, who didn't have a light show—they actually had to play their instruments and try to look good without the benefit of all the production (laughs). And, as I recall, we did all of this on the back of a flatbed truck.

But yes, Roy's songwriting is very personal and sometimes with very adventurous lyrics, which got him into a little trouble here early on. He was a very important part of that world, and amongst people outside of his musical genre who were huge fans were members of Pink Floyd and Led Zeppelin, for example, and me. I guess at one time or another, we've all played with Roy and guested on an album track or something of that sort. So we have a history of taking him under our separate wings. We hugely admired him and wanted to give him some wider publicity opportunities.

King Crimson, *In the Court of the Crimson King*

The first prog album that would come to mind is King Crimson, **In the Court of the Crimson King** because they first started performing on the stage of the Marquee Club, as did Jethro Tull. That was the beginning of something, the start of what became prog rock. I mean, Jethro Tull, King Crimson and Yes, were three of the bands, I suppose. And The Nice sort of oddly morphed into Emerson, Lake and Palmer. That was really the beginning of prog rock.

By 1969, the term progressive rock was being used in the British music press. And I was very happy to be included in that new genre description. King Crimson were probably the first truly prog band, with Yes coming along very soon behind. Some people would cite the Moody Blues and the album **Days of Future Past** as being progressive rock, but I think really it was more progressive pop rather than hard rocking, and they had a niche because of the use of orchestra and conceptual ideas.

The King Crimson vibe was very much driven by the strangely static Robert Fripp who, as a front man for a band, just kind of sat there on a chair and didn't really look at the audience. And that, in a way, was great and riveting because you were struck by the fact that he seemed to direct the band from this very static sitting position. He didn't move around and talk or do anything, just kind of played and nodded to the band.

Various Artists, *Stanley Kubrick's A Clockwork Orange*

I first really took notice of Beethoven's "Ninth Symphony" in the 1971 Kubrick classic, **A Clockwork Orange**. The scherzo was played on early synthesizers by the then Walter (later Wendy) Carlos. I wasn't too keen on the synths but got hold of the Berlin Philharmonic's version conducted by Von Karajan on the Deutsche Grammophon label. At the time, I was buying a Spanish motocross racer bike, the Ossa Phantom, and so that machine and Beethoven were forever oddly linked in my memory.

VINNY APPICE
BLACK SABBATH/DIO

Bassist Kenny Aaronson, guitarist Rick Derringer, guitarist Danny Johnson and Vinny Appice of Derringer, 1976. PHOTO BY FIN COSTELLO/REDFERNS

Vincent Samson "Vinny" Appice, younger brother of Carmine, first came to fame through hot rockin' Rick Derringer vehicle, Derringer, before winding up as the replacement for Bill Ward in Black Sabbath. At this point, Ronnie James Dio was fronting the band, who were making a bold return with 1980's *Heaven and Hell* album. Vinny drummed on the tour for that record, and then made his recording debut with 1981's *Mob Rules*, following up with the double live Live Evil record. From there, Vinny left with Ronnie and the two started Dio, along with guitarist Viv Campbell and bassist Jimmy Bain. On hit records such as *Holy Diver, The Last in Line and Sacred Heart*, Vinny's big beat can be heard along with his groovy, often extended fills, to the point where Vinny and his trademark drum performance added an extra persona to the band—certainly not unheard of but hard to do from behind the kit. Since then, Appice has kept busy with a host of projects and supergroups—over 20 recording bands!—along the way also returning to Black Sabbath for 1992's *Dehumanizer* and then Heaven & Hell, the rechristened version of Black Sabbath in operation from 2006 that was to be Dio's swansong.

PHOTO BY PAUL ARCHULETA/FILMMAGIC

Vanilla Fudge, *Vanilla Fudge*
My brother's first album, and his playing on it, kicked me in the ass. It wasn't an album that was just a bunch of hit songs. It was like performances on each song, and these were rearrangements of songs they didn't write. It was amazing the way they made the songs sound so different from the original and you went from one great song to another great song. But yeah, my brother's playing was very inspiring to me.

The Jimi Hendrix Experience, *Are You Experienced*
Very raw for the time, and very interesting, almost establishing that idea of the three-piece power trio. They looked great and Mitch Mitchell played some amazing stuff on that. Yeah, very, very cool performances on that record.

Cream, *Disraeli Gears*
That was an influential album because they had their own sound and Ginger Baker played totally different, making more use of double bass when all these other drummers were single bass. It was very cool to listen to his approach to those songs. "Sunshine of Your Love"... it's almost played backwards. The way he emphasized the one and the three in that song, it inverted the feel.

Blue Cheer, *Vincebus Eruptum*
A really heavy three-piece band record and the guys looked cool as hell. I remember it said on the second record that they recorded it on a pier because they were too loud. I love that–too loud to go into a studio. Holy shit. But the first one, I listened to that album a lot.

The Beatles, *Sgt. Pepper's Lonely Hearts Club Band*
The Beatles records were always around, but when that came out, it was like a trip, a journey. You wanted to listen to the whole record because it made sense as an album, one big record from start to finish. Back then, I didn't appreciate the drum parts on it. Now I listen to it and I go, you know, they're brilliant drum parts. Anybody could play through those songs; they're easy to play, simple 4/4. But when the drummer thinks up a part that makes the song happen, makes it different, and then doesn't play all the way through, maybe that's a fresh way to be creative, you know?

Yes, *Fragile*
Not the early stuff, but ***Fragile***, and especially "Roundabout." That was another one with different sounds. Like you had a Rickenbacker bass sound going on and this loud voice that was kind of pretty. And then [drummer] Bill Bruford is playing some crazy, beautiful stuff. So that album was a big influence.

Led Zeppelin, *I*

That was a whole new sound, and a little heavier and more rock than Vanilla Fudge, which was almost orchestral. John Bonham's playing was fantastic, doing so many things to listen to on the drums that I wanted to learn, such as "Good Times Bad Times," with that triplet thing he did with his foot. But yes, that, and the riffs, the production, the riff structure of the songs.

Led Zeppelin, *II*

The first one was cool because it was less production, more playing. The second one had the playing *and* a bit more production, with additional different guitar sounds; it was brilliant the different ways Page used the guitar, they had progressed. And then there was "Moby Dick." Usually a drum solo is a drum solo, but this was a musical drum solo done in the studio. You usually heard them on live albums, but this was something different, a drum solo as part of a great song, "Moby Dick." The riff is a cool riff for a drummer to play behind, but then all of a sudden it goes into a drum solo, which was very musical, but he was also playing as much as he can and as fast as he can.

Black Sabbath, *Black Sabbath*

When I heard the first record, I went over to a friend's house and he said, "Hey, check this out." They put it on and I listened too and went, "Wow, that's really scary" (laughs). Really different guitar sound than Zeppelin and the drums were just really dead on it. And then Ozzy's singing was also different–and scary. The whole album was just dark and heavy and scary. But I wasn't a big fan of the drum sound. I was used to a big drum sound like Bonham's and [Bill Ward's] were pretty dry.

The Mahavishnu Orchestra, *The Inner Mounting Flame*

Not so much a rock album, but just an incredible album. I heard it on the radio one night, like going to bed and putting the headphones on when I was a kid. And one of the songs came on and I thought they had the turntable on the wrong speed it was playing so fast. "Holy shit, they used the wrong speed. Nobody can play like that." And then sure enough it was on the right speed. Oh my God. And the next day I went out and got that record. Billy Cobham was playing so fast and playing with the riffs. It was hard to comprehend at first; I had to keep listening to it, listening to it. And even now when I listen to it, man, he's just killing it–incredible.

ROD ARGENT
THE ZOMBIES

The Zombies: Chris White, Rod Argent, Paul Atkinson (with fiancee Molly Molloy), Hugh Grundy and Colin Blunstone. PHOTO BY BELA ZOLA/MIRRORPIX/GETTY IMAGES

Rod Argent and his band, The Zombies, created one of the great albums of all time, 1968's **Odessey and Oracle**, a psychedelic rock masterpiece which did much of the heavy lifting in terms of getting the band inducted into the Rock and Roll Hall of Fame in 2019. That record offered the classic "Time of the Season." Of course, before that the group had a No. 1 hit with "She's Not There," a song written by Argent, and another hit with "Tell Her No." Also impressive was the band's return to recording and touring after their success in the '60s, which caught everybody off-guard due to the quality and vitality of the new senior-citizen Zombies, more prolific and arguably better than the quickly gone post-Beatles outfit. After the original Zombies, Rod had a long career with his band Argent, touring America with all the big classic rock acts of the day, starting pop and ending prog. Pioneering keyboardist and consummate songwriter, Argent proves with this ten-record breakdown that he was—and still is—in it for the right reason, namely an intense love of music and music history.

PHOTO BY OLLIE MILLINGTON/REDFERNS

The Beatles,
With the Beatles

With the Beatles was the second album, released only in the UK, November of '63. Obviously they were making a name a little bit before but the first album **Please Please Me** was very thrown together. But I was still in love with the Beatles by that time anyway. But I can distinctly remember putting on **With the Beatles** and I played the first track, thought it was great. And then I couldn't believe it because every single track I played one after another off the album was absolutely fantastic and no denigration in quality at all. That's the first time that I'd heard a rock 'n' roll or pop album that had that effect. Every single track, it elevated rock 'n' roll music, to me, to a completely higher level because every single track was a work of art. And I can still play the album and love it. So that album represents the huge influence the Beatles had on… well, everybody but certainly me.

And in terms of The Zombies, that album represented the quality I wanted in our first single, "She's Not There." Our first album was very much like the Beatles' first album because it was done just by our record producer on the back of the success of "She's Not There." And like **Please Please Me**, it was recorded in two days and it was an album of covers plus a few originals, done incredibly quickly, usually one take a track. Anyway, **With the Beatles** just showed the band spending more time and indulging in more craftsmanship on each track and paying more attention to it. So similarly, certainly, by the time we did our second studio album, **Odessey and Oracle**, we then put in every piece of craftsmanship we could. And we would have done that on our first album but we just weren't given the space to do that.

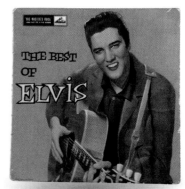

Elvis Presley, *The Best of Elvis*

My first pick was only released in the UK in 1957, a ten-inch HMV album called **The Best of Elvis**. Elvis was the guy that originally had completely changed my life when I heard "Hound Dog" and "Lawdy Miss Clawdy" and after that, even earlier stuff like "Mystery Train" and "That's All Right Mama." I'd always loved music up to that point but I was 11 years old in '56 and I only liked classical music. I didn't like the pop music I'd heard at the time but when I'd heard "Hound Dog" it just spun my world around. I'd bought two or three singles–obviously I didn't have much money–but the very first album I ever bought was this ten-inch HMV album. It just typified how my life had changed at that time. It's really what made me want to be involved with rock 'n' roll.

Miles Davis, *Kind of Blue*

I'd actually heard an EP, which had completely blown me away, when I was about 14. By this time I was absolutely in love with the rawest rock 'n' roll I could hear, but at the same time I heard a Miles Davis track called "Milestones" and I couldn't afford the album, so I bought the extended play record and "Milestones" had a huge effect on me in a way, an equivalent effect to when I heard Elvis sing "Hound Dog." It didn't make me want to stop my interest in rock 'n' roll, but I just fell in love with it. And I can still sing you almost every note of every solo on that record. I just loved it. But anyway, in short order after that I bought **Kind of Blue**, which obviously is the best selling jazz record of all time, which I still adore today and still play.

Wonderful musicianship and also very much following on from "Milestones" because I didn't realize until much later that the track "Milestones" was Miles' first foray into a modal way of playing rather than just straight chords–he's playing modes. That's what he was totally experimenting with on **Kind of Blue**. And actually when I first met Pat Metheny, he said, "Oh man, 'She's Not There' was the song that made me feel I had a way ahead doing what I wanted to do. All that modal stuff that you played…" And I thought, I didn't play any modal stuff on "She's Not There." But I went away and realized that what I thought of as a couple of simple chord changes in the beginning, I actually played a modal sequence over it without realizing what modal sequences were. And that was directly, I think, an input from hearing and loving the early Miles Davis stuff.

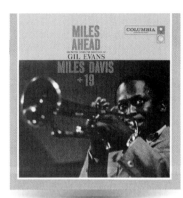

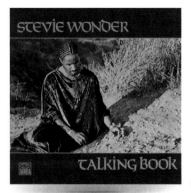

Miles Davis, *Miles Ahead*

This was a wonderful time to buy music, I have to say. There was so much going on that was wonderful around the late '50s particularly, and the Miles Davis group at that time was wonderful. And so right around the time I got **Kind of Blue**, he did an album with Gil Evans orchestrating–orchestrating with brass basically–called **Miles Ahead**. And that was my first exposure to Gil Evans' writing and I was already in love with Miles' playing and I loved that album as well. And that was a pretty sophisticated album for a 14-, 15-year-old because it wasn't even this sort of gritty improvisation that I loved. It was some wonderful, sophisticated voicings within a big band, basically brass, but a big band.

Stevie Wonder, *Talking Book*

Around the time when my second band Argent had a huge worldwide hit with "Hold Your Head Up," I was getting a bit bored with what's around at that point. I don't know why I felt like that, but I just remember a particular weekend going out and thinking, oh, I've got to buy a couple of albums this weekend. I know I looked around and I thought, ah, Stevie Wonder. I remembered some of his early stuff like "My Cherie Amour" and things like that. I'm really liking it and thinking he had a really soulful voice. I thought I'll buy that, which was **Talking Book**. Now for some reason he had a golden period of about five albums started with **Music of My Mind**. For some reason I hadn't heard that, but **Talking Book...** when I put that on, I felt warm from top to toe. I thought this is just inspiring; it's just gorgeous.

The Mahavishnu Orchestra, *The Inner Mounting Flame*

On the same trip to the record store when I bought **Talking Book**, for some reason, the cover of **The Inner Mounting Flame** took my eye, and because I loved jazz anyway, I bought those two albums and this one had the same effect as the Stevie Wonder. It wasn't the brilliance of the individual players so much as the wonderful ecstatic sort of rising themes that McLaughlin had written. And of course the wonderful playing as well–that goes without saying, of Billy Cobham and everybody else involved with the album. But those two albums, in a different way, gave me the same feeling, of feeling very warm and full and inspired. I remember that weekend very, very well.

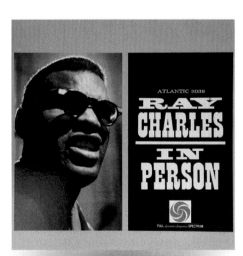

Ray Charles, *In Person*

I'm going back now to 1960 and the first time I heard Ray Charles because I'm still in love with his early period. I must've been about 16, 17 maybe when I bought **[In Person]**, an album I still play now. It's a live album recorded in Atlanta, Georgia with one microphone and it sounds wonderful. Absolutely wonderful. And it was so soulful. And in my early forays to the pub when I was 17, you know, just drinking a couple of pints of beer I would come back and my parents had gone to bed and I would go into our living room and I would lie on the floor and on our radiogram, which is what we had at the time, I would put on Ray Charles **In Person** at a very quiet level so as not to wake everybody up and be in heaven for the duration of that record. He did a version of "Drown in My Own Tears," I remember, and it was so slow that when The Raelets came in on the chorus it felt like about three minutes before they actually came in (laughs), because it was done at such a slow tempo.

Glenn Gould, *Bach: The Goldberg Variations*

Glenn Gould recorded **The Goldberg Variations** twice, once in 1955, and once quite a few years later, I believe in the late '60s. Obviously the one in '55 was in mono. Now that to me is just one of my desert island discs without question. It's just the most wonderful playing. In a classical sense it's incredibly soulful, but it has fantastic bite, fantastic rhythm. Just wonderfully inspired. In 1957 the Canadian government sent him over to Russia because they had to find an exchange for some famous Russian classical musician who was coming over to Canada. Glenn Gould wasn't very well known there, but they sent him over. He played at some conservatory in Russia, in Moscow or Leningrad, and in the first half there were just sort of a dozen people in there; it was very empty. But he played **The Goldberg Variations** and a couple of very famous Russian pianists were there and they were so blown away they phoned everybody in the interval. And to his amazement, he came back after the interval and the place was packed and that started a really wonderful career for Glenn Gould.

Cream, *Disraeli Gears*

I loved Cream. I didn't like their first single, "Wrapping Paper," but everything after that I just thought was fabulous. Great musicianship, great synthesis of three very different players, but wonderfully soulful. And I loved the playing, I loved the material, I loved the writing of Jack Bruce together with Pete Brown. I just thought it was a great, great album. You know, it wasn't any sort of direct influence on us, but the feeling of, I think, all these albums have to me is craftsmanship aligned to genuine feeling and not just trying to be commercial. I mean they all were terribly commercial actually but not being commercial for the sake of thinking we have to get a hit record and this is what we should be doing.

The Beach Boys, *Pet Sounds*

Pet Sounds certainly had at least an indirect influence on **Odessey and Oracle** because, to go back to even our very early songs, certainly the ones that I wrote, I always used to write a bass line that was integral to the song. And it would be part of the composition, like in "She's Not There." One of the earliest things that I wrote was the bass and drum part right at the beginning. So I was always interested in musical bass lines and often bass lines that had a root note that was the root note of the chord that we were playing. Now, Brian Wilson did that as a natural thing as well. But when he wrote **Pet Sounds**, to my ears he took that to another level. And when I heard it, I was inspired by the album as were most musicians that I know that heard it. And I loved the lyricism of the way he developed the bass lines on his songs. It made me want to emphasize that on **Odessey and Oracle**, certainly on my songs, like "Care of Cell 44"–well, on everything, really. It made me excited to just develop that little bit of my style. That was natural to me anyway, but **Pet Sounds** made me feel inspired to take that further.

SEBASTIAN BACH
SKID ROW

Thanks in large part to charismatic front-man, Sebastian Bach, heavy MTV airplay and the good fortune of being opening act on Bon Jovi's worldwide tour, hair metal band Skid Row skyrocketed to fame at the end of the 1980s. The band's self-titled debut album, *Skid Row*, released in 1989, went five times platinum and produced the hit singles: "Youth Gone Wild," "18 and Life" and "I remember You," all of which were accompanied by music videos and heavy rotation on MTV. Born Sebastian Philip Bierk, Bach was a magnetic yet wild lead man whose onstage antics were both captivating and outrageous. Personal differences and changing trends—especially the emergence of Nirvana and grunge—would eventually tear the core lineup of Skid Row apart by 1996, with Bach embarking on a successful Broadway and acting career. In 2016, Bach released a tell-all memoir, *18 and Life on Skid Row*, to enthusiastic reviews. Of the book, *The A.V. Club* wrote "it works because of Bach's puppyish enthusiasm for music, yes, but also for booze, for drugs, and for sex in unusual places."

Sebastian Bach (left) and Skid Row.
PHOTO BY EBET ROBERTS/REDFERNS/GETTY IMAGES

Van Halen, *Van Halen*
I was a huge Cheap Trick fan, and my babysitter, who was, like 10, left her copy of *Van Halen* at my house. It was so much dirtier than Cheap Trick and it freaked me out. I couldn't believe it.

Judas Priest,
Unleashed in the East
I couldn't believe Rob Halford's voice was really his voice. I remember my buddy played me "Victim of Changes" and said, "Listen to him sing!" And I said, "That's not singing. That's the guitar." And he's like, "No, that's his voice." I just couldn't fathom that a human voice was capable of making those sounds.

Metallica, *Kill 'Em All*
I remember going through the record racks at Moondance Records in Peterborough, Ontario, Canada, which is still there—a mom-and-pop record store that you should give a shout out to. And I picked up this album and I turned it around, and they were the ugliest humans that I had ever seen. I had never seen uglier people (laughs). I was like, "These guys are ugly, man. I'm gonna buy this!" So that was a good one.

RANDY BACHMAN
THE GUESS WHO
BACHMAN-TURNER OVERDRIVE

Randy Bachman with Bachman-Turner Overdrive in 1975.
PHOTO BY CHRIS WALTER/WIREIMAGE

Randy Bachman is one of the rare performers to have two No. 1 singles with two different bands in the 1960s and 1970s. With the Guess Who, Bachman had "American Woman" and with Bachman-Turner Overdrive he scored with "You Ain't Seen Nothing Yet." Bachman left the Guess Who in 1970 at the height of the band's success, struggling with the lifestyle choices of other band members that conflicted with his religious beliefs, and formed Bachman-Turner Overdrive. BTO became a classic rock radio mainstay in the '70s with such tunes as "Takin' Care of Business," "Let It Ride" and "Roll on Down the Highway."

"[Bachman] was like my biggest influence when I was a kid," says Neil Young in *Bachman*, a documentary exploring Bachman's life, from his childhood in Winnipeg, Canada, to his conversion to Mormonism to his touring life today. "Watching him play guitar, he had an amazing sense about the way he played. It was more than just chops."

Elvis Presley, *Elvis*
The "Shake That Shook the World" record took all his influences of bluegrass, R&B, gospel, doo-wop, rockabilly and country and the new package heralded the arrival called rock 'n' roll.

The Beatles, *With the Beatles*
The "Shake That Shook the World." Another gift basket that repackaged rock 'n' roll, Motown, country and doo-wop for the next generation of teenagers. This album changed everything. Even drummers started singing to be like Ringo.

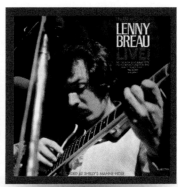

Lenny Breau, *The Velvet Touch of Lenny Breau Live!*
My teenage friend and guitar mentor finally got "discovered" by Chet Atkins who took him to Nashville and recorded this album. I defy anyone to play this album note for note! But if you can, good for you and you should be very famous.

MARTY BALIN
JEFFERSON AIRPLANE/
JEFFERSON STARSHIP

Jefferson Airplane, 1990 (L -R): Jack Casady, Jorma Kaukonen, Grace Slick, Marty Balin and Paul Kantner. PHOTO BY MICHAEL OCHS ARCHIVES/GETTY IMAGES

Marty Balin provided this 10 Albums list to us long before he passed away in 2018 at the age of 76. Balin was guitarist and co-lead vocalist in Jefferson Airplane and Jefferson Starship. A Grammy winner, Balin was inducted into the Rock and Roll Hall of Fame in 1996 along with Jefferson Airplane. He also played with Bodacious DF and KBC band, recorded numerous solo albums and was an avid and accomplished painter. Balin had a hard time narrowing down his 10 Albums list. Besides those listed, he cited The Beatles, The Rolling Stones, The Who, Janis Joplin, Doors, Grateful Dead and Creedence Clearwater Revival as other favorite acts, saying, "I would just put them all on a turntable and play them at the same time; you'll get an idea of how powerful they all were."

PHOTO BY MICHAEL OCHS ARCHIVES/GETTY IMAGES

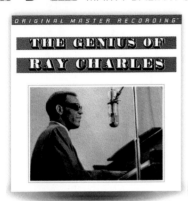

Ray Charles, *The Genius of Ray Charles*

I think this is one of the most beautiful albums ever made, by probably the greatest singer that ever lived. An album that I've worn out ever since I can remember. When I was a kid, it was one of the first two albums I ever bought–this one and Jonathan Winters. **The Genius of Ray Charles** is a soothing, great, wonderful album which I listen to in the car, at home.

Tony Bennett/Bill Evans, *The Tony Bennett/Bill Evans Album*

I just love the mastery of Tony Bennett, but the quality of him alone with a keyboard player shows the range, control. This really just pares it down to him and a keyboard. The Jefferson Airplane were at the original RCA recording studios in LA at Sunset and Vine. In Studio A was the Rolling Stones, in B was us and in C, Tony Bennett. We all wanted to meet Tony Bennett. I figured a good way to meet him was to write a song for him ("Today"). He didn't record it, but we got to meet him.

The Sweet Inspirations, *The Sweet Inspirations*

The Sweet Inspirations sang backgrounds for everyone, and they went in and did their own album and it's just fantastic. I think it's a good training ground for any young singer; a good workout. I used to drive to record stores in the regional soul and R&B areas and buy 45s. I have a great collection of 45s. I knew The Sweet Inspirations from all the records they played on, so when they released their own disc I checked it out. It became a staple of my musical listening diet. I used to practice to it.

The Yardbirds, *Five Live Yardbirds*

I just thought they were one of the better bands; they gave me a lot of inspiration when I was growing up. The songs, the playing, the style that they were doing… it was just a great band.

Robert Johnson, *King of the Delta Blues Singers*

It's something every musician comes across: to hear the man himself kind of hypnotizes and mystifies you as you try to figure out how he did all that with just two hands. The beauty of his haunting voice, haunting songs. When you check out the mythology behind the man, you see why it's so great.

James Brown, *Live at the Apollo*

One of the great albums of all time, shows you the master at work, live, bringing the house down. Makes you want to dance and go crazy. I remember in the early '60s how it was so funky, scary and raw. Before Michael Jackson, he was the dancing man. Sweaty shows. I saw him at the Apollo more than a few times in San Francisco.

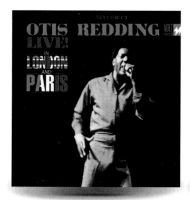

Otis Redding, *Live in Paris*

God, probably the highest performer, highest energy I ever saw come off the stage, and this captures that energy and that kind of performance at its peak. It's just masterful to listen to. We were on the same bill at the Fillmore. I took "These Arms of Mine" to Bill Graham and he booked Otis.

Sam Cooke, *Live at the Copa*

Well, this too, one of the most beautiful voices of all time. Sam Cooke was just a magnificent singer. In concert you could hear the beauty in his voice and the great control he had. When my very first record came out on Challenge Records ("Nobody but You" and "I Specialize in Love") one of my first shows, if not my first show, was with Connie Stevens and Sam Cooke. Sam had on a white cashmere sweater, was real friendly. We all introduced ourselves; it just blew me away.

The Jimi Hendrix Experience, *Are You Experienced*

Well, Jimi Hendrix, monster god of all time. I could say listen to everything he did. Any one of his albums, take your pick, there's nothing like it. It's like listening to Beethoven. The real power and beauty of his guitar playing set standards that have not been toppled, not yet. He made love to every note. He did the thing, the nasty thing, and grooved the note out of the guitar.

Jefferson Airplane,
Surrealistic Pillow
I thought that was a damn good album.

Grace Slick and Marty Balin in Year?
PHOTO BY MICHAEL OCHS ARCHIVES/GETTY IMAGES

FRANKIE BANALI
QUIET RIOT

Quiet Riot in 1983 (from left): Rudy Sarzo, Kevin DuBrow, Frankie Banali and Carlos Cavazo   PHOTO BY CHRIS WALTER/WIREIMAGE

Frankie Banali is a rock 'n' roll whirlwind, a force of nature and one of the best kept secrets amongst the echelon of musicians who know an incredible drummer when they hear one. The go-to session thumper for projects a' plenty throughout the years, Banali has also been a member of a half dozen recording bands. One of those bands is W.A.S.P., for whom he's recorded almost as many albums as he has for his main love and mission, the irrepressible Quiet Riot, who is best known for their *Metal Health* album (1983), which has sold an astounding 10 million copies worldwide. *Metal Health* spawned massive hits in "Cum On Feel the Noize" and the pounding title track, which gave rise to the phrase "bang your head." Follow-up *Condition Critical* also scored platinum and the band has been in operation on and off to this day, as explained in acclaimed documentary, *Well Now You're Here, There's No Way Back.* Need a John Bonham vibe on your record? Only two guys you call: Jason Bonham or Frankie Banali.

Miles Davis, *Vol. 2*
Released in 1953 on Blue Note. The drummers were Kenny Clarke and Art Blakey. Two monster drummers who were front-runners in the bop style of drumming early on. My father gave that to me. He wasn't a musician, but he really loved jazz, big band, swing, all of that. He also gave me a Max Roach, but this one made the biggest impression on me. It didn't have vocals–it was all instrumental–but what really caught my ear was the sound of the drums, the way that they were recorded and the melodies that were being played, especially between the trumpet and the saxophone.

The Beatles,
Introducing the
Beatles
I was one of those kids where I'm sitting at my parents' house in Queens, New York, in Astoria, and my parents were on the couch watching Ed Sullivan like we did religiously. I think Sullivan was, for a Catholic family, just as important as church on Sunday. And I was sitting on the floor and when I saw the Beatles, up to that point, my main concern was playing hockey because I was a goalie in the winter and playing baseball in the summer because I was a catcher. Right after that first performance

on Ed Sullivan with the Beatles, I never picked up a hockey stick again or a baseball bat and I immediately traded them for a pair of sticks. Still, as much as I liked the Beatles and loved the songs and the harmonies and all that, there was also the Stones. And the Stones were like the neighborhood gang kids, you know what I mean? That's the way I heard their music. I equated it more to the kids in the local gang that I was hanging around with in Queens. But the things that impressed me about Charlie Watts and Ringo Starr is that those are the two drummers, starting obviously with Ringo and then Charlie, that taught me how to play songs. They didn't teach me how to play drums–they taught me how to play songs on the drum. That was important to me.

The Jimi Hendrix Experience, *Are You Experienced*
That record is the first time I had ever heard anybody play the electric guitar in that way. And it was the first time that I had ever heard sounds coming up from an electric guitar that I had no idea could come from that instrument. The other thing that impressed me was Mitch Mitchell's drumming. He had a great sensibility. His was such an incredibly difficult job because Jimi Hendrix wasn't just another guitar player. He had to be able to weave in and out of all these crazy things Jimi was doing, yet he had the ability to keep time and at the same time do these avant-garde fills. I don't know if it was if it was by accident or by design, but they married each other perfectly. You have to also say that Noel Redding did an incredible job just solidifying the bottom for the two of them to really be everything they could be.

Cream, *Disraeli Gears*
I was one of those kids that would scream at the top of my lungs, "Clapton is God!" because he had the incredible ability of playing electric blues in a manner that I had not heard before. But then you had the amazing style of Jack Bruce. Jack Bruce was one of my first favorite rock singers because he just had such a unique tone to his voice and such a different way that he wrote melodies. And then of course you have Ginger Baker, who was the first rock drummer that I was aware of that played double bass drums. And he was very much in tune with African tribal music and he married all those things together. That was also something I'd never heard before.

Led Zeppelin, *I*

I was working at a record store after school and on weekends and I got an advance copy with the sticker on it. I was already a Yardbirds fan, but not a fanatical Yardbirds fan. I liked them when Clapton was in the band, when Jeff Beck was in the band and then I started steering away from it for whatever reason. But when I heard Led Zeppelin one, I was aware of Jimmy Page obviously, but everybody else was completely unknown to me. These were new names. Even though John Paul Jones at the time was doing a lot of sessions, that's not something that I knew.

But when I heard that record, it was the complete record. But it was also the individual performances of each musician. It was the dexterity of John Paul Jones, a bass player I had never heard. And I'd never heard a singer hit notes like that ever in my entire life. It was like all of a sudden the bar had been set really, really high–by all of them. John Bonham is my favorite rock drummer. I can't say enough about him. I mean, what a powerhouse. But at the same time, what style and finesse on the quieter things that you would not have expected–something like "Dazed and Confused" had both. Jimmy Page was always stellar, but his production and his use of echoes was just mesmerizing. I couldn't believe it. That album was a turning point in my life in the same way as *Introducing the Beatles* took me from everything that I had done prior to that and dropped me right into music.

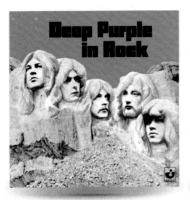

Deep Purple, *In Rock*

When you hear the technical ability that Ritchie Blackmore had back then, I mean his picking was like a machine gun. And then you have Ian Paice who is leaning more towards a jazz sensibility than rock and marries the two effortlessly–just amazing. Those are the records that I would sit there in front of my stereo with a pair of drumsticks and beat holes into the carpet, trying to figure out how these guys were doing it all. And Ian Gillan at the time was a force to be reckoned with. Jon Lord, I had never heard a Hammond organ played that way. Usually the Hammond was through a Leslie [speaker], and in his case it was through two Marshalls with all the treble turned up.

Emerson Lake and Palmer, *Tarkus*

Keith Emerson, the Jimi Hendrix of keyboards. And again, the common thread for me is when I hear musicians doing something that I've never heard anyone do before, on whatever instrument. And even before he really got into the use of the Minimoog and then the larger Moogs and all of that stuff, he was doing it on a Hammond. He really truly was the Hendrix of the organ and keyboard. And then another common thread, Carl Palmer, another jazz aficionado playing technical rock with a jazz sensibility. And then Greg Lake who had clearly the cleanest, most beautiful, most powerful voice. And then the bass playing that he was doing was leaps and bounds ahead of anybody else.

The Who, *Live at Leeds*

Still stands the test of time as being probably the greatest performance of a live rock band that I've ever heard. I have a theory about The Who in their entirety. I think the reason that The Who sounded the way they did comes from Keith Moon. You have Keith Moon, who had a very volatile, very erratic style of drumming that had more to do with how many things can I hit than it has to do with time-keeping. So now because of that, you have Pete Townshend who has to be the single greatest… I mean, he's an amazing lead guitarist, but I think one of his strong points in The Who was being the most incredible rhythm guitarist and coming up with these different chord inversions and all of that. So he was actually the timekeeper, where the drummer's usually a band's timekeeper. But Pete ended up being the timekeeper because of Keith's style. And that allowed John Entwistle to literally become the second lead instrument in the band.

Jeff Beck, *Truth*

The Jeff Beck group **Truth** album with Micky Waller on drums was a huge record for me because this was the platform for Led Zeppelin who then took it to another level. So everybody knows that after Eric Clapton, Jeff Beck came into The Yardbirds and Jimmy Page came in shortly after playing bass and when Jeff Beck left, Page took over on guitar. It's also well known that when Beck would put The Jeff Beck Group together with Rod Stewart on vocals–who was pretty much unknown at the time–and Ron Wood on bass and Micky Waller on drums, they started doing dates.

And at one of the dates, in London I think it was, who was on the side of the stage but Jimmy Page and Peter Grant. So when you take that into consideration, and the fact that both bands did "You Shook Me"… I think at this point in time, I'm pretty sure that Jimmy Page had not secured John Bonham and Robert Plant and possibly not even John Paul Jones. But if you think about the style of Rod Stewart as a vocalist and you look at the people Jimmy Page originally targeted to be singers in what would become Led Zeppelin. His first choice was Steve Marriott. The tale has it that his manager, Don Arden, let Peter Grant know that they should stay away from little Stevie or they were going to break Page's fingers. And so obviously that didn't happen. But you can see the similarities in voices.

His next target was Terry Reid, and that's another singer that was in that same, Steve Marriott/Paul Rodgers/Rod Stewart sort of capable styling. He turned it down because he had just signed a deal and was about to release his solo record, **Bang, Bang You're Terry Reid**. But he was the one that suggested that kid in Birmingham, Robert Plant, and in turn Robert Plant introduced them to John Bonham. When you start putting all those pieces together, including the fact that both bands were a three-piece with a vocalist… you would have to check this, but supposedly when **Led Zeppelin I** came out, Jeff Beck heard it and supposedly he was brought to tears, not because it was so great, which it was, but because of the obvious similarities.

The Mahavishnu Orchestra, *The Inner Mounting Flame*

I had seen Billy Cobham do some jazz-oriented stuff. Miles Davis, Art Blakey, Max Roach, Tony Williams… those are the jazz guys that I was listening to early on and Billy was in that group, but he wasn't as prominent as the rest of them. So all of a sudden **Inner Mounting Flame** comes out and I look at the cover and I'm thinking, okay, it's got Billy Cobham on it.

I was not prepared for what I heard. I mean, when I put the needle down on that record, it was so aggressive and powerful and loud, you could almost compare it to Blue Cheer's first record, although the two of them have nothing in common. But what was amazing about it is I had never heard a four-piece band that was not a rock band that was creating this wall of sound. And that combination of players, with John McLaughlin and Billy Cobham playing together, the chemistry that they had was not dissimilar to what Jimmy Page had created, but in a completely different format. And chemistry aside, no one was creating music that was that far-out and yet that well played at the same time, certainly not in 1971.

Rudy Sarzo,
Frankie Banali,
Kevin DuBrow and
Carlos Cavazo of
Quiet Riot in 1999.
PHOTO BY ANNAMARIA
DISANTO/WIREIMAGE

MARTIN BARRE
JETHRO TULL

Jethro Tull in 1971 (from left): Martin Barre, Ian Anderson, Jeffrey Hammond, Barriemore Barlow and John Evan. PHOTO BY MICHAEL PUTLAND/GETTY IMAGES

Innovative and singular electric and acoustic guitarist Martin Barre has had an astonishing run of well-regarded solo albums late in his career, with five albums of all original music in the 2010s alone. But he is best known for being Jethro Tull's guitarist from the second album, the seminal *Stand Up* (1969), through all the relevant major label releases over the ensuing decades. That run includes ten gold-certified studio albums, topped by 1971 prog rock classic *Aqualung*, which notched triple platinum in the U.S. on the strength of singles such as "Cross-Eyed Mary," "Locomotive Breath" and the intense and rhythmic title track. Other beloved albums of the catalogue include *Thick as a Brick, Songs from the Wood* and *Crest of a Knave*, for which the band humorously and incongruously won a Grammy in 2007 for best Hard Rock/Metal Performance Instrumental, despite, of course, not being a heavy metal band.

Jimi Hendrix,
The Best of Jimi Hendrix

The reason why I pick this one is because I just love all of Hendrix's singles, "All Along the Watchtower," "Purple Haze," "Hey Joe," "Stone Free," "Crosstown Traffic." Although the albums were amazing. I just love all of his singles and they're all put on this ***Best of Jimi Hendrix*** CD that I play all the time now. I first heard Jimi Hendrix when I was playing in Italy. I was living over there. We were playing soul music in… '67? Whenever "Purple Haze" came out. But they played this track and it really blew me away. I don't know how they got it. They had a demo from the studio. It wasn't released. The sound of the guitar and the production was just phenomenal. I'd never heard anything in my life like it before.

The Beatles, *Sgt. Pepper's Lonely Hearts Club Band*

That was the point where, as a musician, you realized something special was going on. I think we were all Beatles fans in our youth, but everybody derided us for being Beatles fans because they were a pop band. And then they turn around and do the most important piece of music ever. And suddenly everybody was focused on what they were doing and how advanced they were in their approach to music. It was literally an album that we listened to almost every day. We lived in London and were a struggling band and it was just a turning point, a pivotal point in music.

And it sort of changed me as a guitar player. Not that I wanted to play like him or copy him or play his songs but there was a whole direction of guitar playing that I was not aware of. And I wanted to be a part of it. It was a real life-changer. And then of course, as we all know, the demo became the single, because he tried to rerecord it, but he preferred the demo version, and that's what became the official recording of "Purple Haze." But I didn't try to play guitar like Jimi Hendrix or Eric Clapton. Anybody who copied Hendrix, in my book, would be crazy. Why would you? No, I just loved music and always listened to everything. I would listen to music to try to get better in what I do. But a direct relationship with how I played? No.

Neil Young, *After the Gold Rush*

When I was in America, in the early days, this was an album I just played and played. I loved the music, loved the songs, loved the atmosphere. It just sort of personified what Californian and American music was all about. Great songs and sort of an earthiness that nobody else was getting. It was really simple, straightforward music, but to make simple music sound that good is a challenge and he did it—it was a wonderful thing.

Cream, *Fresh Cream*

Fresh Cream was another album where there was no comparison. It was music and playing like nobody else was doing at the time. I was still living in Birmingham at the time and we were all out playing in bands and sort of discovering what music was all about. And then Cream come along, and you go, "Oh, okay." And we were out buying the vinyl not understanding how this sounded like that and how the guitar could play music like that. ***Fresh Cream*** had a real impact on musicians in the UK. And from them, you discovered where they were getting their influences from, most notably American blues.

Crosby, *Stills, & Nash*, *Crosby, Stills, & Nash*

The sound of the vocals was just a beautiful thing. Graham Nash had played with The Hollies in England, so I knew of him from The Hollies, and they were sort of a very successful pop group. And he moved to America, when I was in England, I thought that was the end of it. But of course, playing in America with Jethro Tull, I picked up on the fact that he was in Crosby, Stills & Nash and that was sort of my link with what he had done in the past. And he was bringing that to an American band, that vocal sound that The Hollies had in the '60s in the UK, this fantastic layering of sound with great songs and just fantastic vocals.

Donald Fagen,
The Nightfly

Just because of its amazing production and great sounds. You play that CD–and I've got it in front of me–and it's timeless. Everybody raved on about the English sound, and how all the best music was coming out of the UK, but when you hear that studio production, the quality is just absolutely superb–it's a milestone in production.

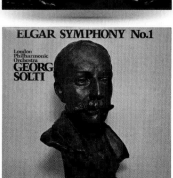

The London Philharmonic Orchestra/George Solti,
Elgar: Symphony No. 1

A group called Gentle Giant introduced me to classical music. Classical music had that aura of being old-fashioned and irrelevant to rock music But one of the guys gave me a cassette of Elgar ... and that was the beginning of me loving pretty well everything Elgar ever wrote and recorded. And led me to listen to Brahms and to many, many other classical composers. So I would say *Elgar: Symphony No.1* would be my favorite.

Mountain,
Nantucket Sleighride

I liked Leslie West, but more for his personality and his attitude and outlook on music. Mountain, and *Nantucket Sleighride*, were both truly great. Mountain were the first band that came out and we all made friends and travelled together a lot. They're just nice people, good people, playing good music, powerful music, and they had this great affinity on stage, this great rapport. And I learned that rapport and the togetherness that a band should have from them.

Paco De Lucia, Al Di Meola, John McLaughlin,
The Guitar Trio

Nylon string playing and stunning. Just virtuoso guitar playing. An amazing album. But having said that, I'm actually not sort of glued to guitar players and what they're doing, thinking, "Should I be like that?" In general I've always listened to other players as a reference. But it's not really going to change what I do. I see myself as a music writer. The guitar is a vehicle that I use, but it's the writing I really enjoy.

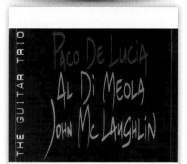

Jethro Tull, *Stand Up*

That was the music that changed Tull. They were a blues band, I joined, and we learned the music of *Stand Up*. And it was the success, both with the album and with the tour, playing that music, that kick-started Tull's career. And so that's the most important thing that ever happened to me, that album. It opened us up, first, to touring in America, and second, now 50-odd years on, my band is playing a lot of the music from *Stand Up*, and we're sort of relearning it and reinterpreting it. It's timeless. But historically, that was the album that made me be able to be a musician for the next 50 years.As to why we went in this new direction, I just think it's a realization that the blues was, at the time, a fad. Music changes. R&B, soul music, Tamla, folk music ... all these sort of fashion changes in music happened in England all the time. Everybody was playing the blues–but badly. Everybody was trying to do Albert King, Freddie King, B.B. King, but nowhere near the quality or the emotion that the American blues musicians were putting out. So I never wanted to be a part of that business of people cloning music and doing it, really, secondhand and badly. And Ian [Anderson] was the same. So we both, without really stating it, knew that it wasn't for us.

GERRY BECKLEY
AMERICA

Gerry Beckley (far left), Dan Peek and Dewey Bunnell of America on a BBC television show in1973. PHOTO BY DAVID WARNER ELLIS/REDFERNS

Founding member of the early '70s light folk-rock band America, Gerry Beckley is known for writing and singing hits like "I Need You," "Sister Golden Hair" and "Daisy Jane." Vocalists/guitarists Dewey Bunnell, Dan Peek and Beckley met while they were still in high school in the late '60s; all three were sons of U.S. Air Force officers stationed in the U.K. As America, the three released a string of hit albums and singles. Beckley grew up in a household surrounded by music. "My mom had the classics playing constantly in our home outside of London in the '50s," Beckley recalls. "She favored the romantics: Tchaikovsky, Rachmaninoff and Prokofiev. They were a wonderful early education about melody. 'Swan Lake' is probably my earliest memory of any music."

42

Lionel Bart, *Oliver! Original Soundtrack Recording*

My family would often attend musicals in London's Shaftesbury Avenue, London's Broadway. *Oliver!* has always been my favorite. Lionel Bart wrote the music and the lyrics, which is rare in stage productions. The songs are incredible– "Where Is Love" and "Who Will Buy"–but I love the whole score.

The Beach Boys, *Surfin' Safari*

This was the first album I personally bought with my own money. I transferred this album to 1/4" tape on our home hi-fi system and learned to play the guitar by starting and stopping the tape after each section of the songs. Dewey Bunnell and I became very close friends with all of The Beach Boys but probably the closest with our dear friend Carl Wilson, who was responsible for a lot of that guitar work.

The Beatles, *Meet the Beatles!*

When The Beatles came to the US in 1963, this album was the first we heard. The album recorded before this, called ***Introducing the Beatles***, came out about the same time but it was ***Meet the Beatles!*** that really changed my life. People probably tire of hearing just how big a deal it was but I'll never tire of the memory or of the music.

A son of a U.S. Air Force officer, Gerry Beckley grew up in a home filled with classical music. PHOTO BY MICHAEL PUTLAND/GETTY IMAGES

The Beatles, *A Hard Day's Night*

The Beatles were releasing numerous albums per year so it can be hard to fathom just how many great songs they were writing. I particularly love the songs from both of the films, **Help!** and **A Hard Day's Night**. I remember thinking that this was their turn towards a more acoustic approach in their writing. There was a lot of strumming on Gibson J-160s. I loved it.

The Beatles, *Help!*

Help!, compared to **A Hard Day's Night**, was a much sillier film but an equally great album. We've all read since that they were smoking pot through the entire production. Whatever they were doing, it worked.

The Beach Boys, *Pet Sounds*

Who doesn't think that this is one of the best albums of all time?! The leap that Brian Wilson made on this recording rewrote the rules and raised the bar… pick your own cliché. But I can tell you that popular music was never the same. From George Martin's quotes about how heavily it influenced The Beatles to Leonard Bernstein's own accolades upon hearing it, **Pet Sounds** was groundbreaking.

The Beatles, *Abbey Road*

I guess it's the ultimate summation, this album. We all know the stories. Dew and I had the honor multiple times to work with both George Martin and Geoff Emerick but it's still hard to wrap your head around the immensity of The Beatles. "And in the end…" well it was the end, but what a finale!

The Beach Boys, *Smiley Smile*

Most of us didn't hear even a rough assemblage of **Smile** until years later but what we did have was still wonderful. I personally think that what Brian and Van Dyke Parks were working on was, is and shall remain the high watermark of popular music in the 20th century. When we signed with Warner Bros. UK in 1971, Derek Taylor had on his office wall a large hand-inked, framed copy of the lyrics to "Surf's Up," including lines like "columnated ruins domino." We've never got close since.

Kate Bush, *Hounds of Love*

I had missed the phenom that was Kate Bush before this album. Fans of **Wuthering Heights**, please forgive me, but it was **Hounds of Love** that converted me. We were touring Australia at the time and from the opening bars of "Running Up That Hill," I listened to that album–and only that album–for the entire tour. It's a shining example of how good a concept album can be. I don't go to many live shows anymore but I truly regret missing her run of comeback shows in London recently.

yankee hotel foxtrot / wilco

Wilco, *Yankee Hotel Foxtrot*
There are so many great Wilco records but it's this one that I hold as a reminder that great music is still being made. Great tunes, great quirky production and the documentary, *I Am Trying to Break Your Heart* is equally good. I've only been to two shows other than our own in the last two years and they were both Wilco!

Gerry Beckley (left), Dan Peek and Dewey Bunnell, 1975. PHOTO BY MICHAEL PUTLAND/GETTY IMAGES

Gerry Beckley and Dewey Bunnell, 1972.
PHOTO BY GEMS/REDFERNS

BEV BEVAN
ELECTRIC LIGHT ORCHESTRA

A must-see in concert, ELO was inducted into the Rock and Roll Hall of Fame in 2017. PHOTO BY MICHAEL OCHS ARCHIVES/GETTY IMAGES

Birmingham, England, drummer Bev Bevan has had a long and distinguished career, opening for the Beatles July 5, 1963 with Denny Laine & the Diplomats before hitting the big time with England's beloved The Move. Then it was on to rock 'n' roll fame—and The Rock and Roll Hall of Fame—as part of the Electric Light Orchestra. Bevan played alongside Jeff Lynne for all the touring and all the albums, many of which went gold and platinum in the U.S. Inducted into the Hall of Fame in 2017, ELO created modern rock and pop songs with classical overtones. Bevan continues to record and play live, but amusingly, one of the things he will always be remembered for is his stint as touring drummer for Black Sabbath during the notorious and short-lived Ian Gillan era, banging out the songs from 1983's ***Born Again*** album, and, most fondly remembered by Bevan, "Heaven and Hell" from the 1980 album of the same name.

PHOTO BY MICHAEL OCHS ARCHIVES/GETTY IMAGES

The Everly Brothers, *A Date with the Everly Brothers*

This is their third or fourth album, when they moved to Warner Bros. from London. I love the harmonies, obviously. Warner Bros. had some terrific session musicians. I don't know if they were credited on the album; I don't think they did that back then. But I loved the drumming, I loved the drummer, and it was Hal Blaine, I think, mainly, who played drums on it. And that again was pretty inspiring. I was lucky enough a few years later, about '68, '69, the Everly Brothers came to my hometown, Birmingham, and they showed up at this nightclub. And myself and Roy Wood were in this club and they were

Elvis Presley, *Rock and Roll*

First album I ever bought, '57 or so. Up to that point, I hadn't the slightest interest in music at all; it was all middle-of-the-road, really. Well, "Heartbreak Hotel" was the first thing I heard and I went, wow! And it inspired me to go and buy the album. But it wasn't really rock 'n' roll; It was sort of more country rock. His voice, to begin with, was very high, really, and quite sweet. And when he started singing more rock 'n' roll, "Hound Dog" and that sort of stuff, he got a rougher sound. He, to me, was inspiring because I loved his music, I loved the way he dressed, the way he looked—everything, really.

our absolute heroes. We got talking to them and we ended up going onstage and jamming with them for about an hour. So that for me was like a dream come true, really.

Dusty Springfield, *Dusty in Memphis*

I think she's our best British female singer, maybe our best singer ever. I was lucky enough to meet her too, lovely lady. Tragically died way too young. But **Dusty in Memphis** is just a classic album. It's Dusty with all these fabulous American session players, in Memphis, and there's not a bad track on the album.

Various Artists, *A Christmas Gift for You*

Again, early influences, a bit of an odd one, but the Phil Spector Christmas album. The drumming on that is inspirational–it's so high in the mix, with lots of tambourine. And I was a real fan of Phil Spector's production, and this was the first album that I could buy where every track had been produced by him. It was a variety of different bands and singers but mainly I was listening to the drumming. And again, I think it was mainly Hal Blaine who played on that.

The Who, *My Generation*

These guys changed the landscape. I was a big Beatles fan, but these guys came along, and the drumming on it, I didn't think you could do that! Keith [Moon] was seemingly out of control but still holding it together. I got to know Keith–crazy, crazy character; a definite one-off (laughs). And not the greatest drummer technically by all means. He didn't keep time that well and I think John Entwistle held it together. But his drumming was just so exciting, even though a lot of tracks really sped up badly. But yeah, I think, between John and Pete Townshend, they kept it pretty much in time. But being in time is not that important as long as it doesn't go crazily out of time. But the fact that they held it together was unique for music.

Chicago, *Chicago V*

I had American influences, too, and probably my favorite American band was Chicago. And when ELO started touring in America, I remember I didn't get to see them for ages and ages. Danny Seraphine was the drummer, very light, jazzy, not like me at all, a very light touch, but a fabulous drummer. And the brass section was just out of this world. Something I've never really done in my career is work with a brass section. And if I ever did, I'd want to work with Chicago.

I finally got to see them when they came over to Birmingham and they played a big arena. And the sound wasn't that good, but they called everybody–2,000 or 3,000 people–to the front for a better atmosphere, and I think they were pretty surprised at the people who were there, how much we loved their music because we had bought their albums. I loved the complicated arrangements that they did, the way they went from one section of a song into another and I loved Peter Cetera's voice. They weren't the sort of band that would suit me to play in, but I would've loved to. I would've loved to sit in even for a couple of songs.

Led Zeppelin, *II*

"Whole Lotta Love," that opening riff still sends shivers down my spine. I would pick this album over the first one. John Bonham was a very good friend of mine, and before he joined Led Zeppelin, he used to come and watch me play. And I think at the time I was the loudest drummer around (laughs), certainly in the area we were growing up in. And I think he actually learned things from me to begin with. People loved our band, but the main criticism was the drummer was too loud. And I was loud. So I think if anything, John would've picked up on the power that I played with. This was pre-Keith Moon, sort of '63, '64, and most drummers just 'played with the wrists, really. They didn't put that much energy into it. I tended to hit the drums as hard as I could and that's what John did and his power became extraordinary.

The way John developed was just extraordinary. I would go and watch him play, usually from the backstage, almost behind him, watching what he was doing. What he could do with one foot pedal was absolutely extraordinary. He became the most influential heavy rock drummer probably of all time. And he was my pal. I'd go to his house and we'd jam together. At the time, Jason, his son, was only about 4 or 5 or so, and John had a little drum kit especially made for him, by Ludwig, I think, and the three of us would actually play together. I saw Jason a couple of years ago and we played again together and he's developed into an amazing drummer.

Robert [Plant] was the all-time rock god, wasn't he? The way he looked on stage, fantastic. Jimmy Page, some of the riffs are so original. Something like "Rock and Roll" is like out of time, and I'm thinking, how on earth can he come in with that guitar riff? And how can John Bonham follow what he's playing? And John Paul Jones too. Talk about a tight rhythm section. I recently reviewed the reissue of the soundtrack to ***The Song Remains the Same*** and I think that was their peak. I mean, what a live band they were.

Allman Brothers Band,
Beginnings

What influenced me particularly with this band was having the drums and percussion, and sometimes two drummers and percussion. And it's a fabulous sound. I've only recently started playing percussion myself on stage. There's a band that I'm with now called Quill, and there's a very good drummer in Quill, but between us, we get a really lovely groove going. So I'm really, really into all this massive percussion on stage. And I still listen to Allman Brothers tracks to see what their percussionist was doing because he and the drummer would just be so tight.

Drummer Bev Bevan with ELO mates Jeff Lynne and Roy Wood performing on the BBC program "Top Of The Pops" in 1972.
PHOTO BY MICHAEL PUTLAND/GETTY IMAGES

The Beatles, *With the Beatles*

I'm not going to say **With the Beatles** is their best album by a long shot, but they came along and changed rock 'n' roll music completely. For one thing, they wrote all their own songs. On the first album they do a lot of covers, but then as each album went along, they started writing, and by the time I think it was **Revolver**, everything was self-written. And that inspired so many people to write songs. People like Roy Wood would say you have to learn how to write your own songs; it wasn't good enough to do covers anymore. And the fact that we worked with them as well, Denny and I, and opened a show for them and got to meet them; they were such lovable Liverpudlians. It was a place called the Old Hill Plaza, and it was Beatlemania, and what an atmosphere. So I really liked them. And any new Beatles release, it was like you were waiting for it. People were queuing up to buy it, you know? That stuff doesn't happen anymore.

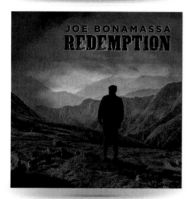

Joe Bonamassa, *Redemption*

I'm so obsessed with it. I do reviews for a local newspaper, and I was sent Joe Bonamassa's new album, **Redemption** and I was so… I mean, I love all his albums as well, but he seems to be getting better and better and better. I wrote such a fantastic review that his management guy got in touch with me, to thank me, and set up a couple of great seats to go and see him play. Seeing him live, playing his new material, and actually watching Anton Fig, his drummer… I think Anton Fig is now my favorite drummer after seeing them live. The album is just stunning. It's rock and blues, and I think the main influence in there is Led Zeppelin. I'd rank Joe as the best guitar player in the world right now.

BOZ BOORER
THE POLECATS/MORRISSEY

The Polecats in 1981 (from left): Phil Bloomberg, Tim Worman, Martin 'Boz' Boorer and Neil Rooney. PHOTO BY FIN COSTELLO/REDFERNS

Depending on which crowds you run with, English guitarist Martin James "Boz" Boorer is most renown for his esteemed and prolific authentic rockabilly act, The Polecats, in business since the late '70s. But in one of rock's cooler second lives, Boorer was hired on by Morrissey to tour the ex-Smiths crooner's 1991 solo album *Kill Uncle*. Moz and Boz have never looked back. Boorer has become not only the co-writer of so much kaleidoscopic and musicologist-level Morrissey solo material over the course of nine albums, but he's also become Moz's musical director, helping to make Morrissey not only an engaging, tough and guitary experience on record, but a juggernaut on stage as well. Boorer also has a clutch of fine solo albums to his name and has worked with Adam Ant, appearing as lone guitarist and co-writer on every track on Adam's *Wonderful* album of 1995.

After years of playing authentic rockabilly with The Polecats, Boz Boorer, shown here in 2008, effortlessly transitioned as guitarist with Morrissey. PHOTO BY RICHARD ECCLESTONE/REDFERNS

T. Rex, *Electric Warrior*

I loved the singles, "Get It On" and "Jeepster," and when I bought the album it had the lovely inner sleeve. And all the lyrics are on the back sleeve, which I couldn't understand from the songs. I loved every single track on it. This was glam rock, which at the age of nine years old I was infatuated with. I was a fan of music basically, but **Electric Warrior** basically made me want to be in a band, made me want to play the guitar. I didn't start playing guitar until about '74, which would have been a year or so later.

The Beatles, *The Beatles*

I learned all my chord sequences from the Beatles. And I had **The Beatles Complete** songbook and I would devour the Beatles albums and learn how to play the chords on every one. And I used to buy albums when I was at school off people in my class. I'd say, "Have you got any Beatles albums? I'll buy them off you." A buddy sold me his bad condition white album album for 50p. And it was a mono copy. I just think every song on it is a little rough around the edges, but there's things like the avant-garde "Revolution 9," the little short tracks, the backwards guitar on it, you know, the social comment of "Revolution" and the polished Beach Boys of "Back in the U.S.S.R.," the humming at the end of "I Will"—it's a great collection of songs.

The Faces, *Ooh La La*

This would be the next of the early albums, after hearing Rod Stewart live and with The Faces. There was only one single on the album, but I loved the track "Ooh La La," I loved "Borstal Boys," I loved "Silicone Grown." I thought it was a great mixture of fast, slow, sad, acoustic, rocky. It was good, and the sleeve had the funny face with the eyes that moved and the gatefold sleeve with the can-can dancer in it. I bought the Faces album because of what I'd seen with Rod Stewart. I had "Maggie May" on a single and I loved "Stay with Me," but it wasn't on the album. The Faces record is quite raggedy around the edges. It sounds as though it was recorded in a weekend and put together in the studio. Funny, looking back on it now, I didn't know that when I was a kid. I just loved the feel of the record.

Alice Cooper, *School's Out*

Well, opposite to The Faces would have been **School's Out** by Alice Cooper. It had the desk design as a sleeve and had a pair of panties that went 'round the record and again, I loved "School's Out" but I didn't have it on a single. And that was on the album with a different ending. And all the other tracks, they were more polished. They had brass on it and there was a kind of **West Side Story** feel to the whole record. So I was introduced to the album and when I played it and I liked every song on it; every song I thought was great. And the production by Bob Ezrin I thought was tremendous. That was another fascinating thing–a man called Alice. I'd seen him on Top of the Pops and he was getting loads of press with snakes and babies and he had dolls on stage and the shock horror effect of it was very impressionable to me as a ten-year-old.

Sex Pistols, *Never Mind the Bollocks, Here's the Sex Pistols*

I had the singles, but I raced to get that record when it came out. I learned to play all the songs on it. The sound on **Never Mind the Bollocks** was like a proper rock record, but it was a punk rock record. I liked every song on it–I still do. I still love all these records. Other than that for punk, I loved the first Buzzcocks album, but it wasn't that important to me where I would know every track. Maybe something like the **New Wave** compilation, the red one, with The Damned on it, Patti Smith, the New York Dolls. I could say the first New York Dolls album was quite important to me, with "Jet Boy" and "Trash." I was gonna say was Live at the Roxy London WC2 as well, because I loved Johnny Moped, who I think were the first punk band that I saw. That also had X-Ray Spex, Buzzcocks and Slaughter and the Dogs, who I loved and saw in '77. That version of "Boston Babies"… they never got better than that, that version that's on there.

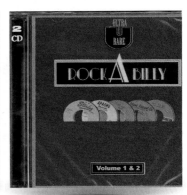

Siouxsie and the Banshees,
The Scream

This is Siouxsie and the Banshees' first record. It was a bit more avant-garde compared to the rock-ness of the Pistols, with the tom-tom drumming and the spiky hard guitar, some strange time signatures and really simple bass on it. The whooping vocal wasn't just singing a tune; it would slide around. For songs, again, there was social commentary and things I didn't know about. I'd never heard of Nietzsche and it's got a dedication to him on there. I went and saw the Banshees in '77 and I had all the John Peel sessions and I remember when John Peel first played the album, I taped it. I had it on cassette and then as soon as it was out in the shop I raced out and bought it and loved every song.

Elvis Presley, *The Sun Sessions*

I played a lot of rockabilly, and another album that I devoured and learned to play was **The Sun Sessions** by Elvis. That was as important to me as anything else. Other punk stuff and post-punk… I didn't really like bands like The Exploited or Cockney Rejects. It wasn't like first wave of punk, which wasn't so art school. Really, I stopped listening to a lot of chart music then and I got immersed more in rockabilly. And **The Sun Sessions** album, it was the birth of rockabilly, really. No drums. Bass, acoustic guitar and lead guitar. And the lead guitar was a perfect mixture of blues and country, with fingerpicking and blues licks as well. Expertly played by Scotty Moore. And I just felt as though I had to manage to play them all.

Various Artists, *Rare Rockabilly Volume 1*

Yes, one of the MCA compilations. That was full of Hank Garland. Well, I didn't know it was Hank Garland playing guitar, but he plays on a lot of the tracks. And that was the first time any of those songs had been released in England. Everyone had a cassette of that record and it was copied off the same cassette because in the middle of "Morse Code," you can hear in the background someone say, "Paul, Gerald's on the phone." Everyone's copy had that on it because we all copied it the same way. It must have been copied about 15 times. But all of those MCA rockabilly records were great. There was always a new rockabilly record coming out every month that would have new stuff on it. Well, new to us.

Rolling Stones, *Sticky Fingers*

I'd seen and bought "Brown Sugar" on a 45. When would that have been, '71? And I got it for Christmas I think from my granddad. The production on it is great right to the last drum beat. "Bitch" I thought was great. And then I learned to play "I Got the Blues." I was definitely listening to stuff and learning how to play it around that time. Again, an album where I love every track.

Tupelo Chain Sex,
What Is It

In terms of new rockabilly, it all came together when The Stray Cats came over. We'd been playing rockabilly for quite a long time, but it wasn't 'til they came and got lot of press and started selling out shows that enabled us to get a record contract for The Polecats. Also part of the revival was The Cramps–**Songs the Lords Taught Us**, 1980, was the perfect mix of rockabilly and punk for me. And then a couple years later, there was a band called Tupelo Chain Sex, that came from Los Angeles. Tupelo Joe Altruda was the bass player

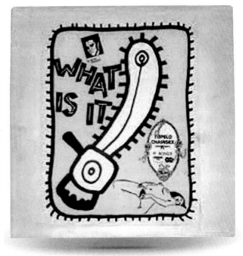

who later became the guitar player and Limey Dave Dahlson was the singer. And their first record, **What Is It**, is a great mixture of dark rockabilly, jazz, ska… really un-together but it has this great soul to it. Great playing and weird sounds, and that was very important to me. A friend sent that to me in the post. It's got a great bass sound on it and it's a lot of fun. They made four albums and I like them all, but that's the main one for me. When I first heard it, I thought it was an Elvis bootleg.

MICK BOX
URIAH HEEP

Uriah Heep at the London Music Festival 1973 (from left): Mick Box, David Byron, Lee Kerslake and Gary Thain. PHOTO BY MICHAEL PUTLAND/GETTY IMAGES

Mick Box, king of the wah-wah, has been the only member of British institution Uriah Heep that has been there since the first album back in 1970, a proto-heavy metal classic called *Very 'Eavy Very 'Umble* in the UK and just plain ol' *Uriah Heep* in America. But it was a couple years later, back in 1972 and 1973, that the band had their heyday, scoring three gold records in a row with *Demons and Wizards, The Magician's Birthday* and *Sweet Freedom* along with their well regarded double-live album from January of '73. Singer Bernie Shaw, nearly 30 years as Heep's circus leader, is widely regarded as one of the very best heritage act front men on the scene, and recent records like *Wake the Sleeper* and *Living the Dream* find the band shot full of energy, heaps of Hammond, washes of wah-wah and shots of the patented high-speed Heep shuffle.

Mick Box with Uriah Heep in 2016.
PHOTO BY HARRY HERD/REDFERNS

54

Jeff Beck, *Truth*

I always thought Jeff was on the cutting edge. Even when he was with the Yardbirds, you know, he's doing all the feedback stuff and he always had that… how can I explain it? There's people that play guitar that just wear the guitar and there's people that wear the guitar and it becomes part of them, and Jeff Beck's one of those guys. He's the complete guitar. It's just not an instrument on a body. He is the guitar; the guitar is him. And of course, he turned me on to the wah-wah, didn't he? Especially on the *Truth* album, he made it growl and talk. And I was thinking, wow, these are areas that I've never even considered. But when I first heard it, I went, "That's for me" and I got my trademark Jim Dunlop Cry Baby. It spoke to me that strongly. And of course with Rod Stewart singing, it was the greatest combination ever. He'd never sung better, in my view.

The Beatles, *Sgt. Pepper's Lonely Hearts Club Band*

That whole idea of it starting off as being a theme album, if you like, I think that's what got to me. The fact that it opened up almost as if you were opening up a show and then they took you through all the different avenues of music, with great crafted songs through to theatrical musical stuff almost and back again. It was just groundbreaking and has stood the test of time. And the playing on it was superb as well. I mean, George Harrison as a guitarist, not many people cite him up there, but he should be up there because it was just amazing what brought to the band.

The Crickets, *The Chirping Crickets*

Now Buddy Holly was a major influence on me. Great songs there: "Oh Boy!," "Not Fade Away," "Maybe Baby," "That'll Be the Day." I can remember the cover with the Fender Stratocaster on the front, the sunburst Stratocaster, and then you had the horn-rimmed glasses, and of course in those days we had The Shadows, where Hank Marvin had the horn-rimmed glasses. And I thought, wow, how can anybody be cool with glasses like that? At the end of the day he created something; there was something cool about the guy. And when I saw old footage of him playing, he had an energy about him that was really cool. And for the songs he was singing, he made you believe them–that was the important thing.

Eddie Cochran, *12 of His Biggest Hits*

Now Eddie Cochran, when he came along, he took the Buddy Holly thing further in my eyes, because he brought the rock into it. And he was the real deal and a super-talented guy, you know; he could play, he could play everything. When he was in the studio, I mean this is all hearsay of course, but from what I heard, in the studio he could go up to each musician and tell every one of them what to play. So he was super-talented apart from everything else. But he brought in some great rock songs. "C'mon Everybody" and "Summertime Blues" and all that stuff, "Somethin' Else" with that sort of attitude and fire in the belly. It was great–I think he bridged the gap between Buddy Holly and Elvis.

The Shadows, *The Shadows*

Hank Marvin was such a clean, melodic player, and apart from all the suits and the walking, the walk steps they used to do, all those things (laugh), he was just a class player, and a master of the echo and delays. He held you riveted to the guitar lines he was playing. And with the music they were creating as The Shadows–forget the Cliff Richard side of it–he was so exposed but he'd never let anyone down. He was always just spot-on every time. And that level of concentration and then managing to smile at the cameras and do his walk as well, that was quite something. Every player I knew had "Sleepwalk" in his repertoire.

The Small Faces, *From the Beginning*

The Small Faces was quite a thing. There was a TV program called "Ready Steady Go!" on Friday night, and they had all different bands on. And the Small Faces were on and I first heard [Steve] Marriott. I can't remember if it was "All or Nothing," which is on this album, the second album, but it was powerful song. And there was this little guy with a big white Gretsch that looked too big for him, and then the moves he had and the energy he came across with and then that voice. And then they had that Mod image, didn't they? With the haircuts and their clothes style and stuff. That was just amazing. I thought, wow, this guy's absolutely tremendous. In fact, funny enough, we played in London in a place that was actually a swimming pool. They put a board over the swimming pool and it became a concert hall. And we did, as The Stalkers, a show supporting the Small Faces. We were quite nervous, obviously. It was a big thing because the Small Faces were huge in those days. So I look 'round half-way through our set, and Steve Marriot's there giving us the thumbs up. It was one of those moments where it really encouraged you, a moment that lives with you forever.

Led Zeppelin, *I*

That to me was the extension of **Truth**. Jeff [Beck] was first and then Jimmy Page came in and created a bigger production. He just took it a bit further, I think. And of course Plant's vocals and you can't not mention John Bonham on drums; he was just immense, wasn't he? The drummer on **Truth**, Micky Waller, he had a great feel too, but Bonham came out and just put it between the eyes. I saw them in a tiny club in London and was right in front of that big bass drum of Bonham's all night.

Deep Purple, *Made in Japan*

Come on, that was one of the all-time great live rock albums, wasn't it? "Child in Time," what a great song. I mean, people say to us we had "July Morning" and Purple had "Child in Time." And Zeppelin's was "Stairway to Heaven," you know what I mean? Everyone had their big song. In fact, there's a live version somebody recorded in Germany of "Child in Time" where they just took it to another level. And Ritchie Blackmore's solo was amazing. He took a really extended solo and it was just an incredible. What a great song. And then Ian [Gillan]screaming over the top, and that great rhythm section, Roger Glover and Ian Paice.

And Jon Lord on that album was very exciting, wasn't he? He came from a sort of jazzy background, with The Artwoods. I remember seeing him in The Artwoods back in London before the Purple thing. But, you know, live with Purple, first of all, he started off very politely sitting down. Next minute he's standing up and rocking it and doing a whole Keith Emerson job on the organ. And he was just very exciting and got into it. And he was an equal player to Ritchie on the keyboard, is what I'm saying, so they were the perfect pair to trade off licks.

Vanilla Fudge, *Rock & Roll*

Certainly Vanilla Fudge, the ***Rock & Roll*** album. And what I loved about them was that they had everything but original songs (laughs). You know, they did all these great arrangement of other people's songs but not much original of their own, until later, really. But the template they created inspired us with Heep to get the Hammond organ and everything. Mark Stein was definitely gifted on the Hammond organ. And the voices, of course; you know, that vibrato is something that Heep got up to as well.

Box with Uriah Heep in 1970.

PHOTO BY FIN COSTELLO/REDFERNS

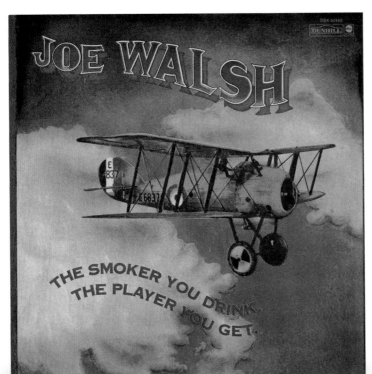

Joe Walsh, *The Smoker You Drink, the Player You Get*

Joe Walsh I loved from The James Gang, and the thing about this album is it's so organic. They sound like they're just in the studio, and they put the mics up–or even put one mic up in the middle room–and played it. You know, and that makes it great, along with the fact that it's got "Rocky Mountain Way." And the guitar sound he gets is just amazing. It sounds just so natural. And that's probably how they did it to be honest (laughs). He's such a laid-back, in-the-pocket player, but he plays everything right, if you know what I mean.

57

RICK BUCKLER
THE JAM

The Jam's Bruce Foxton (jumping in the air), Paul Weller and Rick Buckler in action circa 1975. PHOTO BY ERICA ECHENBERG/REDFERNS

When drummer Rick Buckler joined the England-based band The Jam in 1973, they were playing mostly local gigs in venues like working man's clubs. But through hard work and persistence, the band, which also included singer-guitarist Paul Weller and bassist Bruce Foxton, broke through and released their debut album *In the City* in 1977. From that point, the next six years for The Jam were packed with activity that included five more studio albums, many TV appearances and concerts all over the map from London to New York to Tokyo. Buckler's terrific and crisp drumming is highlighted on such Jam tracks as "Town Called Malice" and "The Modern World." While they could barely get noticed in the U.S., The Jam became genuine superstars in Britain, with an impressive string of Top Ten singles in the late '70s and early '80s. Following The Jam's breakup in December 1982, Buckler performed with the bands Time UK, The Gift and From the Jam.

PHOTO BY MICHAEL OCHS ARCHIVES/GETTY IMAGES

The Beatles, *A Hard Day's Night*
I heard this album when it first came out and it was given to my older brother as a Christmas present. He was playing it all the time while my twin brother and I played with our Scalextric set on the floor. The songs have stayed with me and always remind me of those days. Music–and more so, particular songs–always has the power to invoke memories.

Dr. Feelgood, *Down by the Jetty*
This band had such an influence on us. Wilko Johnson's style of guitar playing solved a problem for Paul–that you did not have to be a Ritchie Blackmore virtuoso to be a guitarist. They also reaffirmed that strong R&B songs and a straightforward approach could work for us

Deep Purple, *In Rock*
This came out when I was still at school. When I first started to play drums, I would always listen to the drummer of whatever band, and Ian Paice was an idol of mine when I was growing up and trying so hard to improve my skills. At times, it seemed to me to be an impossible task to try and be as inventive as he was. Nevertheless, I learned a great deal from just listening to him play.

The Beatles, *Revolver*
In my opinion, the best album The Beatles ever made. You just have to listen to it. If it's not in your collection, be very ashamed!

The Who, *Meaty Beaty Big and Bouncy*
This album is full of great, short and to-the-point songs. Storytelling songs in a very British style before they got into the "enormadome" (to quote Spinal Tap) mindset of later albums.

The Beach Boys, *Pet Sounds*
Again, this was an album I first heard from my older brother but I never really appreciated it until I was older. The production and recording ideas are just groundbreaking. Even today it stands out; fabulous vocals arrangements and I just love the songs. Although I have always disliked the front cover.

The Jimi Hendrix Experience,
Are You Experienced

Like most music-lovers, discovering new things was a pleasure. Especially when you found something like this. At first, I did not understand it. How could anything appear to be so free of structure yet so powerful? It still surprises me to this day!

Fleetwood Mac, *Rumours*

In 1977, the mantra in Britain was rebel against everything that had gone before. So to find an album that was full of great songs, all under five minutes long, an album that was sweeping America from a band only known to us at that time because of one song ("Albatross") was a wake-up call as we first went to America to tour. It was on every radio station along with songs from the newly released **Star Wars** film.

XTC, *Drums and Wires*

I always felt an affinity with XTC. They were not really a punk band and did not seem to rebel against anything, but they were very inventive and musically non-conforming to a still chart-based industry. One of Britain's great studio bands with strong production–and I loved the drumming!

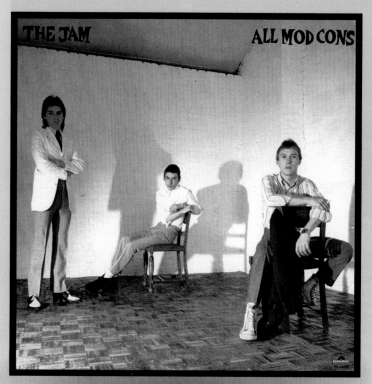

The Jam,
All Mod Cons

I have to put this in my list as it was a game-changer for us on the global market. More importantly, this was a studio album created by a predominantly live band. It was a coming of age in a modern recording studio. We had always approached recording in a live way, getting the instruments down and then overdubbing vocals, percussion, etc. But here it was stripped back to the drum track and we overdubbed nearly everything else.

Buckler with an exhibition of The Jam band photography, 2007.

PHOTO BY BEN STANSALL/GETTY IMAGES

CLEM BURKE
BLONDIE

Blondie in 1976 (from left): Gary Valentine, Clem Burke, Debbie Harry, Chris Stein and Jimmy Destri. PHOTO BY MICHAEL OCHS ARCHIVES/GETTY IMAGES

Fronted by the visually arresting Debbie Harry, Blondie became the most commercially successful band to emerge from the New York punk/new wave community of the late 1970s. During the late Seventies and early Eighties, Blondie had eight Top 40 hits, including four that went No. 1. As a founding member of Blondie, Clem Burke's massive percussive skills are on display on such Blondie tracks as "Dreaming," "One Way or Another," "Call Me" and "Heart of Glass." In addition to playing with Blondie, Burke has also drummed for Eurythmics, The Romantics, Ramones, Pete Townshend, Chequered Past, The Split Squad and The Empty Hearts, among others. In 2006, Burke was inducted into the Rock and Roll Hall of Fame as a member of Blondie. He received an honorary doctorate in 2011 from England's University of Gloucestershire after participating in an eight-year study on drumming. A documentary film about Burke, titled *My View: Clem Burke*, was directed by Philip Sansom and aired in the UK in 2018 and was selected for 2019's NYC Independent Film Festival.

62

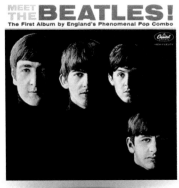

The Beatles, *Meet the Beatles!*

Like most musicians of my generation, seeing The Beatles' first appearance on The Ed Sullivan Show in February 1964 was the impetus for starting your own group. And I do personally feel I owe a tremendous debt to The Fab Four for a lifetime of musical inspiration. This record is actually their second album, named **With the Beatles** in the UK. But at the time, who knew? The Beatles were four individual rock 'n' roll stars with Ringo being one of the greatest drummers of all time!

The Rolling Stones, *England's Newest Hit Makers*

This album really made an impression. Like The Beatles' Vee Jay LP, it introduced a wide range of American R&B and rock 'n' roll to a new generation of listeners. Mostly cover songs, although the classic Jagger/Richards song "Tell Me" is included, it opened up my young mind to artists such as Muddy Waters, Buddy Holly and Rufus Thomas. To this day, this might actually be my favorite Rolling Stones LP.

The Four Seasons, *Golden Hits of the Four Seasons*

Before and after The Beatles, you had New Jersey's own The Four Seasons. This may be the first album I ever owned. The production, vocals and musicianship were all fantastic, and what great songs! Once The Beatles showed up, I remember there being endless arguments at school over who were the superior group! I've been trying to Google the drummer on all those early hits to no avail. Who is that amazing mystery man? With Blondie, we would sometimes cover their song "Big Man in Town." That was always fun, with Debbie boasting about one day being the big "man" in town!

The Beatles, *Introducing the Beatles*

What a fantastic surprise to realize The Beatles already had another album available in the States. Once again, who knew that this LP on Vee Jay Records was actually their first album in the UK, entitled **Please Please Me?** What a great discovery this was to have two Beatles albums available so soon after their first TV appearance! From the opening track "I Saw Her Standing There" to the closer "Twist and Shout," a truly amazing life-changing experience for this boy.

The Who, *My Generation*

Now this was something altogether different. As far as I'm concerned, The Who are the original punk rockers. "Hope I die before I get old," indeed. This heavily R&B-based debut really made a big impact on this young drummer. I remember bringing this record to my weekly drum lesson and trying to play along to the explosive ending of "My Generation" while my drum teacher's jaw was on the floor. To this day, I'm still trying to get that ending right. Thanks to Mr. Moon for showing me what to do on the drums and what not to do on the rock 'n' roll roller coaster of life.

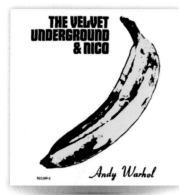

The Velvet Underground, *The Velvet Underground & Nico*

When I first met up with my partners in Blondie, one of the first things we bonded on was our love of The Velvets. Of course, the influence of the amazing Nico was not lost on us. In fact, one of the first songs we covered was "Femme Fatale" from this LP. Truly great songwriting from Lou Reed with his great sense for a pop song mixed with some very dark subjects. To this day, whenever I'm in a writing session, someone will inevitably say "Let's make it sound more like The Velvet Underground."

The Stooges, *The Stooges*

Actually both the first and second Stooges albums were tremendously influential and experimental in their own way. I really didn't know too many kids that were into The Stooges in 1969, only to find out later that four of them were the teenage Ramones who bonded over their mutual admiration for the band. Ron and Scott Asheton on guitar and drums, respectively, laid down the blueprint for the musical punk rock explosion of the mid '70s. As with the Velvets, their minimalist approach to their instruments, especially Scott "Rock Action" Asheton's Detroit deep rock 'n' roll groove, was a touchstone for future punk rockers. I don't how many times and with how many bands I've jammed with on "I Wanna Be Your Dog."

The addition of saxophone on the 1970 **Fun House** album took those crazy punk rock jams to a whole other place, especially on the extended lunacy of the song "Fun House." By the way, did I mention their lead singer? The irrepressible Iggy Pop, still going strong well into the 21st century. We can add Iggy to the cockroaches and Keith Richards' survival list!

David Bowie, *The Rise and Fall of Ziggy Stardust and the Spiders from Mars*

I quite possibly might have to say that of all the records I've mentioned so far, this David Bowie album was for me the most life-changing. David, for me, connected the dots and influences to all the things I was listening to at the time. The most important concert I ever attended was the Ziggy performance at Carnegie Hall on September 28, 1972. I was 17 and had just graduated high school. Talk about life-changing! It turns out that a few of my future CBGB cohorts were also in attendance, including Debbie Harry, Chris Stein, Joey Ramone and, oh yeah, Andy Warhol, too.

If the Beatles on Ed Sullivan in '64 seemed to have come from another planet, then David appeared to be from an entirely different solar system. The **Ziggy** album, to my mind, totally informed what was on the musical horizon with great songwriting, great musicianship and amazing otherworldly presentation. I would say you had to be there but in reality, who doesn't know how special David's time on this earth was for all of us?

Ramones, *Ramones*

From the very first time I saw the Ramones, I got it and I knew they were special. They are probably only second to The Beatles as the most influential rock 'n' roll group of all time! Having seen and shared bills with the band at numerous times prior to the release of their eponymous debut album, I knew what to expect and I wasn't disappointed. Producer Craig Leon's tight production is right on and what about those songs? The Ramones were a hybrid of The Stooges crossed with The Beach Boys mixed with The 1910 Fruitgum Company. Life-changing? Johnny, Joey, Dee Dee and Tommy changed the whole damn world!

Blondie in the empty pool of the Bel Air Sand Hotel in Los Angeles in 1977.
PHOTO BY SUZAN CARSON/MICHAEL OCHS ARCHIVES/GETTY IMAGES

Blondie, *Parallel Lines*

On a personal note, this record really did change my life. Although we had some success in Europe with our two previous albums, this is the one that got us to No. 1 in the USA with "Heart of Glass." The record was a worldwide success for a number of reasons. We had a new producer, two new band members and had just come off a six-month international tour. Our producer Mike Chapman had written and produced loads of hits in the UK/Euro market. Frank Infante and Nigel Harrison were seasoned pros and great players. All this came together to make an album full of international hit singles and an album that's in the *Rolling Stone* top 100 albums of all time!

FREDDY "BOOM BOOM" CANNON

Freddy Cannon and Dick Clark during one of Freddy's 110 appearances on "American Bandstand" circa 1960. PHOTO BY MICHAEL OCHS ARCHIVES/GETTY IMAGES

From the first guitar blast of "Tallahassee Lassie" in 1959, Freddy "Boom Boom" Cannon served notice he was a true rock 'n' roller, releasing one big blast from Boston after another. If he ever recorded a ballad, he kept it well hidden. He reached the Top 10 three times with his singles "Tallahassee Lassie," "Way Down Yonder in New Orleans" and "Palisades Park." Cannon registered a total of 23 singles on *Billboard's* Hot 100 chart and cracked the Top 40 on eight occasions. A crowd pleaser, he appeared on Dick Clark's "American Bandstand" 110 times, more than any other artist. Of note, he began listening to rock 'n' roll during the heyday of the 45, which accounts for the music he says changed his life as well as the compilation nature of his list.

Freddy Cannon, here in 2012, continues to tour.

PHOTO BY LARRY MARANO/GETTY IMAGES

Chuck Berry,
Chuck Berry Is on Top
Chuck was the greatest lyric writer. He could rhyme anything. I don't know how he did it with that many songs, but that's why he's a legend. To this day, I've never seen anyone else play lead, rhythm, sing and dance all at the same time. Who can do that? He was the ultimate rock 'n' roll artist. My favorites were "Roll Over Beethoven" and "Too Much Monkey Business."

Big Joe Turner,
The Best of Big Joe Turner
He was my idol along with Chuck Berry. I only knew of his singles. I worked at a record store in Revere, Mass., and the owner gave me the 45 "Shake, Rattle and Roll." I couldn't believe the sound on that record. That and "Flip, Flop and Fly." There was something about that sound. Whatever it was, it got me hoping and dreaming I'd get into the music business some day. It inspired me.

Jackie Wilson,
My Golden Favorites
"Reet Petite," "Lonely Teardrops"… he made some great dance records. He was one of the greatest live performers I've ever seen. I worked with him once for eight weeks, and he got three to five standing ovations every night. And he was one of the nicest people I've ever met.

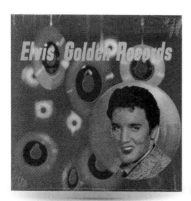

Elvis Presley,
Elvis' Golden Records
His early records, from 1955-56 to the beginning of the '60s… what talent. He had just three guys (Scotty Moore, guitar; Bill Black, bass; D.J. Fontana, drums) backing him, and they made such great, hot records, like "Jailhouse Rock," "That's All Right," "All Shook Up" and "Hound Dog." What an incredible artist. And it's like he never passed away. He's still around.

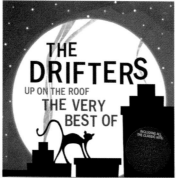

The Drifters, *Up on the Roof: The Very Best of the Drifters*
This was a great doo-wop group. I never worked with Clyde McPhatter, but I did work with Ben E. King, and "Stand by Me," which he did on his own, is one of my favorites. I loved all their songs. The black artists really knew how to make records. There wouldn't be anything today without them.

The Four Tops,
Greatest Hits
I have to put a Motown group in here, and the one that stands out the most for me is The Four Tops. Levi Stubbs was such a great singer, and he was such a nice guy backstage, talking with me. I love all the black acts and commend them all. We copied them.

Little Richard,
Here's Little Richard

He's one of those as well known as the national anthem. He just stands out. You mention his name and everyone knows who you're talking about. I worked with him a few times. He'd have 11, 12 guys on stage, play all his hits. Then he'd play them again with just him and his piano, and they sounded just as good. He could really play. If I had to pick a favorite, it would be "Long Tall Sally."

Fats Domino, *Fats Domino Sings Million Record Hits*

I worked with Fats, and here's something a lot of people don't know: He loves to cook. When he played, every song was a hit. There were no misses. He didn't even talk to the crowd. It was just one hit into the next. And then he would finish by pushing the piano across the stage with his stomach!

Jerry Lee Lewis, *Greatest Hits*

I loved "Great Balls of Fire" and "Drinking Wine Spo-Dee-O-Dee," but there was a song he did later that I absolutely loved more than any. I don't even think it was a hit. It was called "Boogie Woogie Man from Tennessee." I didn't like the movie they did on him. That wasn't him. He was friendlier toward me than anyone. Any time I worked with Jerry, he'd greet me with a big hug and invite me to come sit with him in his trailer, and we would talk and talk.

The Five Keys, *The Best of the Five Keys*

One of my favorite doo-wop groups. One of the favorites of my wife, Jeanette, and myself is "Close Your Eyes." They were so good, other groups admired them. There was something about that sound. I really liked "Ling Ting Tong" too.

Freddy Cannon, here in 1961, had three Top 10 hits and 23 singles on the *Billboard* charts.

PHOTO BY MICHAEL OCHS ARCHIVES/GETTY IMAGES

BUN E. CARLOS
CHEAP TRICK

Cheap Trick in 1977 (from left): Tom Petersson, Bun E. Carlos, Rick Nielsen and Robin Zander. PHOTO BY MICHAEL PUTLAND/GETTY IMAGES

Brad M. "Bun E." Carlos is the Keith Moon-type drum tornado who played the accountant-looking guy in Cheap Trick, the iconic Rockford, Illinois band formed in 1973. Cheap Trick burst into prominence with their 1979 triple platinum *At Budokan* live album, also doing brisk business with *Dream Police* and *Heaven Tonight*, which hatched their evergreen hit "Surrender." While lead guitarist Rick Nielsen played the clown and singer Robin Zander and bassist Tom Petersson both served as the band's heartthrobs, Carlos adopted the look of a bespectacled white-collar worker. But his playing was anything but: Carlos provided a sense of energy verging on chaos, that made the band's pop songs and hard-hitting rockers alike come alive like The Who. Cheap Trick saw second life when power ballad "The Flame" became a massive hit, sending 1988's *Lap of Luxury* platinum. The band was inducted into the Rock and Roll Hall of Fame in 2016. Carlos remains a dedicated record collector and musicologist with an encyclopaedic knowledge of '60s and '70s rock.

PHOTO BY RON POWNALL/CORBIS VIA GETTY IMAGES

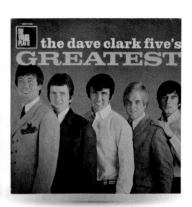

The Rolling Stones,
The Rolling Stones

Okay, the first will be the Stones' first album. When I was 13, in 1964, I bought mostly singles, and my parents got me a couple records for Christmas, this one and **12 x 5**, both of the Stones' first albums. I liked that they weren't the Beatles (laughs), and their stuff was a little harder rocking, and bluesier. And they looked cool, but all the bands looked cool back then. I saw them in '65 and '66 and '69. The Stones kind of peaked with **Exile On Main Street**, I thought, and those three, four records before that were highlights of mine for years.

The Beatles, *Meet the Beatles!*

The Beatles were always around. I bought their singles mostly until later in the '60s, and then I got the albums. But yeah, the Beatles were always there. "I Want to Hold Your Hand" was the very first song I heard. I remember being in the family station wagon and it coming on the radio and it was just like something completely different. I'd seen their picture in Life magazine in November 1963 and it was just like, those guys look weird, couple of them got big noses. They had those haircuts. I saw the first Ed Sullivan Show and I remember my mother going, "You know, you won't remember those guys in six months." And then she denied that the next 40 years. Yeah, I was hooked. I got some drums that summer, 1964. It was all over.

The Dave Clark Five,
Greatest Hits

I bought all the singles and bought all their albums. The killer one, of course, would be the first **Greatest Hits** album. The drums were featured on the records. And being a drummer, it made perfect sense to me. They always had big drum licks, snare drum licks and stuff. And they did good cover songs. When they didn't do originals, the cover songs were good ones. "Do You Love Me" and things like that. It was rocking stuff. And they were cool live too. The Beatles and the Stones were good rock bands, and the Dave Clark Five was a good rock band that featured a drummer. Yeah.

The Beach Boys, *Party!*

The first one I bought. I had an older brother and older sister who had Beach Boys records and I was already big fan. And I went down to the local store, and that was the brand-new record and I bought it, and it was really influential, just because it didn't have drums on it. It had acoustic guitars and stuff like that. So something different. And it was neat to hear all the cover tunes on there, "Barbara Ann" and Beatles tunes.

The Ventures,
On Stage Around the World

My first band was '66, so the next few influenced that. I know this all sounds like '64 and '65, but of course, the first half of them are because those are the first albums I got that I really just sat down and soaked in. The first concert I went to was The Ventures, and I had their album. It had some U.S. tracks, some Japan tracks, and they do "Wipe-Out" and "Walk Don't Run." Big influence too, of course, because of Mel Taylor, the drummer. He did the classic drum licks, like "Walk,

Don't Run," which was a big hit on the radio and "Slaughter on 10th Avenue," and the guitar player did a thing where they run their finger down the neck when they're picking. I know the Stones did that on like when they did "I'm Alright" by Bo Diddley and for "Mona" and stuff like that. And you'd hear other bands imitate those licks.

Cream, *Fresh Cream*

One word would be "Toad," the first long drum solo ever heard on a record. It was only five minutes long, but that was forever back then. And that got me into more of the three-piece stuff and it also got me more into vintage stuff. I started to go looking for all these blues tunes that are on the Stones and Cream albums, the original versions. The Stones took me back to Chuck Berry and Bo Diddley, and Cream, Skip James and Robert Johnson. Clapton was in John Mayall's band, and he had a Marshall with him, the four 12-inch speakers and a Les Paul, and that got all the guitar players going. It's like, what's this guitar sound? And Cream took it a step further. I saw them in March 1968 in Beloit, Wisconsin, right up the road, and when Clapton walked out on the stage, he had two stacks of Marshalls, and he walked up to them and turned them all the way up. And we were just like, "Oh boy, here we go."

Them, *Them*

The first album and of course the one after it. Loved "Gloria," but then also "Baby Please Don't Go" and "It's All Over Now, Baby Blue." I liked it because it reminded me of the Stones, but then as the years went on, I liked it because it was Van Morrison.

The Who, *My Generation*

I saw Rick Nielsen's band, The Grim Reapers, do "My Generation" and I went down to the store and dug the record out; that would be like '66, '67. Keith upped the ante for all the drummers. He played a lot and he played good and he played fast and the band was a great band. And you may notice by all these records, I'm a big "band" fan. I like bands. The front stuff on "Ain't That a Shame" I stole from Keith Moon, from "I Can See for Miles." And from The Who, I learned things about production. Like that song "I Can See for Miles," I remember listening to the stereo version, and it was a drum track on the right and it was an overdubbed cymbal and a snare drum on the left, and it was like, oh, a case of double drums.

The Jimi Hendrix Experience, *Are You Experienced*

In 1968–I totalled them up–I saw Hendrix four times, saw Cream three times, saw all these bands; would buy the records and then I'd go see them. And it would help me understand the record more or vice versa. And I would always bring a pen and paper and write the set list down. I started doing that when I was like 12 or 13. And it helped me remember the gigs. First song we heard was "Hey Joe" on KAAY from Little Rock, early '67 or late '66. It was a whole new sound, a whole new way of playing guitar. And the drumming was really active, behind the guitar. It took me a couple months to get into the record. When I first got it I liked "Hey Joe" but the rest of the stuff seemed a bit noisy. And after a couple of months it kind of became clear what he was doing, and I ended up being a total geek on Hendrix. Mitch Mitchell had five drums, while Ginger Baker had an extra bass drum. Mitch Mitchell on the first record sounds a lot like Keith Moon. I remember seeing something in **Crawdaddy** or one of the magazines and they went, you know, Keith Moon and Mitch Mitchell, you can almost swap them for each other. I remember thinking, yeah, that's kind of true. And then when I went and saw both of these guys later that year, it's like, no way, two *way* different guys.

Patto, *Hold Your Fire*

One prog album that kind of like made prog make a bucket of sense for me—which it never really did for before—was Patto's and the second album. Rick [Nielsen] brought it back from one of his trips to England, '71, '72; we just couldn't get enough of it. It was like Led Zeppelin with humor and with a little jazz thrown in. The guitar player was just unbelievably killer, the drummer, killer, and the singer, Mike Patto, was cool, like Roger Chapman or Bon Scott would later be. He had a good talking/screaming/singing voice. Just a massive influence on me when I was like 20 or 21.

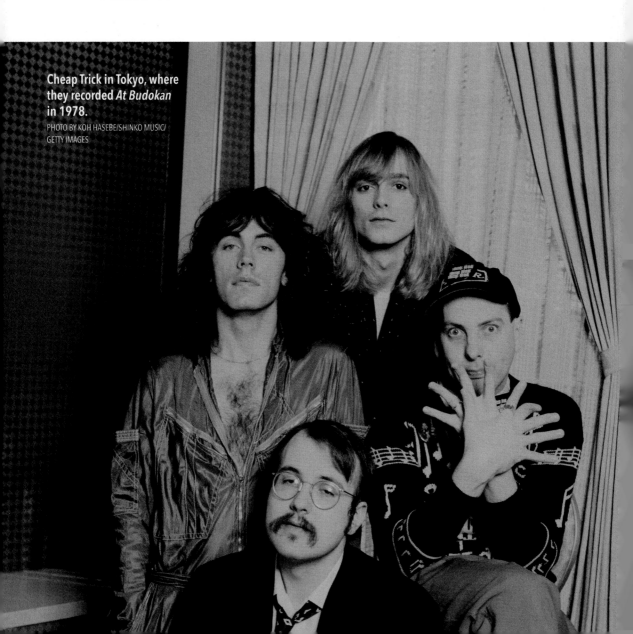

Cheap Trick in Tokyo, where they recorded *At Budokan* **in 1978.**

PHOTO BY KOH HASEBE/SHINKO MUSIC/ GETTY IMAGES

GERALD CASALE
DEVO

One of the more innovate new wave bands, Devo scored a massive hit with 1980's "Whip It," an MTV staple. PHOTO BY CHRIS WALTER/WIREIMAGE

Gerald "Jerry" Casale has been the bassist for Akron, Ohio, nuclear age punkers Devo since the band's Kent State incubated inception in 1972. He also sings and plays keyboards in the band, as did his brother Bob, who died in 2014. Devo entered public consciousness through their Brian Eno-produced, gold-certified debut album *Q: Are We Not Men? A: We Are Devo!*, which hatched underground hits in "Mongoloid," "Jocko Homo" and the band's herky-jerky cover of "(I Can't Get No) Satisfaction." It was, however, the band's third album, 1980's *Freedom of Choice*, that made Devo a brand, the record selling platinum through the radio play afforded synthpop anthem "Whip It" and to a lesser extent "Girl U Want."

Whether it was the "Energy Dome" red flowerpot hats of the *Freedom of Choice* era or the blindingly yellow PVC jumpsuits from the early days that commanded your attention (or perhaps the frenetic vocals of Mark Mothersbaugh, the David Byrne of the band), there's no question that for a couple years there, Devo were America's favorite nerd scientists of fearless and futuristic music-making.

Rolling Stones, *12 x 5*

Right around when I was 15 or 16, the Beatles and the Rolling Stones, exploded onto the American scene from the British invasion. In terms of actually paying attention to vinyl, I just came of age at that point, scraped my part-time job money together to buy vinyl LPs and put them on my little record player. So it was definitely for me the Rolling Stones. And it would be hard, the first seven records (laughs). Certain **12 x 5**, but also **Now!**, **Out of Our Heads**, **Between the Buttons**, everything up to **Their Satanic Majesties Request**. But I love their blues covers. Of course, they started out just covering classic American urban and rural blues. And white kids in America didn't know that, that the Rolling Stones were bringing us that. The next year when I entered college, I met people who knew a lot more than I did about the history of blues music, and that led me to buying the real blues records.

Bob Dylan, *Highway 61 Revisited*

I become aware of him just before I leave high school and the album is **Bringing It All Back Home**, and **Highway 61 Revisited** solidified that. He was a rock 'n' roll poet and the lyrics were just mind-blowing. Of course, **Bringing It All Back Home** is Dylan's manifesto, right?, where I'm going electric, I'm abandoning my folk credentials here. I'm gonna piss everybody off at the Newport Folk Festival. And so these were the first batch of songs that he did with Al Kooper and the new band and so it has a fantastic urgency and a consistency to it. But then he keeps going with that new thing into **Highway 61 Revisited**, and he gets more deep and more into the tapestry of different styles and tonalities. So I love **Highway 61**.

The Jimi Hendrix Experience, *Are You Experienced*

This was psychedelic acid-head blues and it was incredible, like nothing I'd ever heard. I saw him in 1967 in Cleveland, Ohio, and I saw The Cream the very next year. And those two records, Cream's first record, **Fresh Cream**, and Jimi Hendrix, **Are You Experienced**, we were off and running. This was all pre-Devo, but it's laying the groundwork for the expression we would find to be original.

James Brown, *I Got You (I Feel Good)*

I Feel Good was almost like listening to humans playing so tight that it seemed like it was sequencer lines in electronic music, except you got James Brown over the top instead of a European guy with an accent. It was powerful, and that dance-ability was fantastic. I mean, look, our album, **Freedom of Choice** only had, believe it or not, one song with a click track on it (laughs). The rest was Alan Myers acting like a machine. He played like a human metronome. In fact, when we had to redo "Whip It" for a parody version of it, we went back to the original tracks and we beat-mapped Alan Myers' drum parts off of the **Freedom of Choice** record masters. He varied, somewhere in the middle of the song. The song finished at the same BPM as it started. It was unbelievable. And that's because we revered James Brown and the Flames, and Alan Myers was as good as that.

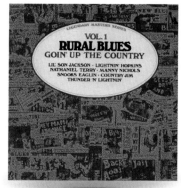

Various Artists, *Rural Blues: Vol. 1: Goin' Up the Country*

Vol. 1 and **Vol. 2** as well, and that was put out by Liberty Records. **Vol. 1** had obscure guys like Snooks Eaglin, Nathaniel Terry, and Country Jim but also Lightnin' Hopkins. **Vol. 2** had Boozoo Chavis and Slim Harpo. I'm hearing all this stuff and it's a revelation, definitely changed me. And I started copying that music. That's when I learned how to play bass guitar based on that. So that was my early passion.

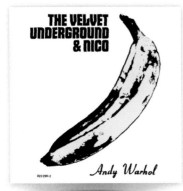

Velvet Underground, *The Velvet Underground & Nico*

Right after Bob Dylan, all hell breaks loose. I get Velvet Underground and Nico's first record, with the banana on the cover. That did it. That solidified it for me. It was completely just pure art. I mean, it sounded like noise at the time to most people. I recognized it was very carefully manicured noise, and really well recorded, really cool, and nothing sounded like it. They were basically psychedelic beatniks. And I wanted to be Lou Reed. I thought I was my own version of Lou Reed in my mind. And that inspired me to go beyond copying 1-4-5 blues progressions and start thinking creatively. Like, okay, let's make music for me. Like, what's *my* blues? What is my version of expressing my dissatisfaction with the world? And the Velvet Underground gave me a road map for that.

David Bowie, *Diamond Dogs*

In '73 and '74, I started collaborating and experimenting with Mark [Mothersbaugh], in a rudimentary way where the foundation for Devo, musically, was being formed. And we'd have these rules like you can't make a musical change unless you can justify it. You can't play the same lines as the other guy. Everything has to be interconnected and polyrhythmic. And it has to sound crude like a caveman making music, but with a spaceman mentality over the top. And about the time we were doing that, David Bowie comes out with **Ziggy Stardust** and then **Diamond Dogs**, and **Diamond Dogs** was actually, for me, much more influential. At that point, I'd not only bowed down to David Bowie, I was jealous, because he was so much beyond us. In other words, he was so far ahead of us, and he'd done so much more work and honed his aesthetic.

Diamond Dogs was my Bible. And the fact that then we would, by '77, be in direct talks with him and have him endorse us and want to produce us was just completely a life-changing thing–eventually it fell through and we worked with Brian Eno on that album. But here's your idol and now he's giving you his blessing. So that's validated you. And of course, a young artist who is still in a garage or basement needs validation. Any artist that says he doesn't care what people think, that's just bull. You don't really want to create in obscurity and in a vacuum forever. You're looking to connect with the culture and be validated.

Captain Beefheart, *Trout Mask Replica*

This album showed me true experimental freedom and innovation, and just unhinged, whacked-out creativity. Just played it over and over and over. And once again, that was another polarizing record. So all this stuff was revolutionary and polarizing. Certainly Velvet Underground was polarizing. Bob Dylan was polarizing–it's hard to understand that now. Early Rolling Stones was polarizing. Captain Beefheart, you know, separated the men from the boys. I mean, my God, Captain Beefheart is a singular, unique, unbelievable artist. You've never heard anything like it and you never will. And the musicianship and the interplay of sounds is insane. It's like jazz meets acid-head blues rock. And then Captain Beefheart's surreal lyrics put you in an alternate reality, basically. It was a lot to take in. In other words, **Trout Mask Replica** was like eating three or four meals in one sitting. But ultimately, it drove most people out of the room. But the creativity, that's what was inspiring. This was what was life-changing about him. Like, you can do this. If you think of something, you can do it. And you just have to get really good at doing it, figure out why you're doing it, and figure out a way to do it in another way that other people can possibly digest.

Ramones, *Ramones*

We were in the midst of doing what we were doing when that came out. We felt like, okay, now we're part of the zeitgeist–now is the time. And what they already had together, they had stripped everything down to the most fantastic minimalism. And the BPMs [Beats Per Minute] that they were playing at were defining what punk was about in America. I saw them in New York City when we were there. I was blown away by the professionalism, you know, where it's only the illusion of chaos or being rebellious. And really, they were well rehearsed and had their sound down, had the BPMs down, had the songs that were just riveting and catchy.

And I realized we had to up our game and take what we were doing to the next level of a professionalism. And it definitely changed the speeds we played at. But again, you felt like you were fellow travelers at that point. I didn't feel like I had to be a fan. I was being inspired and I was competitive. Devo is fully formed at that point. I was no longer listening as some kind of a fan or anything religiously. We were being inspired to be that good, as good as the Ramones, but stick with what we do.

Johann Sebastian Bach, *The Brandenburg Concertos*

I had this anthology of Johann Sebastian Bach, which was put out in the late '60s, a double record set, and I would just be transfixed listening to it at the time. Hypnotized. And it's basically pre-electronic electronic music. It's like listening to sequencer lines that are complex and melodic, right? And I listened to that over and over. So when Georgio Moroder came along, we were like, okay, we didn't see this dichotomy that a lot of people did. Like, oh, that's bullshit. That's disco or whatever they called it. You were either in that camp or rock 'n' roll. We didn't see it like that at all. And in short order, we were incorporating, not just synth parts, but synthesizer lines, sequencer lines, repetitive parts that we overdubbed onto our early records.

Devo co-founders Casale and Mark Mothersbaugh were art student pals at Kent State University in Ohio. PHOTO BY ED PERLSTEIN/REDFERNS/GETTY IMAGES

HARRY WAYNE "KC" CASEY
KC AND THE SUNSHINE BAND

MICHAEL OCHS ARCHIVES/GETTY IMAGES

Harry Wayne "KC" Casey is the face and driving force of one of America's most beloved disco and funk bands, KC and the Sunshine Band. Formed in Hialeah, Florida, in 1973, the band had hits with "That's the Way (I Like It)," "(Shake, Shake, Shake) Shake Your Booty," "I'm Your Boogie Man," "Keep It Comin' Love," "Get Down Tonight" and "Boogie Shoes." The band took its name by mashing up lead vocalist Casey's last name ("KC") and the "Sunshine Band" from KC's home state of Florida, the Sunshine State. While the Bee Gees may have dominated disco during the 1970s, KC & the Sunshine Band were not far behind. The group had six top 10 singles, five number one singles and one number two single on the Billboard Hot 100 chart. KC earned nine Grammy nominations and won three awards. Besides its music, the band was known for its interracial makeup. "I was raised in a gospel church and my mother loved R&B music," Casey said. "It was all I ever heard from a young age, growing up. Music is really a wonderful thing. It brings people together. I never looked at people as different; I saw them as different people, but not as different colors."

Three Dog Night,
Three Dog Night
Their vocal sound is so tight and fresh, and it also has so many great songs. Many nights were spent at one of my girlfriend's houses sitting in the dark with black lights on, listening to "One."

Blood, *Sweat & Tears*,
Blood, Sweat & Tears
David Clayton-Thomas had an amazingly soulful voice, and the brass and arrangements were like none other. They were the first group I ever saw live. My mother took me to their concert. I'll never forget that experience.

Pink Floyd,
The Dark Side of the Moon
The stereo sound and the concept were amazing. It is a great album to put on and just allow yourself to detach from reality.

LEE CHILD
NAKED BLUE

Author/musician Lee Child with Tom Cruise, star of *Jack Reacher: Never Go Back*. PHOTO BY JOSH BRASTED/GETTY IMAGES FOR PARAMOUNT PICTURES

Millions have enjoyed the Jack Reacher novels that author Lee Child has written for almost three decades. Now Child's creative force is also being directed into songwriting for the musical group Naked Blue. Naked Blue is a band moniker for the songwriting team of Jan and Scott Smith. The duo's seventh release, *Just the Clothes On My Back*, developed into a musical collaboration with Child, based on the author's iconic Jack Reacher character. Naked Blue's rootsy rock 'n' roll style (some would call it Americana nowadays) works seamlessly with the Lee Child's lyrics in each song on *Just the Clothes On My Back*. It's uncanny, really. According to Child, "Making this record was three things in one for me; first, intense fun with my friends Scott and Jen, who are two of the nicest people a guy could hope to meet; second, a fascinating peek at how creativity works in a different medium than my own; and third, it gives me an album I can listen to for the rest of my life and think, hey, wow, I had a part in this." The release of *Just the Clothes On My Back* happened to coincide with the publication of Child's 23rd Jack Reacher novel, *Past Tense*.

Various Artist, *Blues Anytime*
Vol. 1: An Anthology of
British Blues

Record albums were very expensive, and at first I couldn't afford them. I depended on the radio and ex-jukebox 45s. Then the label started selling "sampler" albums for not much more than the price of a single. This one had John Mayall, Eric Clapton and Jimmy Page, plus others. Finally I had music that I owned, in both senses of the word.

Iron Butterfly,
In-a-Gadda-da-Vida

The world wasn't linked back then like, it is now–strange stuff would filter in, like a secret. Someone's older brother would have a weird album he'd gotten from somewhere, like this one, with its long title track on side two. I loved it. It made anything seem possible.

Jefferson Airplane,
Surrealistic Pillow

The West Coast was a long way from Britain, but when I heard this, I wanted to go there, wherever it was. "Somebody to Love" is still one of the greatest songs ever, and "White Rabbit" one of the cleverest–no chorus, no repeated lines. Maybe the incipient writer inside me responded to it. Plus I was a teenager, and Grace Slick was really cute.

Cream, *Wheels of Fire*

In particular, I love the live half of this double, industrial-scale volume, with its long, long improvisations. I was entranced by the idea of three guys on stage in front of thousands, basically making it up as they went along. On the other hand, the solo on "Crossroads" is perfectly concise and to the point–a focused piece of musical narrative, like a great short story.

Led Zeppelin, *I*

Their first album arrived like a hydrogen bomb–loud and proud. It was tight and heavy, but also subtle and wildly exuberant. If a Martian came to visit and asked, "So, what exactly is rock music?," you'd give her this album. Or maybe Zep *II*. It's the perfect example of four musicians together adding up to about 11.

The Jimi Hendrix Experience,
Electric Ladyland

Was there a better year than 1968? Didn't seem possible at the time. Hendrix's masterpiece was on fire with scope and sophistication and wild, wild imagination. "All Along the Watchtower" is surely the best cover ever. Hard to believe all this came only five short years after the first sparks of Beatlemania.

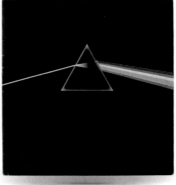

Mike Oldfield, *Tubular Bells*
This was out when I started college, and it was played constantly, for its hypnotic unravelling and its surreal humor, the perfect undergraduate record. When I listen to it even now, I immediately feel cold; it takes me back to freezing student accommodations in the North of England. It was empowering–some kid had recorded himself on a lot of instruments and made a record. Maybe we could do stuff too.

Pink Floyd, *The Dark Side of the Moon*
The other great album for my college years. Hundreds of hours were spent inside its lush soundscapes. Much weed was consumed. It was a fabulous album to have sex to–the idea was to keep it going until the fourth track, "The Great Gig in the Sky." Its sound was so hi-fi, that people would buy a new copy whenever they got a new stereo, as a test record. I have about eight copies myself.

Dido, *Dido Live*
I got this CD bundled with a DVD of Dido's 2004 gig at the Brixton Academy in London. I'm a big fan of her writing and singing, but it's her band that puts this album on the list. Presumably, they're halfway through a never-ending tour, but they rock and swing and groove with total joy and enthusiasm. They're playing like it's their last show ever. A great lesson–always do the best work you can.

Naked Blue with Lee Child, *Just the Clothes On My Back*

Maybe I shouldn't include this one, but hey, it's an album and it changed my life, because it's the first one I ever made. I wrote the lyrics and my friends Naked Blue wrote, performed and produced the music. It is mostly their album, so I can be objective enough to say it's really good. I put a lot of myself in the lyrics and it's amazing to hear them come back at me.

FAST EDDIE CLARKE
MOTÖRHEAD

Fast Eddie Clarke on stage at the Electric Circus, a nightclub in the East Village neighborhood of Manhattan, New York. PHOTO BY PAUL WELSH/REDFERNS

Fast Eddie Clarke (1950-2018) came to prominence in Motörhead. The records Motörhead did together—*Motörhead, Overkill, Bomber, Ace of Spades, No Sleep 'til Hammersmith and Iron Fist*—will live on in heavy metal lore as a bunch of the baddest ruff 'n' roll ever—barely contained on vinyl. But Clarke is also known for forming Fastway, an '80s supergroup that originally featured UFO bassist Pete Way and ex-Humble Pie drummer Jerry Shirley. Fastway scored a couple of hits with the hard-rockin' "Say What You Will" and "Easy Livin'" back in 1983. In 2012, Clarke got the band back together (this time with vocalist and bassist Toby Jepson) to release *Eat Dog Eat*, Fastway's first studio album since 1990. In April 2014, Clarke released the solo LP *Make My Day (Back to Blues)* on Secret Records. As for Motörhead, sadly, all three members of the classic lineup—Phil "Philthy Animal" Taylor, Lemmy Kilmister and Fast Eddie—are gone. Clarke died in 2018 at the age of 67.

Photo by Philip Dethlefs/picture alliance via Getty Images

Jeff Beck, *Truth*
This had a great lineup and some great moments on it. I think it is his best rock album. The later solo stuff, like **Blow by Blow**, was a different animal, and you had to be into guitar only, which I was not. I like vocals, so the solos have their place.

John Mayall, *Blues Breakers with Eric Clapton*
By the time this came out, I was well on my way with my guitar playing. I was lucky to see John Mayall live many times. This is how I wanted to play guitar and how I wanted it to sound. I played most of this album in my second band, Umble Blues. So sure, I guess in a way my roots are in the blues, which is probably why Lemmy and I got on so well writing songs.

The Jimi Hendrix Experience, *Are You Experienced*
I was blown away by this. The guitar playing was out of this world. I was still in the Eric Clapton camp, but you could not help but be influenced by this great album. I was lucky enough to have seen Jimi live three times in small venues. It really was something. So I always have to go back to Jimi Hendrix. "Purple Haze" for me, when he first did that, it blew me away, took me head off. These are the people I look up to, Jimi, Jeff Beck and Eric Clapton.

Deep Purple, *In Rock*
The guitar solos on this album are amazing, and every one of the tracks has its own signature guitar solo. The variation and themes of the solos helped me always try and make each solo unique. We had the first song with double bass all the way through, with "Overkill," but Ian Paice deserves credit for what he did on "Fireball. But Deep Purple, they never kicked in that way, the way we did it. The drums in those days were still a little bit back in the mix. And to have two bass drums at the center of the song was fucking brilliant. But these things, they come about just by accident. It's like Phil saying, 'Hey, let's do a song like this. It's got two bass drums.' Because he never had two bass drums before. We could never afford them, you see what I mean? It was little things like that that just added that bit of spark to do something a bit out of the ordinary.

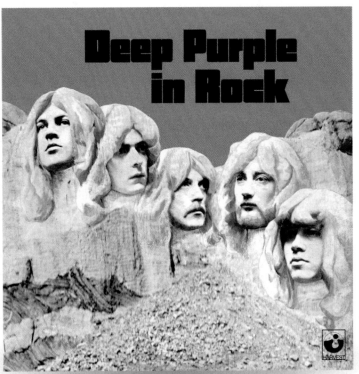

Classic Motörhead lineup in 1978: Phil "Philthy Animal" Taylor, Fast Eddie Clarke and Lemmy Kilmister.
PHOTO BY ESTATE OF KEITH MORRIS/REDFERNS

Cream, *Fresh Cream*

I had followed Eric Clapton to the ends of the earth with John Mayall, and the first Cream album didn't disappoint. I was at their first gig at the Windsor Jazz and Rock Festival and saw them many times. There were some great solos on that album. So I was a '60s guy really. I had come up on John Mayall, Eric Clapton, Jimi Hendrix, early Deep Purple, '69, '70, Led Zeppelin–that was my diet. Lemmy's was that with a little tad earlier, because he's a bit older than me. He had a little bit more of the rock 'n' roll thing–Buddy Holly–whereas where I came into it, I was listening to the Stones and the Yardbirds, Jeff Beck and Clapton

So we had these three tiers, really, like Lemmy going back to Little Richard, me starting at the Yardbirds, and then you had Phil starting five years later. So it was quite nice, because you had these three eras–that might've been one of the secrets: three sets of eras in one. Because of course eras in those days... nowadays, it wouldn't matter so much, but this was all happening so fast back then. Five years back in the late '50s and '60s, was a long time–a lot happened musically.

The Yardbirds, *Five Live Yardbirds*

This was the first album that drew my attention to lead guitar and also Eric Clapton.

I borrowed it off a friend's older brother and it became my bible. I played most of this album in my first band, The Bitter End, although we played mostly in our garage. So to qualify, I'm not really from the blues but from rhythm and blues, from the Yardbirds and all the local bands in England, really. I think of myself as a third generation blues player whereas people like the Stones and the Yardbirds are second generation, because they copied the old masters, as it were. I copied the Stones and the Yardbirds, so it's not from the root, you know? Heavy metal came along later. The album **Five Live Yardbirds** was quite rocky and has quite heavy shit going on in it, like build-ups and stuff like that. So I was brought up on that, and that was the start of heavy metal, really. Because they were all thrashing out a bit, and the volume was up. Lemmy always thought of us as sort of a rock band. I always thought of us as a metal band.

Led Zeppelin, *II*

When I heard this for the first time, I had just been told I had lost my gig. The solo in "Whole Lotta Love" haunts me to this day.

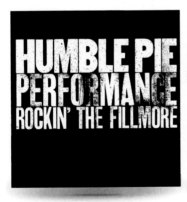

Humble Pie, *Performance Rockin' the Fillmore*

When I heard this for the first time, I thought to myself, "This is the best album ever," and whatever anyone may say or think, Peter Frampton is a very fine guitar player.

Santana, *Caravanserai*

Now this really surprised me. I loved it from day one and still play it regularly today. I loved the first two albums, but the third was a disappointment, so this was very welcome.

Joe Walsh, *So What*

I loved the way Joe Walsh found so much space. I was a big fan of the **Yer' Album** by the James Gang, but **So What** really struck a chord with me. Shortly after this, I joined Motörhead and the landscape completely changed.

DAVID CLAYTON-THOMAS
BLOOD, SWEAT & TEARS

Singer David Clayton-Thomas and Blood, Sweat & Tears at the Metropolitan Opera House in 1974. PHOTO BY STEVE MORLEY/REDFERNS

Second only to Chicago, Blood, Sweat & Tears were one of the biggest brass-based rock bands in music history, with their self-titled second album from 1968 certifying at four times platinum (and selling ten million copies worldwide), flanked by a clutch of gold records. David Clayton-Thomas was the legendary lead singer on the 1968 release ***Blood, Sweat & Tears***, which won a Grammy as Album of the Year. Clayton-Thomas was the voice on all the band's big hits through 1972, including "Spinning Wheel," "And When I Die" and "You Make Me So Very Happy." Indicative of the enduring nature of the band, their ***Greatest Hits*** album went on to sell seven million copies worldwide. Clayton-Thomas, a Canadian born in Surrey, England, was the son of a Canadian soldier and a musician mother. He was honored with a star on Canada's Walk of Fame and is an inductee in the Canadian Music Hall of Fame. Aside from his work with Blood, Sweat & Tears, Clayton-Thomas issued more than a dozen solo albums.

PHOTO BY STEVE MORLEY/REDFERNS

The Beatles, *Revolver*

The Beatles were considered a nice, middle-of-the-road pop kind of thing. And then I was walking down Avenue Road here in Toronto one afternoon and this sound was coming out of a club. I ran inside and I said, "What the hell is that?!" And they said it's the new Beatles album, **Revolver**. I went, oh my God, what are they doing? Really, that was a seminal point.

Albert King, *Born Under a Bad Sign*

The big song on this one was "The Hunter." Albert King, who I met several times during my life before he passed away, was always my favorite blues guitarist. He just had a tone and a sound and the songs were great. And you can listen to Cream and hear where Eric Clapton got his stuff from.

Jimmy Reed, *Jimmy Reed at Carnegie Hall*

This was probably the first album that I ever had that I learned every song from the album—double album set—from beginning to end. Just the best funky blues and roots blues ever. Great album.

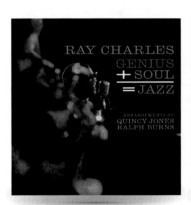

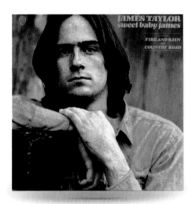

Ray Charles,
Genius + Soul = Jazz

This has to be one of the seminal albums for me. It was like 20 hits on that record (laughs). It was just amazing. Everything that came off that record was a hit single. Ray Charles I think is probably the most important person to my singing style. I idolized Ray and saw him every chance I got. To me he was the perfect blues singer.

Aretha Franklin, *I Never Loved a Man the Way I Love You*

Aretha's Atlantic sessions; this one or any of those, **Lady Soul** with "Natural Woman." They had Aretha pretty much singing kind of syrupy ballad stuff at Columbia. And Ahmet Ertegun came along and took her into Atlantic in New York and he took her down to FAME in Muscle Shoals and put her in the studio with a piano and some funky players and just let her go. And, you know, not a lot of strings, not a lot of orchestration, just Aretha. I thought this was a tremendous, tremendous album.

James Taylor, *Sweet Baby James*

James was another guy I knew. I used to hang out with him on Bleecker Street in New York City in the early days. I always thought he was a brilliant songwriter, beautiful lyricist. His lyrics were unpretentious and very, very honest. They weren't contrived at all and they weren't too wordy—they just flowed.

The Rolling Stones, *Exile on Main St.*

One of the great rock albums of all time. I opened for the Stones here in Toronto, at Maple Leaf Gardens before I joined Blood, Sweat & Tears, with my band, the Shays. So I got to meet them and we spoke the same language. It was the blues. And they were all blues-obsessed as I was. And I think ***Exile on Main St.*** really took them to another level. It was very raw, very real. You could tell that they were in the studio sittin' there playing it live. You could tell there was not a lot of overdubbing. You know, maybe some fixes here and there, but most of it was just played live off the floor. And I really got an appreciation for that band for the first time when I heard that, just as I was late to the Beatles, with ***Revolver***.

The Jimi Hendrix Experience,
Are You Experienced

Still one of my favorite albums; hugely influenced by Jimi. I knew him. We hung out together in New York. We had a lot of mutual friends. And I went to Electric Ladyland many times and watched them record in there. When he came back from England with the ***Are You Experienced*** album, it blew me completely away. His guitar solos were a complete sexual experience (laughs). And he was a decent singer, a blues singer. I don't think he was one of the great singers of all time, but he was Jimi. He was what he was. But that guitar. Oh my goodness. Nobody ever played like that before or since.

The Band, *Music from Big Pink*

When we're talking about writers, I have to put Robbie Robertson in here. Of course Dylan showed everybody that rock 'n' roll didn't have to be "Ooh baby, oo-ee (laughs); it didn't have to be cutesy-cutesy, "Wooly Bully" kind of lyrics. You could really make a statement and be very politically astute. He just touched an entire generation and hit it right on the money. Every single song was exactly what everybody was talking about in the coffee houses. ***Blonde on Blonde*** was a good one but I liked everything he did. And of course Lennon and McCartney, post-***Revolver***. John Lennon in particular.

But yeah, I would have to say I like the way Robbie Robertson writes, and that The Band's ***Music from Big Pink*** was one of the most important albums in my lifetime. I worked with these guys on Yonge Street. We played together in the Ronnie Hawkins band and so I knew them all. They were all personal friends. And when they came out with that album, I just loved it, particularly the songwriting.

The Rolling Stones,
Exile on Main St.

One of the great rock albums of all time. I opened for the Stones here in Toronto, at Maple Leaf Gardens before I joined Blood, Sweat & Tears, with my band, the Shays. So I got to meet them and we spoke the same language. It was the blues. And they were all blues-obsessed as I was. And I think ***Exile on Main St.*** really took them to another level. It was very raw, very real. You could tell that they were in the studio sittin' there playing it live. You could tell there was not a lot of overdubbing. You know, maybe some fixes here and there, but most of it was just played live off the floor. And I really got an appreciation for that band for the first time when I heard that, just as I was late to the Beatles, with ***Revolver***.

Blood, Sweat & Tears,
Blood, Sweat & Tears

I didn't really get into the horn band thing until I joined Blood, Sweat & Tears, and you could put the second Blood, Sweat & Tears album on the list if you want (laughs), if I'm not being too presumptuous. Of course that changed my life forever. Working with that band and those calibre of musicians, it was like going to college and learning music. I had to learn to read music for the first time to work with these guys. They were all very educated, most of them Julliard and Berkeley masters graduates. I know they've been credited with bringing horns into rock, but they didn't really do that. We didn't really do that. Ray Charles had horns. Little Richard, Fats Domino… they were all using big horn sections. But I think what Blood, Sweat & Tears brought in were sort of New York City, Basie, Ellington, Broadway show band kind of arrangements.

Blood, Sweat & Tears and David Clayton-Thomas (left) won a Grammy for Album of the Year in 1968.

PHOTO BY MICHAEL OCHS ARCHIVES/GETTY IMAGES

STEWART COPELAND
THE POLICE

The Police in 1983 (L-R): Sting, Stewart Copeland and Andy Summers. PHOTO BY ROB VERHORST/REDFERNS

Stewart Copeland is one of the industry's preeminent composers of music for TV, film and video games. But he'll always be most famous for being the drummer of The Police, duking it out creatively with Andy Summers and Sting, three strong writers jostling for position across the band's hallowed five albums. Such singles as "Roxanne," "Message in a Bottle," "Don't Stand So Close to Me," "Every Little Thing She Does Is Magic" and "Every Breath You Take" made superstars of the Police by 1983. Their final studio album, *Synchronicity* (1983), topped the American charts for 17 weeks. Stewart was inducted into the Rock and Roll Hall of Fame as a member of The Police in 2002, but he is also in the Modern Drummer Hall of Fame and has been ranked by *Rolling Stone* as the tenth greatest drummer of all time. Perhaps there is no higher praise than the fact that Rush drummer Neil Peart cites Copeland as a big influence on his playing in the late '70s through the mid-'80s.

PHOTO BY ETHAN MILLER/GETTY IMAGES

The Beatles, *Help!*

Let's start with *Help!*, although with *Help!*, there'd have to be Kinks' first album and the Stones' first album because they all kind of mushed together. But of those three, I'd have to put *Help!* on the top because it was the first album that I personally owned, even though the Stones and The Kinks were equally impactful. See, my favorite was the Kinks, but there wasn't a definitive album. "Tired of Waiting for You," "You Really Got Me"… they're just sort of spread out over several albums. I would have first heard those songs at the American Embassy Beach Club parties in Beirut or the British embassy beach parties.

Stones, my brother Ian had their first album and I listened a lot to that. That was kind of the talk on the playground when I was ten. Who's your favorite singer? Is it Elvis Presley? I mean, I wasn't into singers. I was into bands. There's this new concept called a band. It's not one guy; it's like four guys. And for me it was the Stones, The Beatles and the Kinks. The Kink soon jumped the shark. I never listened to another record after that period, although "Dedicated Follower of Fashion" was kinda cool. But I sort of lost the plot with The Kinks. The Stones also–I pretty much gleaned everything that I needed to know about what they had to offer on the first couple albums. And they deliver that perfectly 50 years later. You gotta give them props for that.

The Buddy Rich Big Band, *Big Swing Face*

This was important as an antidote by my father who was a jazz musician and raised me to be a jazz musician. I had discovered Sandy Nelson and it was all over. Sandy Nelson, my father said, "Hang on a minute, you've got to check out Buddy Rich." He was trying to steer me on the correct path for a musician not realizing that… a couple of things. First is he cured me of jazz for life. Second of all, that having been cured of jazz, I never went down that wrong path into obscurity. Which is why I'm not a teacher at Julliard today. Along with Buddy Rich would have to be Stan Kenton, Harry James, one or other of the Dorsey Brothers, for whom my father played trumpet and other wrong white big band jazz. But really it was Buddy Rich and his drums that just stood up beyond Louie Bellson, beyond Gene Krupa, all of them. And people will curse my name to hear that, because there are parts of them in all the above mentioned.

The Dave Brubeck Quartet, *Time Out*

I'd have to say the next one that actually changed my life was Dave Brubeck–of all people–*Time Out*. And the reason for that was just walking down the road with that music thrashing through my head. If it was in 7/8 time, it forced me to discover–or it induced the discovery–that if I kept walking, it would come back around (sings a beat) Wow! So the subdivision of rhythm… there's the different units that actually come around and do a circle again. You know, if you're walking in 2/4 or 4/4 time, rhythms will come back around, but odd ones like five or seven will put you on the upbeat every other bar–interesting! And so that kind of loosened up the relationship between four-on-the-floor and strange time signatures. And to note, Dave Brubeck is absolutely wrong jazz, except for "Take Five" which is absolutely one of the most *right* recordings ever made.

Maurice Ravel, Orchestre Des Concerts Lamoureux, Vladimir Golschmann, *Concert Ravel*

Meanwhile, my mother was just listening to her own music without any agenda, which was the 20th century composers, Stravinsky, Carl Orf, Debussy, Ravel–those really struck emotionally and really left a mark. I would sit in a darkened room and just listen to them. And, you know, at the age of seven, I could just see the music. I now realize the music that I was seeing was in fact the designs on the Persian carpets that she got before I was born in Isfahan as a diplomat's wife. "The Rites of Spring" are perfectly expressed in a Persian carpet, through those shapes, the combination of anarchy and structure. But I guess of all those I'd have to go with Ravel, and also Debussy, for that wash, that emotion. Unto to this day, I still have their scores on my desk because that's what I do now is write music for big orchestras stealing techniques from the masters, which is what every orchestral composer does just as a matter of education.

The Jimi Hendrix Experience,
Are You Experienced

Suddenly I was a teenager with raging hormones. Jimi Hendrix was there, Jimi was my daddy, and that was all there was to music. Everything else was laid waste and irrelevant. But then there was the mental struggle of, "Am I the guitarist or am I the drummer?," walking down the street with that music in my head. Am I fantasizing that that's me on guitar or is that me on drums? Both! Shouting out, "Oh God! Oh God! Is there any way I can do both?!"

I was a late developer, a skinny, scrawny little teenager with dreams of grandeur, but very much wishing that I was a giant 800-pound silverback. And Jimi Hendrix, the power of it, the passion of it, the anger of it, it made me feel like an 800-pound silverback. As in, "I may be a skinny little… but turn this motherfucker on!"

And Mitch Mitchell, I loved the fire. Mainly the fire. And the technique, which is weird because he's a weedy little guy. I suspect he got into the drums for the same reason I did: because he was a weedy little teenager. But man, he exploded on the drums. He had all the technique and I don't think there's another rock drummer that has matched his technique. John Bonham was a mountain, an incredibly important figure and people will hate me for not having him at the top, but Mitch Mitchell just had more chops going on. Ginger Baker was critical too. That thumpy sound, which is all about the tom toms. That was really powerful and empowering too for a skinny, you know, early teenager, but Mitch just had that sizzle. Also he was playing with Jimi Hendrix.

The Doors, *Strange Days*

Now I'm a teenager and I'm playing in bands but I'm still turning off the lights staring off into space, moving inside the music as just a soundscape and an emotional escape. And so The Doors served that purpose well. The beginning of "People Are Strange," with "People are strange when you're a stranger"… oh my God, I get all shivery even today, 50 years later, just thinking about it.

Leo Kottke, *6- and 12-String Guitar*

Then I went to college and discovered Leo Kottke and all of the beauty that can come from one instrument. It's about harmony and it's about the complexity of counterpoint. Now you'd think I would have gotten that from Stravinsky and Ravel, but actually just hearing music on one instrument really clarified where the actual notes are and how they add up and what they do when you add these ones. And, the first album, *6- and 12-String Guitar*, just had all these harmonic elements really plainly to see. And it was mostly feeling. At that stage, I didn't have the sensation of learning anything. It was just absorbing it and coming to an understanding of, wow, there's a lot you can do with cascading notes.

The Mahavishnu Orchestra, *The Inner Mounting Flame*

Then I almost took a wrong turn with Mahavishnu Orchestra. And fuck me, that first opening drum riff with Billy Cobham… I was the first kid on my block who could actually play that sucker. And all of my friends, many of my friends, were ruined by trying to play that and blew many a' session and got fired from many a' band by playing too much drums. I was that guy who should have been fired because of the inspiration of Billy Cobham, but fortunately I was dating the singer. So the band leader couldn't fire me. And by the way, I was strenuously trying to not have the singer fire the bandleader. Because then we would have all been on the street. And that was Curved Air and Sonja Kristina, the wonderful mother to three of my sons.

Steve Reich, *Drumming*

So I was a prog musician, of course. Sonja ordained me as a prog musician. I had the boots, the hair, the whole deal. I was a member of Curved Air for God's sake! I yam prog! But that was sort of what I did for a living–although I liked Yes and so on, that wasn't ever what I really listened to. The next thing I listened to, which was beyond prog, prog in the next universe, was Steve Reich. He was even beyond the uber-prog, I guess you could say. And so there's **Drumming**, and that with the other minimalists, Philip Glass and John Adams, that was another life-changing turning point where the structure of music is completely cast aside and a new way of doing it has arrived.

The Wailers, *Burnin'*

I was saved by Bob Marley and the Wailers. **Burnin'** was the album that I heard when I was a disc jockey at Berkeley, the station there, KALX. It was like a ten-watt or one-watt radio station. I was the guy listening to English music. Somehow reggae landed on my desk, as an English phenomenon. And wow, that's completely fucked-up. And listening to the drums, they're just backwards. How is he doing that? Why is he doing that?! Why is snare drum and kick both landing together on three?! Why would you do that?!

I realized that you couldn't do it without the bass and the guitar. The interdependence of those three elements was another kind of breakthrough that this doesn't work unless that's in place. And if that's in place, I don't have to do those things. I can do this other end of the rhythm and be counter to that. And the interlocking parts of a reggae–guitar, bass and drums–that was a big breakthrough. And by the way, I'm telling you all this really intellectually. But at the time I was just emotionally engaged by the music, and only in sober moments thinking exactly what the hell's going on there. As a musician, pretty much I've always been moved by emotion and fascinated by analysis.

Copeland and Sting (born Gordon Sumner) formed the Police in 1977, with Summers joining shortly after. PHOTO BY MICHAEL PUTLAND/GETTY IMAGES

DAVID COVERDALE
DEEP PURPLE / WHITESNAKE/

Whitesnake in 1987 (L-R): Vivian Campbell, Tommy Aldridge, Adrian Vandenberg, David Coverdale and Rudy Sarzo. PHOTO BY GEORGE ROSE/GETTY IMAGES

Northern soul greenhorn and aspiring haberdasher, David Coverdale's life changed the minute he was named to replace Ian Gillan in one of the biggest bands on the planet circa the mid '70s. With Deep Purple, Coverdale would record *Stormbringer, Come Taste the Band, Made in Europe* and most pertinently, *Burn*, his debut with the band, one of classic hard rock's finest records. Incredibly, post-Purple, Coverdale would go on to even greater commercial heights fronting Whitesnake. With Whitesanke, Coverdale established himself as one of hard rock's finest vocalists with 1980's *Ready an' Willing* and the 1984 commercial breakout, *Slide It In*. The band's self-titled 1987 album sold 12 million copies worldwide on the strength of "Here I Go Again" and "Crying in the Rain" (both re-recordings), plus "Still of the Night," which features what some consider one of the greatest guitar riffs of all time. Inducted into the Rock and Roll Hall of Fame in 2016 as a member of Deep Purple, Coverdale still records and tours regularly.

SATISFACTION 10 ALBUMS THAT CHANGED MY LIFE • 93

The Academy of St. Martins-in-the-fields, *Sir Neville Marrner,*
Mozart: The Early Symphonies

Especially "Symphony No. 11," but any Mozart. That's one thing my love of classical music gives me. I arrange symphonically a lot of times. A lot of people won't be aware of that. One of my guitarists, Joel Hoekstra, is such a master musician and he's totally aware. Most rock songs are what you would call concertos, three movements with a solo, you know? Whereas symphonies are four movements, with the solo. And if you look at a lot of the epic Whitesnake songs, there's usually four parts to the songs, or at least the ones that have independent hooks or dig a bit deeper or change colour or tone.

Bob Dylan, *Bob Dylan*

Bob Dylan, Bob Dylan, Bob Dylan, Bob Dylan! (laughs). Oh, for fuck sakes, that's some real poetry. I was an art student. I trained to be a teacher and a graphic design artist. And so Dylan was played in the '60s. Are you kidding? He was our first poster boy for… well, you know, we weren't really activists, but nuclear arms protests, stuff like that. He just resonated with me. And not a lot of people rate Bob Dylan as a singer, but I do. It's the same with a lot of the early blues, country blues people. Very difficult for young ears to hear, but that certainly never was that way with me. When I first heard Lead Belly in those Alan Lomax field recordings, it just made the hairs of my neck stand on end. I don't know whether it's past life connections that light up little synapses or whatever, but that's what this music did to me.

Miles Davis, *Kind of Blue*

Miles Davis taught me to caress, not just grab. So much rock is aggressive and rough, darling (laughs). So, you know, Miles Davis whispered in my ear on that record, which is definitely a desert island disc.

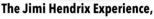

The Pretty Things,
The Pretty Things

Actually, we were blues snobs. I was more Pretty Things and Yardbirds than pop. In the North of England, we were very aware of some of the familiar blues songs that bands like Zeppelin would do, or Peter Green's Fleetwood Mac, Cream, Bluesbreakers. So Muddy Waters, Sonny Boy Williamson, Buddy Guy, Willie Dixon, who Pretty Things cover here… it's very interesting. And Jimmy Page and I spoke about that when we worked together. The first thing he heard that blew his mind was "Baby Let's Play House" by Elvis, Scotty Moore on guitar. And that's when he knew this is what he wanted to do. In essence, we're all magpies. We see something shiny that we like and we take that back to the nest, you know? But Pretty Things were just mind-blowing, and their songs were very Chuck Berry, who they also cover here.

The Jimi Hendrix Experience,
Are You Experienced

Hendrix is definitely a muse to me. He harnessed soul, blues, rock, sex, and you know, that was basically the blueprint of any Whitesnake song. That's what, for me, Hendrix was the most successful at. And then taking it another step further. Even though I know there's an enormous amount of Buddy Guy and Albert King in his playing, just the way he packaged it all together–breathtaking. I still have it playing in my car; it's my favourite things from that time. I saw Hendrix when I was 15, and that's when I thought, I think I'll concentrate on singing (laughs).

Coverdale is that rare performer who experienced
fame with two bands, Deep Purple and Whitesnake.
PHOTO BY FIN COSTELLO/REDFERNS

The Temptations, *Greatest Hits*

You know, as I said earlier, we're all magpies. I try to think of it as, you put all the stuff into the blender, run the blender and spit it out and hopefully you get something that is in your voice. So all my stuff, if you take some of the pounding drums and the guitars out of there, and stick Four Tops on, you know, "Always & Forever" could be a Temptations song, from the new album. I'm very much inspired by the Stax Volt '60s and Tamla Motown '60s. Huge, as well, of course, is Chess Records, all of these things.

So yes, soul music—Stax and Tamla was the underground music when I was growing up, when I was a student and started in bands. I loved Otis Redding's first album, Aretha Franklin's first album.

The Rolling Stones,

Sticky Fingers

A girlfriend got me into the Beatles, but for some reason, I was drawn to the grittier stuff, the early Stones. I love Chuck Berry, so the Stones doing that stuff, they did it more convincingly than the Beatles, I thought. Now while I think Brian Jones was an amazing catalyst, God rest his soul, in that time, once Mick and Keith were forced into a corner to write, it was the beginning of one of the most potent, juicy—still—writing teams in the world, well up there with Lennon and McCartney. Just marvelous stuff. And I suppose more than anything, the reason that I love this stuff is hearing these bands harness their influences.

Yardbirds, *Five Live Yardbirds*

A bit of a musicologist, I was (laughs), I was more into the Yardbirds and other blues things. I would always be looking where the record was pressed, not that I knew what it meant. And I wanted to see who wrote the songs. And I'd see, okay, well, all of the Yardbirds names are there—who is Elias McDaniel? And then you find out that's Bo Diddley. They didn't have the Internet at that time. It was cave drawings for me at that time (laughs).

The Beatles, *Beatles for Sale*

I came to the Beatles after seeing Shea Stadium, broadcast on, probably black and white, BBC television. And it was just overwhelming; and the second time I had that experience was watching Woodstock. It was just like, oh my God, all these people love this kind of music. I had a girlfriend who I was with that time, who would play me **Beatles for Sale** and I think *Revolver*. And that was the beginning of an adoration, playing them and admiring them. And I got to meet George quite a lot, actually, in later years. And he gave me an amazing guitar, which I still have, and have written a lot of the Whitesnake songs on. As much as I love the Beatles, I hear more related to American girl groups of the '60s in their early songs. Their arranging was very much like The Chiffons. A lot of the early Beatles I think were influenced by The Crystals, The Ronettes, all that stuff.

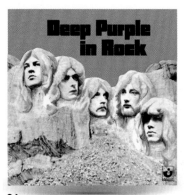

Deep Purple, *In Rock*

I can remember thinking, "Wring That Neck" (laughs), which is one of their early things, was really cool. The thing I got with them first was the singles, because suddenly they started having hits, when the Mk II came together, with "Black Night" and "Strange Kind of Woman." "Strange Kind of Woman" was the only Deep Purple song I sang at my audition, and I sung it in a more bluesy way, and Ritchie actually came up to me and said, "That's exactly how I heard it when I was writing it." But I actually didn't hear a Deep Purple album until a couple days before my actual audition. I said to myself, you'd better learn something! But *In Rock*, I still think is a classic rock album—and it was initiated by Ritchie. Because the first album Roger and Ian did was **Concerto for Group and Orchestra**. So everywhere they were going, Ritchie told me, the promoters are going, "Where's the orchestra?" So he was particularly pissed, as you could imagine. And he said, if we don't do a straight rock record, I'm out of here. And that's what we have to thank him for—that fabulous pivot into an incendiary rock band.

KEVIN CRONIN
REO SPEEDWAGON

With Kevin Cronin as lead vocalist and rhythm guitarist, REO Speedwagon experienced their greatest success, most notably with 1980's **Hi Infidelity**, which featured four U.S. Top 40 hits and sold more than 10 million copies. On the strength of the hit singles "Keep on Loving You" and "Take It On the Run," the album remained on the charts for 65 weeks, 32 of which were spent in the top ten, including 15 weeks atop the **Billboard 200**. Growing up in the Chicago suburbs, Cronin first joined REO in 1972 but left after one album. He rejoined the band in 1976, helping to kick-start the REO's hit parade. Cronin has written or co-written many of the band's biggest hits, including "Keep on Loving You," "Can't Fight This Feeling," "I Do' Wanna Know," "Keep Pushin'," "Roll With the Changes," "Time for Me to Fly," "Here With Me," "In My Dreams," and "Don't Let Him Go." Cronin started playing guitar because his parents wouldn't let him have a drum set. "I was in sixth grade," Cronin says, "and my dad said the guitar was the perfect instrument because I could take it with me to parties. I guess he was right."

REO Speedwagon, 1981: Neal Doughty, Alan Gratzer, Gary Richrath, Kevin Cronin and Bruce Hall.

PHOTO BY MICHAEL MARKS/MICHAEL OCHS ARCHIVES/GETTY IMAGES

Elton John, *Madman Across the Water*
Singing, songwriting, arrangements, this album has it all. "Holiday Inn," which opens side two, is the song that got me the gig in REO.

The Beatles, *Rubber Soul*
This was the first album I ever owned. I am partial to the US version, which opens with "I've Just Seen a Face," a song I still love to play. The second cut, "Norwegian Wood" has perhaps the best opening line in rock history: "I once had a girl, or should I say, she once had me."

Sting,
The Dream of the Blue Turtles
I had been a fan of all four Police albums, so I was skeptical about a Sting solo project. When I heard this record, I ditched my solo career.

DENNIS DEYOUNG
STYX

Styx (L-R): Chuck Panozzo, John Panozzo, Tommy Shaw, James "JY" Young and Dennis DeYoung. PHOTO BY WARING ABBOTT/GETTY IMAGES

Dennis DeYoung is a founding member and key visionary of Styx, who hit it big time with a string of arena rockers and power ballads through the late 1970s and 1980s. Sharing lead vocals with Tommy Shaw and James "JY" Young, DeYoung is also the band's keyboardist and writer of some of the band's biggest hits, in fact, seven of the band's eight Billboard Top Ten singles were written by DeYoung. After 15 years with the band, DeYoung went solo, recording and touring and reminding tens of thousands of fans about his band's impressive run of five platinum albums in a row, four of them multi-platinum. "Come Sail Away," "Suite Madame Blue," "Lady," "The Best of Times," "Mr. Roboto"... these songs are part of the pop culture and rock 'n' roll fabric, and classic rock fans have Dennis DeYoung to thank for them.

Various Artists, *RCA: 60 Years of Music America Loves Best: Vol. 1*

This was important because I was 11 years old and I had no ambitions of being a professional musician and I just loved music. In the Sunday newspaper supplement they would advertise all these records for like a penny or whatever it was, RCA Record Club. But the catch was that then you had to buy an album from them every every month or something. And so they got you on the back end. But as a young person I didn't know that. I just wanted to get some music in my house. And at this time when I was 11, in '58 or so, rock 'n' roll was brand new and I just bought that album not having any clue what it was. And when I got it, I just listened. I didn't even know what I had gotten. And there was this myriad of musical styles only recorded by RCA artists. I listened to this record and there it was, from jazz to classical, the hit parade, everything. And it just made me curious about music in all its permutations.

The Beatles, *The Beatles' Second Album*

First of all, okay, I didn't buy **Meet the Beatles!**. My friend Dave, he had Beatle boots and I had heard "The Beatles are coming! The Beatles are coming!" and I guess I was one of those people resistant to hype. Because the first song they released was "I Want to Hold Your Hand." Didn't like it then; I don't like it now. It wasn't a favorite of mine. If they'd released "She Loves You" or "All My Loving" or any of those things, they would have had me. But it was "I Wanna Hold Your Hand." It was the only song I really heard.

And then Dave and I, we were going to a Sunday night dance, the same dance that I would go to two weeks later and meet my wife. And so I listened. I said, okay, let's go to the dance. No, he's got to see Ed Sullivan [and The Beatles]. We were standing in my mother's kitchen watching it. It came on and then my life was changed. Just like that. Isn't it funny? It was like somebody turned on a light switch, or opened the window and the spring air came in. It was that for millions and countless musicians of my era who saw it. But when I formed the band, when John and Chuck Panozzo and I got together in '62, I didn't know that. There was no such thing as rock bands. And seeing that, I said, "Anything's possible." My friend, Dave, had "Meet the Beatles," but I didn't become a fan until Ed Sullivan, night one. After that, and until this day, they have been the greatest influence on me. The Beatles held no songwriting boundaries – much like that RCA album above.

The Animals, *The Best of the Animals*

I didn't like "House of the Rising Sun." Now I do. I didn't like it then, but I was in college and I went to see them, my first concert. They played in this little area in like a cafeteria almost, at the University of Illinois where I was going to school. I studied, of all things, journalism. I was blown away and I went and bought **The Best of the Animals** and I love, love, love their music. It was completely different from the Beatles, and I never liked the Rolling Stones. I know when I say that, all I do is open myself up to millions of people saying I'm a douche-nozzle. I appreciate the Rolling Stones' songwriting as probably the best rock 'n' roll songwriting duo in rock 'n' roll or blues-based rock 'n' roll that's ever existed. But no offense to Mick: I get it, but I wasn't a fan of the singing. But I liked Eric Burdon's singing and music and songwriting fine. Music is, by and large, singers and songwriters. That's it, baby. First, singer, second, music–and I just loved Eric Burdon's singing.

The Beatles, *Rubber Soul*

I said goodbye Beatlemania, hello future. I mean, the first listen to **Rubber Soul**, I thought that, you know, these guys, they screwed up. They went and they broke the mirror and now we see the other side–they screwed everything up. Beatlemania–what happened?! **Hard Day's Night** and then suddenly it's "Norwegian Wood." I listened to it like four or five times and I realized it was the future and I better get on board, and I did. Whether this period–**Rubber Soul**, **Revolver**–marks the rise of George or not, truth be told, I was not into the investigation of how the stew was made. I was listening to the songs and sometimes… because a lot of the time John and George and then John and Paul would sing. They would double the melody line. And for a while, on some records, I couldn't figure out which guys were really singing. But I'm not into awarding prizes to those people who are breaking out. "Oh look, there's George." No, it was the group; it was not the individuals. It was the group. But you listen to those two records, **Rubber Soul** and **Revolver**, and you go, well geez, how about that?

DENNIS DEYOUNG // **STYX**

Yes, *The Yes Album*

JY had just joined the band and we started playing on stage live, before *The Yes Album*, they did that Richie Havens song, "No Opportunity Necessary, No Experience Needed." We did that live. I played that on an organ, just like they did when they played it live without the orchestra. And then when *The Yes Album* came out we went, oh wow. "All Good People." You know what I mean? And of course "Lucky Man," because Emerson influenced my synth playing forever. Genesis… we opened for them at the Aragon Ballroom when Peter Gabriel was wearing the white face makeup thing. I watched them. I thought, wow, what was that?! You know, it was something. I think the first album I had was *The Lamb Lies Down on Broadway*, then I went back and bought *Trespass* and then of course *Selling England*. We were already making records before I heard them. Still, I guess *The Yes Album* would it be included in there, 1970, when we're formulating what kind of a band are we gonna be. Because when we did cover tunes, we did everything from "Foxy Lady" to "Helplessly Hoping." We did Grand Funk. We did what was popular. "Wooden Ships;" you name it, we did it. I used to sing "Whole Lotta Love" but I can't say Led Zeppelin had any influence on the Styx records we were making. People tried to categorize us for years and when the hardcore prog people say, well, Styx is not prog enough for us, I understand that. But we didn't intend to be, so go pound sand. I wasn't trying to be Emerson Lake and Palmer or Yes. At our heart we were still an American rock 'n' roll band.

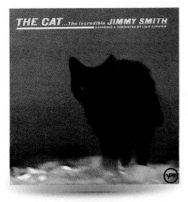

Jimmy Smith and Lalo Schifrin, *The Cat*

Let's face it, rock 'n' roll at its essence is to show off with your guitar players. They've got the best instrument, no question about it. You can see what people are playing. It's expressive like no other instrument; it has variation and possibility that far exceeds anything I can do on a piano or an organ–it's the instrument for rock 'n' roll. Well, I'm an accordion player for God's sake. Where do I fit in? I only chose it because my neighbor, who was like six years older than me, played accordion. God forbid he played the oboe, right? So to me, Jimmy Smith was a magician. Every jazz keyboard player that's come after him is really doing their take on Jimmy Smith. He's the godfather. He's an Adam and Eve the way McCartney and Lennon are Adam and Eve. Hendrix invented modern guitar playing and Jimmy Smith was that to the Hammond organ.

The Beatles, *Sgt. Pepper's Lonely Hearts Club Band*

Robert Hilburn was the tastemaker for the West Coast out of the LA Times. He wrote a piece, an essay, about how *Sgt. Pepper* ruined rock 'n' roll. You find me one musician who would concur with that. He wrote that 20 years ago. I read that and I thought who gives you a job? He was making the case that the Sex Pistols' album was more important. Not on any planet in the solar system. You know what *Sgt. Pepper* said? All you guys can do whatever you want. No boundaries. No limits. Let your freak flag fly. Create whatever it is you want. Just make sure it's good. That's what *Sgt. Pepper* said to every musician. I can remember the day I opened that gatefold, in the living room, hot, no air conditioning, it was rainy and muggy. We sat there, we listened to it and we looked at it. Then we looked at each other and said, "We got work to do."

Three Dog Night, *Three Dog Night*

They didn't write their own music. The Beatles made up the new rules, right? If you want to be taken seriously by people who write about music and really, the public at large, you have to create your own songs. They were just singers and fine musicians. You know what? Styx's three-part harmony is based on the three-part triad power vocals of Three Dog Night, only higher and whinier. The power of three people sitting and making something together… obviously like so many bands–and probably people feel this way about Styx and every band–they'll say the same thing: the earlier stuff is better than the later stuff. At the very end, Three Dog Night were just making pop records. But you've got to listen to some of the early stuff.

The Beatles, *Abbey Road*

Greatest ending of an album of all time, right? "And in the end the love you take is equal to the love you make." I played that on stage with my band. Now, if you want to talk about George Harrison, okay, he's got "Here Comes the Sun" and "Something." Well, that puts him up there with McCartney and Lennon. Prior to that it's "While My Guitar Gently Weeps." ***Abbey Road*** affected me. ***The Grand Illusion, Pieces of Eight*** and ***Paradise Theatre***… if you look at that, those are all titles and concepts for the band to work with where I was trying to recreate that album–good luck with that, Dennis. Essentially, I'm saying that's the goal. So if I only get halfway there, it's still going to be pretty good. Yeah. I was trying to make an album that felt connected. Some people maybe think ***Abbey Road*** isn't, but it's just something about that whole "Golden Slumbers" thing 'til "The End"… I don't know that it gets better than that as a piece of art. Hey, there are Beatles albums that had maybe more better individual singles on them, but there's something about the totality of that album that makes it a masterpiece.

The Who, *Who's Next*

If you're talking about the ultimate punks, it's not the Sex Pistols. The Who were the original "wanna die before they get old" band. And Pete Townshend invented the power chord. Where would music be without that, for God's sake? If you listen to "Come Sail Away," when it gets loud, that's Pete Townshend, even though I wrote it on piano. I said, "What would he do?" And I told the guys, "This has got to be Pete Townshend." And listen to "Won't Get Fooled Again:" the greatest scream in rock 'n' roll. And smart lyrics, synthesizers, guitars. So when people talk about punk bands, most of them are just plain crap compared to The Who. Pete and John [Entwistle]–and especially Keith–played like they were in the same band but completely detached from each other.

Tommy Shaw, Dennis DeYoung and James "JY" Young of Styx play The Spectrum in Philadelphia in 1981.

DENNIS DIKEN
THE SMITHEREENS

The Smithereens in 1990 (L-R): Dennis Diken, Jim Babjak, Pat DiNizio and Mike Mesaros. PHOTO BY GIE KNAEPS/GETTY IMAGES

D ennis Diken is best known as drummer and founding member of New Jersey hard popsters The Smithereens. Over their career, the Smithereens opened for a mix of artists ranging from the Ramones and the Pretenders to Tom Petty to Lou Reed as well as fellow New Jersey rockers Bruce Springsteen and Bon Jovi. The Smithereens scored hits with "Only a Memory," "Too Much Passion" and "A Girl Like You," as well as the fabulous "Behind the Wall of Sleep" across their approximately ten albums. In addition to their conventional catalog, the Smithereens have done covers albums reflecting their deep love of '60s music, including an entire record examining Beatles B-sides. It's no surprise then that Diken has served as a fill-in DJ at the legendary WFMU, in Jersey City, New Jersey, the longest running freeform radio station in the U.S. Diken's latest gig has been drumming for Dave Davies of The Kinks.

PHOTO BY DEBRA L ROTHENBERG/GETTY IMAGES

The Beatles, *A Hard Day's Night*

The American version of this album was the first Beatles album I owned. When you're talking about albums that changed your life, in addition to the music, you've got to consider the covers. When I was young, the graphics made a big impression on me. We were all trying to imagine what the Beatles were really like, trying to gain any insight, any clue as to what their personalities were like. And the pictures on this record actually did quite a good job of that. The photos on the back from the movie, they're all in these different poses. But also the music is great. The British album is probably my favorite Beatles album; it was the original album. Here the songs are interrupted by the instrumentals, by the George Martin Orchestra. And as hip as George Martin was actually, it was a great juxtaposition between the hipness of the Beatles and the adult square interpretation of their music. You know, if you listen to the instrumentals on this album, there's something Lawrence Welk Show about it, next to the swinging London of the mid-'60s that the Beatles embodied.

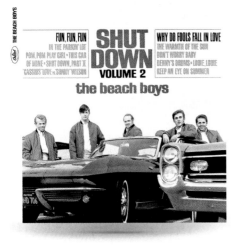

Beach Boys, *Shut Down Volume 2*

My first Beach Boys albums was technically Beach Boys *Concert*, but this was my first Beach Boys studio album. Even though this album doesn't rank high on a lot of lists, it's way up there for me. I think it's a fabulous record and it contains at least two of my favorite Beach Boys songs, "Don't Worry Baby" and "The Warmth of the Sun." Two other points about this record, there's a cut called "'Cassius" Love vs. "Sonny" Wilson" with the quote marks. It was a fake staged argument between Brian and Mike, commentary with the rest of the guys. And it really offered insight into the personalities of the band. It was very valuable–it's them speaking. But another very important point on this record, I remember even before I owned it, standing at the A&P and looking at the album cover at the supermarket, I saw there was a track on here called "Denny's Drums" and I was seven at the time and I knew I wanted to play drums, but I didn't at the time know that the drummer in the band was named Dennis or Denny. So that really made a big impression on me, that the drummer in my favorite band at the time shared my name–very inspiring.

Various Artists, *Good Guy Jack Spector Presents 22 Original Winners*

Long title. This came out in '64. Jack Spector was a DJ on WMCA radio in New York and it's on Roulette and it's 22 songs mostly from '63 and earlier. It was just a great collection and introduced me to The Coasters and Little Eva. Little Richard's on here, Chuck Berry's on here and it just exposed me to a lot of different styles and rhythms in particular. First time I really got to sink my teeth into Earl Palmer on "Long Tall Sally" by Little Richard and really dig into Chuck Berry and get a good feel for his music as well.

The Temptations, *Greatest Hits*

The main reason I chose this one is because I'd heard all the Motown records on the radio, but this was a chance to own an album where I could really dig into the Motown drummers' playing. And it really had a profound influence on the way I played drums. As it can be said for a lot of players, my playing is an amalgam of all the different styles I listened to, but I guess I learned to play a shuffle listening to this record and it informed me of certain fills that I still use, and an attitude more than anything. It's almost intangible, hard to describe. But there's an attitude to the playing that stays with me. And I just loved the songs and the fact that there were different lead singers too. I love David Ruffin and Eddie Kendricks, but also Paul Williams on "Don't Look Back." There was awful lot to like on here.

Kinks, *Face to Face*

First Kinks album that I owned, so that's why it's so influential to me. The Kinks became a very important band to me, to my friends, to my musical thinking and attitude. And this probably remains my favorite Kinks album, although that's hard to say as much as it is with the Beatles or the Beach Boys. But I love every tune on here. I love the immediacy of the album, the way the band played. It sounded like a lot of them were first takes. I just loved the fresh, raw feel of this and the songwriting. It really spoke to me, still speaks to me.

And the cool thing is, I started listening to The Kinks with "You Really Got Me," and then when I got *Face to Face*, it made me realize how important this band was to me. And at the time when I got it, if you had told me that I would ever end up playing with any of the Kinks, it would have blown my mind. And I've been Dave Davies' drummer I guess now for three or four years and I still have to pinch myself when I get on stage sometimes that I'm actually playing with the guy that I've been admiring so much since I was a kid.

The Lovin' Spoonful, *Do You Believe in Magic*

What can I say? When I was a kid, my parents didn't have a lot of money to buy LPs—or me—but they always made sure if I nagged them enough I would get at least The Beatles albums, the Beach Boys albums and the Lovin' Spoonful albums. The Lovin' Spoonful were real important to me. And this album, as much as the next two Spoonful albums, really gave me a sense of the roots of American music. The Spoonful took so much from jug band and country blues and old jazz and early rock 'n' roll. And they were the first band to really—and I think this gets overlooked—to really introduce country forms into rock 'n' roll. I didn't know that when I was eight years old listening to this, but when I grew up and started listening to Johnny Cash and Robert Johnson and The Memphis Jug Band, I already had a great grounding in all that music from listening to the Spoonful. Plus they just had such a sense of fun that I try to keep within my musical spirit. And I'll just add that Zal Yanovsky is my favorite guitarist.

Small Faces, *There Are but Four Small Faces*

I just love this record so much, but in terms of changing my life, it made me realize how much Kenny Jones' drumming meant to me, and starting from when I first listened to this album, how much of a role model he became for me and my playing. There's a wonderful band feel to what they did on here. And I love how they make concise little psychedelic cuts like "Green Circles" and... I don't know, the music really spoke to me and opened up my thinking about band playing. Small Faces didn't have as much of a profile in the States as The Kinks or The Who. I think most people will think of The Faces rather, probably, with Rod Stewart rather than Small Faces with Steve Marriott singing lead. So maybe it gets short shrift in terms of importance in history. But they typified to me what it meant to have a great band. All the pieces fit together. It seemed like a great boy's club to be part of. I think any band is defined by their songwriting. So without getting into specifics, the songwriting was just different than The Kinks or The Who.

The Who, *Tommy*

Not my favorite Who album, but it was the first Who album that I owned. And it just opened my ears and soul to The Who and made me want more and more. And it gave me a chance to really study Keith Moon's playing and dig on the whole spectre of The Who, which is so important to me and so important to The Smithereens. This was the album that the broke it wide open, where The Who are concerned.

The Who's music is certainly in our DNA. I'll tell you one anecdote. I played in a cover band with Pat DiNizio before The Smithereens. And at my audition (laughs), the song that clinched it for him that he would want to play with me was when we did "Can't Explain." And when I went into high school and I wanted to find musicians to form a band with, my criteria was if I could find a guitar player who could play "Can't Explain" then I felt that I met my match. Then the first day of school, Jimmy Babjak is sitting in row one, seat one, and he opens up his loose-leaf and there's pictures of The Who plastered in his notebook. So I spoke to him that day and we started playing together that day.

The Association, *Insight Out*

The big hits on this album are "Windy" and "Never My Love." I was crazy for The Association. In '67 I got this album and they really had an impact on my sense of vocal harmonies and the way they used harmonics in their vocal arrangements really did something to me. I didn't know what it was that I was ingesting at the time, but they had a touch of modern harmony and it really haunted my spirit.

I have a stereo copy of the album and I was picking apart the tracks. I just loved the way the drums and bass sounded. And I thought, wow, Ted Bluechel from The Association is one of my favorite drummers. Then years later I found out it was Hal Blaine and Joe Osborn. What I'm saying is, before I even knew who he was, Hal Blaine really was an important rhythmic voice to me. [Drummer Hal Blaine appeared on more than 35,000 recordings, including some 6,000 singles as one of music's great session players] And this album, I can't tell you how many times I would listen to just the one channel that had the bass and drums to try and figure out what he was doing and get the feel of what he was doing. This was my big Hal Blaine album when I was a kid.

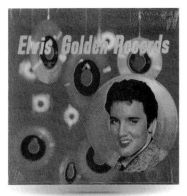

Elvis Presley, *Elvis' Golden Records*

I think the only time in my life I ever babysat was in 1970 when I was 13 years old, for the kid around the corner. And the lady there, Mrs. Gillan, gave me as part of my payment, a copy of *Elvis' Golden Records*. I'd been hip to Elvis at that point from his singles. One of the first singles I ever had was "Return to Sender." But this really opened my ears to music that came before me and kicked me in the butt to go back and listen to Eddie Cochran and Buddy Holly and Little Richard, all the stuff from the '50s. It really expanded my horizons in terms of from whence I came and where I was gonna go. Very important record to me.

The Smithereens' power-pop catalog had a cult following, even influencing a young Kurt Cobain. PHOTO BY MICHAEL OCHS ARCHIVES/GETTY IMAGES

THOMAS DOLBY

With the help of MTV, Thomas Dolby scored a massive hit in 1982 with "She Blinded Me With Science." PHOTO BY ERICA ECHENBERG/REDFERNS

You may know Thomas Dolby best as the bespectacled singer behind the quirky 1980s synth-pop hits "She Blinded Me With Science" and "Hyperactive!!," but Dolby—whose professional surname started out as a nickname given by schoolmates impressed with his musical and computer programming skills—has run the gamut of the business. Dolby directed the music video for the infectious "She Blinded Me With Science" and had the concept for the video well before he had written the song. The video's constant play on MTV assured him of a hit. In addition, Dolby has scored films, served as a sound engineer, played synthesizer in studio sessions for everyone from Def Leppard to Foreigner and built his own computer equipment. Dolby currently serves on the faculty of the Peabody Institute at Johns Hopkins University. Five solo albums, three EPs and a stint as the musical director for the TED Conferences later, what music has influenced this musical Renaissance man?

PHOTO BY PAUL MORIGI/GETTY IMAGES

Elton John, *Honky Chateau*

This was the first album I ever bought. I saved up my pocket money and I was so proud of it. I made a special shelf to hold my future record collection and started out with just one album. I loved Elton's piano playing and was amazed how roots-American he sounded, for being such a blatant Brit. I once waited at the stage door for him before a concert in North London, with a pen and a program in hand. And a big Rolls pulled up and out he got—but my pen didn't work!

Joni Mitchell, *For the Roses*

My brothers and sisters were big fans of *Blue*, but this was the first Joni album I paid for myself. Her poetry and voice and unusual chord sequences and intervals made her a complete standout. These days, she sounds bitter and twisted, but I will always remember her as the sweet hippie painter from the cover of this album. And her later record, *Hejira*, in my opinion, is the greatest rock album of all time.

Dave Brubeck Quartet, *Time Out*

I dabbled in jazz and was attracted to the bohemian lifestyle, but could never stand the endless self-indulgent solos. Along came Dave, who was actually a composer (though I only recently discovered saxist Paul Desmond is credited with the smash hit "Take 5," much to Dave's disdain). There has always been a strong jazz flair in my songs, especially the harmonies. Now you know where it came from!

Kraftwerk, *The Man Machine*

Undoubtedly the patron saints of the UK electronic underground that I cut my teeth on, the famous German mannequins set a standard for electronic pop that has never been equalled. They were the first to truly let machines be machines, and celebrate their inanimateness.

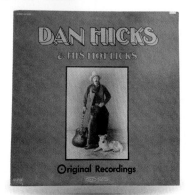

Dan Hicks and His Hot Licks, *Dan Hicks and His Hot Licks*

This is the brilliant album that features Dan's version of "I Scare Myself," which I later covered. It was the soundtrack to a summer I spent at Oxford University–not actually attending (I left school at 16), just drinking in the pubs, going to Ban the Bomb rallies and climbing walls of girls' colleges after curfew.

David Bowie, *Low*

I had always loved Bowie as a pop icon, but when he teamed with Eno and went off to the Berlin Wall to make records with primitive synthesizers, I was completely gaga. And side two was all electronic instrumentals. By a rock artist, that was simply unheard of!

Van Morrison, *Astral Weeks*

The vibe of this whole album has stuck with me all these years. Van often sounds a bit angry and uncomfortable to me, but on this LP, he seemed to discover a temporary oasis of spiritual peace within the music as well as inspired jamming from the group of musicians he assembled. "Without You," in particular, had a huge influence on me–without that track there would have been no "Screen Kiss," possibly my best song.

Soft Machine, *Third*

"Moon in June" was the ultimate 20-minute rock opus from an era replete with 20-minute jams. Robert Wyatt was a true prophet. The chord and tempo changes left us fledgling musicians scratching our heads. Plus, the triple album gatefold sleeve provided a much more solid base for the construction of "Camberwell Carrots." Just try rolling one of those babies on a CD jewel box!

Iggy Pop, *Lust for Life*

This album showcases Iggy's raw power combined with Bowie's songwriting prowess. Add to that their excellence in conducting a rocking band and turning chaos into order and back again, and you've got a classic album of the era. Against a backdrop of the London punk scene of the late '70s, which was fun as hell but had not a lot of musical merit to it. I loved this album above all others from that era.

Talking Heads, *Talking Heads '77*

What a relief when at the end of the '70s a new breed of music emerged that had the manic energy of the three-chord, spike-haired brigade, but also had a thoughtfulness and compositional flair that appealed to my delicate music sensibilities. The Heads seemed otherworldly, with David Byrne's neurological contortions set against a rocking rhythm section. I dutifully headed to New York, to CBGBs and The Mudd Club, to soak it all in, and paid my way with keyboard sessions for the likes of Foreigner and Def Leppard. During that era, I was quietly cooking up my own contribution to the rapidly morphing world of '80s music. What a strange melting pot we all dove into!

K.K. DOWNING
JUDAS PRIEST

The twin-guitar team of K.K. Downing and Glenn Tipton with lead vocalist Rob Halford of Judas Priest. PHOTO BY MICHAEL OCHS ARCHIVES/GETTY IMAGES

K.K. Downing is the blond to Glenn Tipton's brunette in the ground-breaking twin-guitar team that powered the mighty Judas Priest for more that 40 years. Now retired from the band, K.K. manages his real estate holdings, having gotten the bug for the business during the band's early platinum success in the mid-'80s. Emerging from industrial Birmingham, England, Judas Priest date back to 1969, debuting with their first record in 1974. A series of undisputed heavy metal classics ensued, such as 1976's *Sad Wings of Destiny*, but the band would break big in 1980 with *British Steel*, which featured hits such as "Living After Midnight" and "Breaking the Law." *Screaming for Vengeance*, *Defenders of the Faith* and *Turbo* kept the band filling arenas through the '80s, to the point where Priest are considered, arguably, the premier ambassadors for heavy metal music, in part from their considerable success (including a dozen gold and platinum albums), in part due to their championing of the cause, in lyrics, in their studs-and-leather looks and in interviews. If you'd like to learn more about the man's dire but character-building childhood and his positive yet deferential attitude despite early hardship, Downing's memoir *Heavy Duty: Days and Nights in Judas Priest* will engage those curiosities thoroughly.

PHOTO BY PAUL NATKIN/GETTY IMAGES

The Jimi Hendrix Experience, *Are You Experienced*

Obviously that was a game-changer. With "Foxy Lady," "Manic Depression," "Are You Experienced," it didn't get any better than that. It's still the all-time best ever, for me. It was just different in every way. What a lot of people don't realize is, Hendrix, when he first came to England, '67, whenever it was, he was a free spirit in those early days. When he was on that stage, there were no complications. It was like he was totally invigorated, he was totally enjoying himself, full of it, and everything was great. And this is what happened to Judas Priest and every other band in existence. In the early days, you know, there's no money, there's no fans, there's no glory, particularly. You're out there, and just enjoying the view, because that's all you've got. But obviously quite quickly, Jimi started to get pretty much saturated. He got involved with various people, some hard people in the business and the industry, and was being pushed and pulled and it started to get to him in a short space of time. So unfortunately I think that started to creep into his life.

But in the early days, those original performances, you had to see it to believe it. He used to turn around and the crowd frenzied; they went absolutely crazy. And the first time I saw him, it was a sizable theatre, probably seated about 2000, Coventry Theatre. But at least half the audience stormed the stage, including me. We were just in a frenzy–that's what would happen when Hendrix came out in full flight.

Cream, *Fresh Cream*

This goes way, way back to when I'm still in school. "I'm So Glad," "Spoonful," "Cat's Squirrel"… songs like that were going to lead to good things, obviously, with Cream. I saw both the farewell concerts at the Royal Albert Hall. And I saw both the Jimi Hendrix concerts there too. I used to get around as a kid, a lot (laughs). But Cream, a few the kids at school were into them as well; they became very popular very quick. They were blues-oriented, of course, but when Cream went on to their longer solos, that's when they really got my attention.

Skid Row, *Skid*

The original Skid Row with Gary Moore. In fact, I just found a ticket for a show, Judas Priest supporting Skid Row, 50 pence, which is half a pound (laughs). This is West Bromwich Town Hall, and I was born in West Bromwich. I've got it right here. This was in 1971, Priest with Al Atkins and it was us supporting the Gary Moore band. Skid Row, I would put them probably as one of the first progressive rock bands, really. Because they steered away from blues on those albums. They were doing their own thing, which was good–again, I like that–although there are a couple tracks on there that are a bit bluesy. When I first saw them, as a trio, with that first album, Gary used to jump on the drums with his guitar and he used to sing a blues song. Which was good, but the mainstay you'd have to say was progressive rock, I suppose. It was pretty fast stuff, because Gary then, at the age of 16 or 17, had the reputation of being the fastest guitar player in the land, and you know, he probably was. Fantastic.

Free, *Tons of Sobs*

As much as I'm trying to steer away from them, there were all these great bands that had blues backgrounds, and so Free were another great band. I know they would become very popularized with "All Right Now," but when you saw them, like I did, in whatever year it was, '68 or '69, in a club, what a band–Paul Rodgers, great bass player in Andy Fraser, Paul Kossoff on guitar, and just sort of the real great on-the-beat drumming from Simon Kirke. It was just something to behold. They were so locked in, so in tune, so in time, they really were a great band live; unforgettable, really. They were laying it down with that really sharp snare. And **Tons of Sobs**, with like "The Hunter" and "Walk in My Shadows," songs like that, they really started to move away from the archetypal blues stuff.

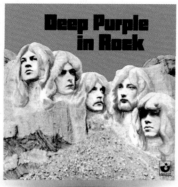

Scorpions, *In Trance*

In Trance, *Robot Man*, *Top of the Bill*. Scorpions is one of my favorite bands, definitely. I could cite all the Scorpions albums, but this is an early one I stuck to like glue and played to death. Great guitar players, obviously, Rudolf [Schenker] and Uli [Jon Roth]. They come from the same stock, both being German, great credentials, great songs, very consistent performers. Similar to Priest, they did have two guitarist but one was rhythm and one was lead. In my book, what I was looking for was two lead players, two good rhythm players, two songwriters and good performers and guys that looked good image-wise.

Deep Purple, *In Rock*

You couldn't ignore that album, because obviously it was a great album for the time, with "Child in Time" on there, the epic, and songs like "Speed King." Obviously, Ian Gillan's vocal performance on there was extraordinary. You had to be drawn to that album, I think. It was a slam-dunk, really, at that time. There are certain guitar players like Ritchie and Jimmy Page that I wasn't particularly drawn to, because I was so into Hendrix already; he set the bar, really. But obviously, these guys were all good at the time and much better than me, so all the guitar players in this list were heroes to me.

Jeff Beck, *Truth*

I remember going around to my mate's house when that album first came out and we just played the vinyl until it wouldn't play anymore (laughs). They just had a difference about them. It was very, very important to the history of the music we know today. **Truth** and the first Led Zeppelin definitely swim together.

Quatermass, *Quatermass*

Quatermass didn't have a guitar player, but they made a great album, with songs like "Post War Saturday Echo" and "Black Sheep of the Family." And when I was in Priest with Al Atkins, we covered a few of their songs, with was something, because in Priest, we never really did cover versions—we did all our own original material. But we did more Quatermass songs than anyone else. I think the only other song we covered was "Spanish Castle Magic" for a while, back with Al Atkins. I don't think we did any other covers—it was all original. But I just really loved that album. I'm sure there's lots of people around like me, but I was into stuff that didn't remind me of the mainstay of what was out there, or any other genres, like jazz or classical or even the blues. I liked stuff that was not very definable to start with, but you'd have to call it rock, I guess. Which was fine by me, because that covered a lot of bands.

D

Budgie, *Never Turn Your Back on a Friend*

Back in the day somebody started playing Budgie on a late-night radio show and I picked up on them and really got to like them, really early on. This was before I was in Priest. When I got to be in the band, obviously we got to know Budgie really well and became friends and did an awful lot of shows together, supporting them. *Never Turn Your Back on a Friend* stuck out because it had "Breadfan" on there, which Metallica covered, and "In the Grip of the Tyrefitter's Hand" and obviously the ballad "Parents." I liked what they were doing because it wasn't blues. It wasn't particularly metal at that point, but it was a diversion from blues or even progressive blues. And so I like that; that suited me.

UFO, *No Heavy Petting*

Yeah, loved the songs, but obvious the guitar playing of Michael Schenker as well. Great feel, and again, just doing something different, out of the ballpark–not blues. And I liked bands like that; you'll see a lot of that in these records. You know, that kind of predicting everything that was to come, really. That's why I really liked bands that looked different, sounded different and did their own thing, that didn't get a piggyback on the blues, particularly. But guys like Clapton and Rory Gallagher are not to be ignored either. I mean, I saw Taste [the band Gallagher founded] a lot of times and they were a great band as well. Same thing as UFO and Scorpions, very consistent performer. I don't think it was in his genetic code to not put on a great performance; he was just sensational all the time. But Rory was a blues man through and through.

Judas Priest in all their black leather and studs glory (L-R): Dave Holland, K.K. Downing, Ian Hill, Glenn Tipton and Rob Halford. PHOTO BY EBET ROBERTS/REDFERNS

DENNIS DUNAWAY
ALICE COOPER GROUP

Alice Cooper group in 1972 (L-R): Neal Smith, Alice Cooper, Michael Bruce, Dennis Dunaway and Glen Buxton. PHOTO BY MICHAEL PUTLAND/GETTY IMAGES

Dennis Dunaway is a founding member of the Alice Cooper group, and a big part of the conceptual visual work that went into making the band so distinct and successful, bringing shock rock to the masses while becoming one of the most influential acts of the 1970s. Such hits as "I'm Eighteen," "School's Out" and "No More Mr. Nice Guy" proved the band was more than the guillotines, electric chairs and snakes that filled their horror movie stage shows. Alice Cooper and Dunaway were art students first, and the pair were the band's biggest visual forces, with Dunaway also writing regularly, on top of handling bass duties. The original Alice Cooper group was inducted into the Rock and Roll Hall of Fame in 2011. For more details on Dunaway's career, check out his acclaimed autobiography *Snakes! Guillotines! Electric Chairs!*

Dunaway and Alice Cooper performing in London in 2017.
PHOTO BY BRIAN RASIC/WIREIMAGE

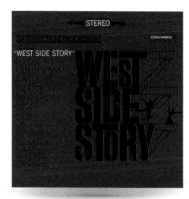

Leonard Bernstein, *West Side Story: The Original Sound Track Recording*

At ages 14 and 15, Alice and I skipped over the sappy girl songs, but those incredibly complex rhythms and the finger-snapping street savvy attitude inspired us to buy white tennis shoes and search in vain for purple T-shirts. We wanted to be cool like those guys. I mean the Sharks and the Jets were dancing around but they still came off as tough, and that was because of the music. It was sophisticated yet it had this finger-snapping street savvy attitude. That attitude was a big influence in the Alice Cooper music and our stage shows.

Bob Dylan, *The Freewheelin' Bob Dylan*

As old high school buddies, Alice and I thought we were incredibly hip. But when our art teacher made us listen to this album, even though we laughed at the froggy voice, the dead seriousness of most of the lyrics made us realize that our art teacher was way hipper than us. Soon after that, we met Dylan's parents at the local mall. Alice had just bought a harmonica and showed it to them saying he started playing it because of Bob. He asked them what they thought of their son's harmonica playing. Mr. Zimmerman said, "I guess he gets what he wants out of it." Dylan's lyrics influenced everybody. I mean he raised the bar way higher than anyone had even thought of. Many years later, we were honored when Dylan said, "I think Alice Cooper is an overlooked songwriter," and mentioned "Generation Landslide" which we wrote as a group.

The Beatles, *Introducing the Beatles*

It was like there was an explosion and the Beatles became all that mattered. Just the sound of their recordings had an unexplainable mystic quality about them. From the ripping scream in "I Saw Her Standing There" to the farewell pleas on "Anna" and especially the guttural vocal performance on "Twist and Shout," overnight the Beatles became all that mattered. We didn't even know what instrument we would play but we started a band. Later on, we got Michael Bruce to join us and his songwriting was very much influenced by the Beatles. Some of that is obvious and some isn't because we would overhaul songs to give them a raw edge.

The Beatles, *Sgt. Pepper's Lonely Hearts Club Band*

Suddenly the world was in color. How could this be the same band of only four years prior? Our generation was swept away in their evolution. There was something important happening on this album and we weren't sure what it was, but it lured us into believing that it was something to figure out and to follow. So we were a band in the wake of the Beatles and the whole British Invasion. Great bands were happening in America too. We had to try harder in that crowd. How do you do that? We were on the same bill as John Lennon up in Toronto, back in '69. So we threw a chicken into the crowd.

The Rolling Stones, *England's Newest Hit Makers*

I was working on my grandfather's farm in Oregon to earn enough money to buy my first bass. I walked past a record store window in Eugene and saw a picture of a band on a 45 RPM single called "It's All Over Now." I thought it was the ugliest band I had ever seen. It was hard not to buy it, but I had to save my money. It didn't matter though because the Stones had won me over anyway. When I got back to Phoenix, Glen Buxton helped me pick out an Airline bass. I had enough money to buy the Rolling Stones album, so we went to Glen's house and he started teaching me all the notes and patterns from every song on the album (plus "It's All Over Now"). And so, with Glen's help, I learned how to play rhythm and blues-rooted bass parts from Bill Wyman's recordings. And when I developed my own style, I'd start with those patterns and alter them into something new.

The Who, *My Generation*

It was all about the excitement in the crashing tone of that guitar, and the explosive power of the bass and drums, and the charismatic singer that had to work hard just to hold his own on a stage that seemed like a rock 'n' roll battleground. I had seen them on television and my parents complained about why they would break perfectly good equipment. But like every teenager, I knew why. And I loved it. All that imagery came through on the album. The Alice Cooper group wanted to do exciting stage shows. Hendrix had to follow The Who so he lit his guitar on fire. We wanted to be the band that nobody wanted to follow.

Pink Floyd, *Piper at the Gates of Dawn*

The Alice Cooper group had a kindred feeling toward the experimental nature of this album. It was as if we were exploring outer space and ran into someone else. Music had become experimental. It still required good song structure, but electronic sound effects could push it into the abstract. Alice and I had become friends in art class, mostly because we both liked abstract art. Forget the paintbrushes, let's do it with music. And we could perform live happenings. We were doing that before we knew about Pink Floyd, but we admired them, kinda like fellow pioneers.

Neal Smith, Michael Bruce, Alice Cooper and Dennis Dunaway in 2011.
PHOTO BY MICHAEL OCHS ARCHIVES/GETTY IMAGES

The Jimi Hendrix Experience, *Are You Experienced*

The Alice Cooper group was dirt-poor and living in Watts during the torch-burning tensions of the equal rights movement. We put this album on our crappy turntable and it ripped the roof off the house. We hung out with those guys. Jimi was nice to everyone. They all were. I think that was a great lesson that a rock star doesn't have to have an inflated ego. We would make fun of how they dressed, right to their faces— and we would be dressed crazy. It was an ongoing joke. Jimi laughed every time.

The Doors, *The Doors*

We were opening two shows for the Doors so I hastily listened to the album and was unimpressed. After watching them give two riveting live performances, I gave the record another listen. It pulled me in. It was the perfect soundtrack for Los Angeles. A lot of the L.A. bands were less likely to be seen around town. They'd be up in Laurel Canyon and you'd hear about some stoned-out jam session or something. But we'd run into the Doors a lot. We'd see then on Malibu beach, or on the Sunset Strip, or even at a bar in a Mexican restaurant. I think that's why their music captured the feel of L.A. so perfectly.

The Yardbirds, *For Your Love*

Paul Samwell-Smith made me realize that I could take my own bass parts to the moon. Without ever meeting him, he set me on my own lifetime musical adventure. We loved their energy. We heard that their British fans would wait for their high-energy rave-ups. Then the crowd would go berserk. I think we had a similar kind of energy, even at rehearsals.

ROGER EARL
FOGHAT

Roger Earl and Foghat were flying high in the 1970s with hits like "Slow Ride" and "I Just Want to Make Love to You." PHOTO BY GAB ARCHIVE/REDFERNS

PHOTO BY LYLE A. WAISMAN/GETTY IMAGES

Shuffling and bespectacled drum legend Roger Earl has had a long and distinguished blues rock career, first appearing on a string of fine Savoy Brown albums with his buddy Kim Simmonds and slaking fully of the British blues boom before looking for greener pastures stateside. In 1971, Earl became a founding member of Foghat, appearing on multiple gold, platinum and multi-platinum albums such as *Fool for the City*, *Night Shift* and *Stone Blue*. Two Foghat classics – "Slow Ride" and "I Just Want to Make Love to You" – are featured in the movie *Dazed and Confused*, the acclaimed 1993 coming-of-age film by Richard Linklater set in 1976 Texas. Earl has kept Foghat rolling, as well as recording an interesting array of albums (covers, originals, live...), both with Foghat and his side-dish Earl & the Agitators.

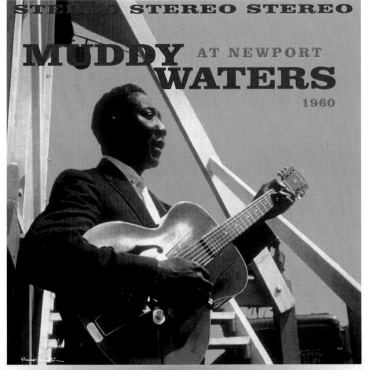

Jerry Lee Lewis, *Jerry Lee Lewis*

My father brought home a Jerry Lee Lewis single, "Whole Lotta Shakin' Goin' On." And Dad said, 'Have a listen to this boy. He can really play the Joanna!' Dad also played piano in the style of Fats Waller–a heavy left hand. No wonder where I get it from. I believe the B-side was "Mean Woman Blues." My father at that time thought that was a far better recording. My older Brother Colin was already a huge fan of Jerry Lee. And his first album on the Sun label never left our record player. It was magic! t

Elvis Presley, *Elvis Presley*

Elvis Presley was on the Sun record label. And my older brother would buy singles and extended players–the music was just incredible. And it's possible Elvis had one of the greatest bands ever with Scotty Moore on guitar, Bill Black on bass, and DJ Fontana on drums. The early Sun recordings changed the world of rock 'n' roll forever. The way the band played, nobody had ever done anything like that before.

Johnny Cash, *With His Hot and Blue Guitar*

My brother, who is four years older than me, turned me on to Johnny Cash. I was probably the only kid in South West London riding my bike to school singing Johnny Cash songs. Even though he didn't have a drummer on his early recordings there was always this rhythm in his songs. I never got a chance to see him, but my wife bought me a compilation of all his TV shows. I also have a Johnny Cash calendar every year beside my practice kit. So you see, I am still a fan.

Muddy Waters, *At Newport 1960*

I actually turned the tables on my brother with this album. I bought it for him for his 21st birthday. In some ways this record probably influenced me more than just about any other. It was a style of music I had never heard played live. I listened to this record over and over and over again trying to cop some of Francis Clay's licks, trying to find this fantastic groove the album had. To me this was one of the greatest recordings of Muddy Waters who was idolized by anyone who had a notion of loving the blues. I couldn't play like Francis Clay, but I played along to this record incessantly. Muddy Waters, James Cotton on harmonica, and Otis Span on piano… to me this was one of the greatest live recordings ever.

Otis Spann,
The Blues of Otis Spann

He came out of Muddy's band and this was his first solo album, 1960. Most blues albums weren't recorded well. But this one was the first I ever heard in what they used to call "high fidelity." He played a Steinway Grand, and it was the most incredible sounding record. And the band was incredible! Muddy played some guitar, and Otis had such a great voice! He's probably my favorite all-time piano player, (except for maybe Meade Lux Lewis). I always wanted to play piano. I can only play a 12-bar in the key of C. This is not much use to current guitar players as they seem to prefer E and A. Oh well, such is life. Also, his album was produced by Mike Vernon. I worked with him in my early days in Savoy Brown and he was a great producer. He just knew how music should sound.

Johnny Burnette, *Johnny Burnette and the Rock 'n Roll Trio*

Johnny Burnett, with his brother Dorsey on bass and Paul Burleson on guitar made up the Rock 'n Roll Trio. It was a ten-inch record. I owned it twice. The first time I found one was on my first tour with Savoy Brown in the United States. The second time I found it was on my first tour in the United States with Foghat. Dave and I would scour the record stores trying to find that record and other rarities. I have it on CD now. I think my first wife probably still has the first one. Anybody who ever loved or wanted to play real rockabilly must listen to this record. Because this is where it all came from.

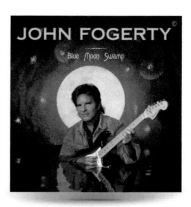

John Fogerty,
Blue Moon Swamp

I've always thought he was the quintessential American songwriter, guitarist and singer. I romanced my wife Linda with it when it came out in 1997. And I picked one of its songs "Joy of My Life" to dance with my daughter Louise at her wedding. Every song he does is an instant classic in my book. Had I not been in Foghat, I would have wanted to be the drummer for Creedence Clearwater. As far as I'm concerned John Fogerty is a national treasure.

Foghat's Lonsome Dave Peverett, Rod Price, Roger Earl and Craig MacGregor, 1980.
PHOTO BY PAUL NATKIN/WIREIMAGE

Chuck Berry,
Chuck Berry Is on Top

Like Muddy Waters and like Willie Dixon, if there was no Chuck Berry there would be no rock 'n' roll. The Rolling Stones would be out of work. We'd all be out of work. I still get chills any time I hear a Chuck Berry record–any number of his songs. When I was learning to play, I would play along to Chuck Berry records. One of the early Chess Record drummers, Freddie Below was one of my favorites. He always managed to make it swing.

Gene Krupa & Buddy Rich,
The Drum Battle: Jazz at the Philharmonic

This was a 78 record in some store when I was a kid. I played it over and over again. I just became fascinated by the drum solos. I would bash on all the furniture with spoons and drove my mother crazy. I wore that record completely out.

Little Feat,
Waiting for Columbus

Actually, every record was great but their 1978 live album ***Waiting for Columbus*** was such a classic. It was just the way they all played, the way they all sang, the way that they wrote. It was probably my favorite band of all time. Over the years I was fortunate enough to play a number of shows with them. And even though they have lost two key members, Lowell George and Richie Hayward, they still remain in my humble opinion one of the greatest bands that ever hit the highway.

Roger Earl lived the rock 'n' roll lifestyle with Swedish actress and girlfriend Britt Eckland, 1978.
PHOTO BY RICHARD MCCAFFREY/ MICHAEL OCHS ARCHIVE/ GETTY IMAGES

DAVE FENTON
THE VAPORS

The Vapors in 1980 (L-R): Howard Smith, Edward Bazalgette, David Fenton and Steve Smith. PHOTO BY GERRIT ALAN FOKKEMA/FAIRFAX MEDIA VIA GETTY IMAGES

Dave Fenton, the singer/guitarist/songwriter of The Vapors, wrote one of the best-known songs of the New Wave era, 1980's "Turning Japanese." The short, spiky power pop tune and its fantastic video made The Vapors darlings of the MTV crowd. The Vapors recorded two albums, 1980's *New Clear Days* and 1981's *Magnets*, before splitting up. It's easy to dismiss The Vapors as a one-hit wonder but overall their punchy Brit-pop sound in the vein of The Jam holds up better than most from the period. Fenton went on to become a lawyer but he reconvened The Vapors in 2016 with original members Steve Smith (bass) and Ed Bazalgette (guitar) along with new drummer Michael Bowles. After many headline and festival appearances in the UK and elsewhere in Europe, The Vapors returned to North America where the band continues to perform.

PHOTO BY GAB ARCHIVE/REDFERNS

Television, *Marquee Moon*

This album always sounds crisp, fresh, pure and powerful, and still gives me the shivers. In the punk era, the guitar usually thrashed chords supported by a growling bass. So I was fascinated to hear melodic guitar and bass parts cleverly intertwining, working together and independently and even leaving room for empty spaces. Still one of my all-time favorite albums. Tom Verlaine – genius.

Talking Heads, *Talking Heads: 77*

David Byrne is another genius. Talking Heads are still a great band, but this album gave me headaches when I first heard it – it seemed that different and complicated–but I found it made more sense the more I listen to. Well worth the investment of time as it has some great songs. "Psycho Killer" just has to be one of the best songs ever.

Captain Beefheart and his Magic Band, *Safe as Milk*

John Peel and the good Captain started my interest in what was going on the U.S. West Coast in the late '60s and early '70s. Me and my mates used to play football in Redhill Rec every Sunday afternoon with radios in the goalmouths, and when Uncle John played the Captain, football would be suspended for a few minutes while we listened/danced in the goalmouth.

Canned Heat, *Refried Boogie*

Canned Heat are probably best remembered for "Going Up the Country," which is a great track and still being used in TV adverts today. I saw them live in Croydon in the late '60s. But this live album, in my opinion, has the best intro of any live album I've ever heard, and still gets me on my feet. It hits something inside that nothing else does, if you know what I mean!

Love, *Forever Changes*

Another album that I grew up with that has gone down in history, and is still being discovered today. I just wish Arthur [Lee, singer/songrwriter] was still here. But then I could say the same about Bowie, Lennon, Cohen, Van Vliet, Wilson, Hite and others referred to here.

Devo, *Q: Are We Not Men? A: We Are Devo!*

I first heard "Jocko Homo" at the Marquee in Wardour Street. I was there to see a support band called The Screens, and the DJ played it in the interval. To an impressionable young person, the wiggly riff and incomprehensible rhythm was a big surprise and I had to buy the single–and then the album–to try and understand it all. The album also reshuffles the Stones' "Satisfaction."

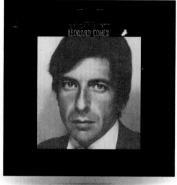

Blondie, *Parallel Lines*

I couldn't leave out Blondie, still playing after all these years. This album has some of the best punk songs ever, and shows the strength of Debbie's [Harry] voice. It was produced by Mike Chapman and engineered by Dave Tickle, who coincidentally went on to produce The Vapors' second album **Magnets**. Dave's the one singing out of tune on the "boys, boys, boys" outro to the title track!

Leonard Cohen, *The Songs of Leonard Cohen*

My introduction to Leonard Cohen came at a party in the late '60s. Everyone was dancing vertically until someone put this on and suddenly everyone was dancing horizontally and snogging. Best disco ever! A classic album and classic timeless songs that The Vapors pay tribute to in our live set with our own song, "King L."

The Beatles, *Sgt. Pepper's Lonely Hearts Club Band*

The Beatles were the first band I ever saw live (Bournemouth Gaumont, August 1963) and **With the Beatles** was the first album I ever bought. I could've chosen other Beatles albums but I used to play "A Day in the Life" on acoustic guitar at folk clubs before I could afford an electric guitar to start a "real" band. So for that reason and others I've chosen **Sgt. Pepper**.

David Bowie, *Hunky Dory*

I could have chosen ten Bowie albums for this list, but this was the first one I bought and I never played anything else for at least two months. I then started collecting Bowie albums both retrospectively and as he released them.

LITA FORD
THE RUNAWAYS/SOLO

The Runaways in 1977 (from left): Lita Ford, Joan Jett, Cherie Currie, Sandy West and Jackie Fox. PHOTO BY MICHAEL MARKS/MICHAEL OCHS ARCHIVES/GETTY IMAGES

From being a "Runaway" to living like one, Lita Ford's life has never been boring. The guitar-slinger got her start at the tender age of 16 in the 1970s with the Runaways, the all-female hard-rock band featuring Joan Jett, Cherie Currie, Sandy West and Jackie Fox. Mistakenly dismissed as a gimmick, the Runaways played loud, straight-up, guitar-driven rock 'n' roll while producing one undeniably classic single "Cherry Bomb." Ford stepped into her own as a solo artist in the 1980s, displaying guitar heroics on the level of any male metal hero. While she is perhaps best known for her single "Kiss Me Deadly" and her duet with Ozzy Osbourne ("Close My Eyes Forever"), Ford has kept busy on the road and in the studio. Her last effort, *Living Like a Runaway*, brought her back to her '80s roots, and gave her the title of her subsequent thrills 'n' spills autobiography.

Elton John,
Goodbye Yellow Brick Road
These songs told stories and made me feel happy. I listened to them while drinking Boone's Farm wine and walking with my wiener dog in the park. Absolutely beautiful songs. Very visual.

Pink Floyd,
The Dark Side of The Moon
The female vocal tracks were amazing on this album, on "Great Gig in the Sky" and also this album in its entirety was life-changing. A journey.

The Jimi Hendrix Experience,
Are You Experienced
Jimi made his songs so different than anyone else: sloppy noise that spoke a thousand words, feedback on guitar channelled into awesome guitar riffs, burning guitars, which no one did.

The Monkees,
The Monkees
These guys were so cute, and the TV show was awesome. Loved their songs, too.

Led Zeppelin, *I*
They brought to heavy rock a completely original sound. Led Zep are the grandfathers of rock 'n' roll. I listened to them in my teen years and was in awe of Jimmy Page, John Paul Jones, John Bonham and his "one of a kind drumming" and, of course, the higher vocal register of Robert Plant.

Grand Funk Railroad,
Grand Funk
Some of the best riffs I've ever heard. Of course this is all before our time. We came up in 1975, and the Runaways days were Sex Pistols and the Ramones. The first tour we ever did with The Runaways was three months on the road with the Ramones. That was pretty cool. I remember squeezing into this station wagon, like nine of us, all squished into this station wagon, driving across the country for three months. So we came from that punk era, but stuff like Grand Funk is what got us there.

The Who, *Who's Next*
This album was truly life-changing because of the aggressive performances this band did live, and their songs were so beautiful and well-written.

Deep Purple, *Machine Head*
Of the girls in the Runaways, Sandy was the biggest metalhead. I remember when I first walked in to see the girls in the Runaways, it was just Joan, Sandy and me, we were the first three, and Sandy and I had jammed on the guitar solo to "Highway Star." She knew the entire drum part, and I knew the entire guitar part, and so we walked in and looked at each other up and down, started jamming. We played "Highway Star" and it was like that's it, she's rockin', she's slammin', I couldn't believe how she played.

Deep Purple, *In Rock*
Deep Purple had the best musicians; all of them were my favorites. Ritchie Blackmore was my first guitar god. I worshiped his playing.

Black Sabbath,
Sabbath Bloody Sabbath
Heavy metal at its finest. Also, some of the best rock riffs in the world. Evil, dark and haunting. The first concert I ever saw was Black Sabbath, Long Beach Arena, when I was 13. I really think your first concert influences you so much musically. And when I saw Black Sabbath at Long Beach Arena, I just flipped out. I thought wow, they are so heavy, and they seemed almost like gods. They seemed untouchable, unreachable. They didn't seem human, you know? Really, it's just a bunch of guys up there, but they just seemed so godlike. And their music, the way the music was making people feel, it was like they were under some sort of spell. And I wanted to be able to do that. I wanted to be able to sound like that. I wanted to be able to make people feel like they were making people feel.

Lita Ford had a successful solo career in the '80s, scoring a hit with "Kiss Me Deadly."
PHOTO BY MICHAEL OCHS ARCHIVES/GETTY IMAGESGETTY IMAGES

STEVE FOSSEN
HEART

Heart in 1980 (L-R): Ann Wilson, Michael DeRosier, Howard Leese, Nancy Wilson and Steve Fossen. PHOTO BY MICHAEL PUTLAND/GETTY IMAGES

Bassist Steve Fossen is a founding member of Seattle classic rock institution Heart and is a member of the Rock and Roll Hall of Fame, due to Heart's induction in 2013. Fronted by sisters Ann and Nancy Wilson, Fossen was aboard for the band's debut album, 1975's *Dreamboat Annie* through 1982's *Private Audition*. Four of the band's first six albums are certified platinum and double platinum, with one additional, *Bebe Le Strange*, certified as gold. While there are many reasons for Heart's success, Fossen credits, in part, the singing of Ann and Nancy Wilson. "The two of them singing together ... that two-part harmony, with an occasional three-part harmony thrown in, is something that is just so appealing to audiences when done right that it is beyond compare," Fossen said. Fossen and classic lineup drummer Michael Derosier now record and tour as Heart by Heart.

The Beatles, *Meet the Beatles!*

Meet the Beatles! was the album that inspired me to become a rock musician. My parents had a record player that was in the bottom of a TV and you pulled it out. So I remember being in the basement and just playing it over and over and over and staring at the album cover and marvelling at the talent and the musicianship and singing ability of those guys.

The Beatles, *Sgt. Pepper's Lonely Hearts Club Band*

Well, by that time it was five, six years later and I was older and had experimented with smoking marijuana. And I think by that time I'd even taken LSD and I know the Beatles were doing that too at that time. So the sonic landscape of *Sgt. Pepper* and the subject matter and the variety of songs… the band's musicianship had progressed from the early days to where they were studio masters at this point. Rather than

Yes, *Fragile*

I loved *Fragile*, and we did "Roundabout" back in the old days. Chris Squire's bass tone was like a revelation for a lot of people. So of course I ran out and bought myself a Rickenbacker. What I liked also about Yes is that they had the acoustic and the electric and the bass and the drums, you know, the big drums going on. So with Nancy playing acoustic and Roger playing electric, we had stuff to emulate and think about–it inspired us to be better all the time.

The Moody Blues, *Days of Future Passed*

That album actually preceded *Sgt. Pepper*, but it was a total "scene" album or concept album from top to bottom. I just loved how Justin Hayward sang songs and his guitar playing and then I was a fan of the bass playing also. And I had always been interested in orchestration and stuff, so that album really struck a chord with me. And then in later years after I'd met Ann [Wilson], I found out that Ann was a huge fan of the Moody Blues also. And then in our first band together that we had back in '71, '72, Ann and I would sing Moody Blues songs together. That band was Hocus Pocus and then we changed the name back to Heart and by the time we changed our name back to Heart, back in April of '72, we used to do "Ride My See-Saw" and a few other Moody Blues songs. And I remember back when Roger [Fisher] and I had The Army, we sang "Knights in White Satin." You don't really hear Moody Blues in Heart, but they were a big influence on me personally, and on Ann as well.

King Crimson, *In the Court of the Crimson King*

Greg Lake was a big influence on my bass playing. His bass tone was very much sought after in the day. He's using a Fender Jazz bass. I'm a Fender guy; I've always played Fenders. A P-bass has a thicker, meatier tone and then the Jazz bass has a little more high end and bite and a little bit different character. But between those two basses you can get almost any tone. I know that Paul McCartney played a Jazz bass on the *White Album*, on some of the cuts, so that was kind of cool. This was a dark album but it was kind of a dark time. America was heavily involved in the Vietnam war and there was a lot of antiestablishment sentiment going on in my generation. And it kind of fed into the vibe of this record, especially "21st Century Schizoid Man." There was a certain element that it evoked, of an older business class that probably still exists today, but fairly cynical in its quest for prosperity and control.

Led Zeppelin, *IV*

I actually wrote down Zep *I*, Zep *II* and Zep *IV* (laughs). But Zep *IV*, with of course "Stairway to Heaven," that was a song that Heart played at clubs back in the day and that was a big showstopper for us. Of course everybody wanted to emulate the bass and drum combination. I don't think that John Paul Jones and John Bonham have ever been surpassed to this day as far as their musicianship and tones and everything else. But that album's got "Black Dog" and "When the Levee Breaks." All that stuff, at the time, you'd put it on the stereo, and of course that was back when you dropped a needle. You'd drop the needle on those things and man, your speakers just went crazy alive, you know? The production on that album was amazing for the time.

Everybody in the band were Zeppelin fans. Roger and Ann, all of us. They were on the turntable at all times. We did a lot of stuff off of *Houses of the Holy*, plus "Kashmir." We did a whole medley of stuff from the first two albums. This was in clubs. Once we got *Dreamboat Annie* out there we stopped, although we'd play "Stairway to Heaven" every once in a while and we'd play "The Rover." "The Rover" was a big song for us to play for encores or just at a rock show. Especially for *Dreamboat Annie*, because with *Dreamboat Annie*, we only had the one album of our own songs to choose from. So we kind of had to fill it up with some extra things and Led Zeppelin was one of them. And "Rock and Roll" was a good encore song that Heart did. But most important to Heart, as big fans of Led Zeppelin, we understood that as long as you scattered enough rock stuff in there, you could do a nice acoustic song on the same album.

The Sonics, *Here Are the Sonics*

Here are the Sonics was very important, with that raw energy. The singer was great. The bass player, Andy Parypa, was a good friend of mine and he kinda took me under his wing a little bit and taught me a lot of stuff about how to get good sounds and how to play and all that kinda stuff. The band I was in at the time, before Roger and I teamed up, we opened up for them. Andy moved into the booking agent part of the business and by that time he was helping book us and everything. So I'd meet with him all the time and sign contracts and we'd talk and he was just very, very cool to me and gave me a lot of advice that really stuck with me. There are lot of bands that will say that The Sonics were an influence on their development and everything. And I know the Sonics are pretty big in England still and Europe still, so yeah, they can go do a tour over there.

Leonard Cohen, *Songs of Leonard Cohen*

That very first album, I don't know if it influenced Heart, but it was a big influence on me personally. Not a lot of people knew about him back in those days. What I liked is his subtle, understated delivery, and his guitar parts, they weren't exactly droney but they were simple. It wasn't like he was a great guitar player, but the guitar parts were very straightforward and they fit the song and his singing and the lyrics. And of course, you listened to the lyrics and it's like you'd get an epiphany every two minutes,

The Beach Boys, *Smiley Smile*

That was a big influence on me even though I think the only hit it had on there was "Good Vibrations." But I remember the sonic-ness of it and everything really captured my imagination. And the lyrics… I don't know, it's just a strange… the Beach Boys were a very different kind of act because at first they had all the surf songs and car songs, and then they went into an era where they had those beautiful, sentimental love songs. And then they got into the era of "Good Vibrations." So every era was so different from the last.

Heart, *Dreamboat Annie*

Finally, I'd say that out of any record here, ***Dreamboat Annie*** changed my life more than anything. Because it did. It changed all of our lives basically, and it's still changing my life to this day because, you know, Mike [Derosier] and I, we play together in Heart by Heart and we still get royalties and everything. With the streaming and the downloading and stuff, this year, "Magic Man" actually surpassed "Barracuda" in that department, and that's off ***Dreamboat Annie*** of course. But what I like about that record in particular, we had been playing together since '72 and we were one of the premiere rock bands in the lower British Columbia/Vancouver area. And back in those days, you would pull into a club on a Monday or Tuesday or Wednesday night and then you'd play all the way through Saturday night. Sometimes you'd just take Sunday off and then you'd play at the same club for another week. And so you really got to hone your chops, so to speak, and learn how to make a set that excited the audience and all that kind of stuff. So the band was like a finely tuned sports car. So by the time we did ***Dreamboat Annie***, we had all that going for us. And the vibe of us playing together for those three or four years and traveling around and experiencing all these things together… everybody was kind of on the same page back then as far as ambition and drive went. It was a special time.

TONY FRANKLIN
THE FIRM

Tony Franklin (left) and Jimmy Page of The Firm onstage at the Milwaukee Arena in 1985. PHOTO BY PAUL NATKIN/GETTY IMAGES

Tony "The Fretless Monster" Franklin might possibly be the best bass player you never heard of, unless of course you are an adherent to the bass, and its envelope-pushing capabilities in the hands of someone like Franklin. Sure, there are great bass players in rock music, and Franklin is one of them, but he's more, very much more. Franklin rose to prominence in the 1980s as the bassist with The Firm, the supergroup that grew out of the ashes of the mighty Led Zeppelin, with Jimmy Page leading on guitar, Paul Rodgers (Bad Company) on vocals, Franklin on bass and Chris Slade (Uriah Heep) on drums. Like Page's early beginnings, Franklin has done his share of session work, appearing as a four-string gunslinger on over 150 albums for such artists as Kate Bush, Roy Harper, Glenn Hughes, David Gilmour, Quiet Riot and of course Jimmy Page.

PHOTO BY PAUL NATKIN/GETTY IMAGES

Queen, *A Night at the Opera*
"Bohemian Rhapsody" ruled the UK charts in late 1975, but it never occurred to me that there was an album it came from. Months later, a close school friend played **A Night at the Opera**. I was transfixed. At 13 years old, I'd never heard anything like it. Symphonic in its scope and musically diverse–from hard rock to vaudeville. Operatic, adventurous and playful.

Abba, *Greatest Hits*
My dad owned the album, and at 13, I played it repeatedly. I still love Abba. I consider them masters of pop music songwriting, production and performance. Even at that age, I was aware of how skilfully they created musical hooks and passages that filled every second with meaningful melodies, sounds and rhythms.

Be-Bop Deluxe, *Futurama*
I was introduced to Be-Bop Deluxe by a school friend in 1976. The band's music was like a stream of consciousness, dreamlike and ethereal, with poetic lyrics and unusual musical landscapes that conformed to no stereotypes. Though Be-Bop Deluxe did not receive the public accolades and success they deserved, this album was a great influence upon me.

Jaco Pastorius, *Jaco Pastorius*
This album was released in 1976 but I didn't hear it until 1979. I'd been playing fretted bass for five years. Jaco's harmonics, his tone, his groove and his compositions spawned a complete paradigm shift in my musical journey. I had to have a fretless bass. Fretless bass has become my signature instrument, and this was the album that ignited the spark.

Weather Report, *Heavy Weather*
This album was a continuation of my discovery of Jaco Pastorius. It showed a different aspect of Jaco – in a full band context, often playing other people's compositions. To me, Heavy Weather seemed closer to rock music than the pure jazz and funk of Jaco's solo album. Jaco's playing seemed more thoughtful, straight-ahead and emotional.

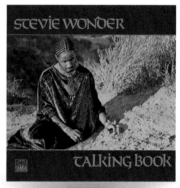

Stevie Wonder, *Talking Book*
This album has appeared at various times in my life, each time presenting me with different inspiration. This might qualify as my sole desert island disc. It covers many aspects of music that are dear to me. It's pure inspiration, offering phenomenal songwriting, great performances, daring creativity, passionate vulnerable love songs and a funk and groove like no other.

Roy Harper, *Work of Heart*

I wasn't sure if I should include this album on my list, as I played on it. But there's no denying its influence and impact upon me. I consider Roy a poet first, who is able to craft his words into emotional, meaningful musical works, supported by masterful acoustic guitar. His use of alternative open tunings opened up a whole new world of possibilities to me.

Stevie Wonder, *Songs in the Key of Life*

Songs carries on where **Talking Book** left off. Stevie is at the height of his creativity and confidence, willing to take musical chances, while crafting some of the biggest hits of the era, like "Sir Duke," "I Wish" and "Isn't She Lovely." Steeped in spirituality, this album has a subliminal timeless quality, which touches me on a very deep level.

Various Artists, *Standing in the Shadows of Motown*

In 2008, I became aware of the powerful and emotional movie **Standing in the Shadows of Motown**, featuring the legendary "Funk Brothers," the band that played on almost every Motown song from 1959 to 1972. It finally shone the spotlight on the little known heroes and innovators of this groundbreaking era in Motown's history.

Led Zeppelin, *Physical Graffiti*

In spite of working extensively with Jimmy Page, my appreciation of Led Zeppelin didn't fully blossom until after working with him. Zeppelin's catalog as a whole has been a major influence, its zenith being **Physical Graffiti**. Here they seemed to be completely at ease with themselves as a band, with nothing to prove, willing to stretch, experiment and have fun.

ART GARFUNKEL
SIMON & GARFUNKEL

Members of the Rock and Roll Hall of Fame, Simon & Garfunkel had 15 Top 40 hits. PHOTO BY RICHARD E. AARON/REDFERNS

At the height of the British Invasion, when U.S. airwaves were under siege by the likes of The Beatles, the Rolling Stones and Herman's Hermits, an unlikely American folk-rock duo not only withstood the offensive but prospered. As Simon & Garfunkel, Paul Simon and Art Garfunkel, childhood friends who grew up three blocks from each other in Forest Hills, New York, connected with listeners of all ages with melodic songs featuring gorgeous harmonies and Simon's exceptional songwriting. Between 1964 and 1970, Simon & Garfunkel released five albums of exquisite beauty and creativity. The duo's *Bridge Over Troubled Water*—which featured the hymn-like title track, sung by Garfunkel—topped the U.S. album charts for ten weeks in 1970 and went on to sell 13 million copies worldwide. The album, the duo's last of new material, won five Grammy Awards and numerous other honors on the strength of the title song and three other hit singles: "The Boxer," "Cecilia" and "El Condor Pasa." Simon & Garfunkel reunited in 1981 for a free concert in New York's Central Park. The ensuing live double album, *The Concert in Central Park* (1982), went platinum and included the duo's 15th Top 40 hit—a spirited rendition of the Everly Brothers' "Wake Up Little Susie." Simon & Garfunkel were inducted in the Rock and Roll Hall of Fame in 1990 and in 2003 received a Grammy Lifetime Achievement Award. "Everyone is younger than me now," said Garfunkel. "So my list covers a whole bunch of decades. You can see a little of American musical history through my list."

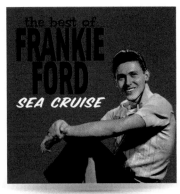

Enrico Caruso, *Aria from the Pearl Fishers*

The Pearl Fishers has a particular melody that I just love. [Sings] 'Da-da-dee-da-dee-dum… la-da-dee-da-dee-dee-da-ee-dummm…' You hear that little twist at the end? That's what got me. It's like a bumblebee stinging you for life. To do that with your voice and do it with finesse, on a melody that's got heart to it, that was the disease I caught – right there. I heard this first when I was 5 listening to 78-rpm records on the Victrola with my dad who would play the Andrew Sisters and some classical things. I fell in love with it. Caruso was a hell of a singer.

Nat King Cole, *Nature Boy*

It was the differentness of the melody that I loved. What an offbeat song from left field. I must have said as a kid, 'you can do that kind of song and get away with it? And the lyric can be so philosophical?' [Sings] 'And then one day, one magic day he passed my way… And while we spoke of many things… ' Isn't that something? Listen to these blue notes: [Sings] 'Fools and kings, this he said to me…' A lot of chromatics. And what did he say? [Sings] 'The greatest thing you'll ever learn, is just to love and be loved in return.' That's beautiful Zen philosophy in the middle of a pop song. It was new to me, and I saw that the art form – the record, the song – could have real dimension."

Frankie Ford, *Sea Cruise*

[Sings]'Won't you let me take you on a sea cruise?'… Nothing rocked quite like this record. It was full of distortion and I loved it. For me, it was the door opening to rock 'n' roll. There are a lot of wonderful examples I could have picked, but for me, Frankie Ford's "Sea Cruise" says it better than anything. It was the groove. It pulled you out of your seat out onto the dance floor more than any other. I loved that groove.

Garfunkel's movie career included playing Jack Nicholson's friend Sandy in 1971's *Carnal Knowledge.*

The Everly Brothers, *Songs Our Daddy Taught Us*

My favorite group, one that filled my teenage years, The Everly Brothers. And this album, the whole album, was definitely one of the records that changed my life. They captured me and my friend who lived three blocks away, Paul Simon. We were students of the Everly Brothers for a year or two, metaphorically speaking. It really was central to our musical growth. That magnificent two-part harmony was fused together so beautifully. In their case, I'll move from songs to albums and pick **Songs Our Daddy Taught Us**. It's a killer.

Sam Cooke, *You Send Me*

This is a record that changed my life. Sam sang with such open-throated force and beauty that as a singer, Artie Garfunkel was really sitting at Sam Cooke's feet. [Sings] "You...send me..." There's a lot to love about this record, but above all, is comes down to this: The singer can really sing.

Johnny Mathis, *It's Not For Me to Say*

You could predict that. You could figure Artie Garfunkel likes Johnny Mathis' singing. [Sings] "It's not for me to say, you love me..." Brilliant stuff. Just a gorgeous singer. When I was 14 I thought he was the one. He was really good. His vibrato was unearthly; it was heaven sent. In his finest recordings he was king. His vibrato was killer. The amount of vibrato, the dialing it in so it was just right is what great singers do. If you're a singer like me, you went crazy the first time you heard the voice of Johnny Mathis.

Ike and Tina Turner, *River Deep, Mountain High*

There's a record that changed my life. It was so f*cking great. Call that Phil Spector's masterpiece. That's really what it is. The artists certainly executed, they delivered but Phil's vision is grandiose in the best sense. When you hear all these elements in a studio record, he threw the kitchen sink at the song, all mixed and balanced artfully. Wow. He worked with quantity successfully. Usually it could be a mess. Phil Spector was the best definition of grandiose. Although the end of "Bridge Over Troubled Water" was a good version of grandiose, too.

The Beatles, *Here, There and Everywhere*

When I heard "Here, There and Everywhere" I was smitten. What a great, great record. This little fluty melody is from the gods. When [Paul] McCartney wrote that his head was up looking at clouds. How I love that. What was going through McCartney's life the week he wrote this? You have to be in some kind of magical mood to come up with something this enchanting. If music can be defined as that which perfumes the atmosphere, then "Here, There And Everywhere" does it like no other single I've ever heard. It's supreme.

Les Swingle Singers,
Jazz Sebastian Bach
An album of Parisian singers taking the notes of Bach's music and singing them with a doo-wop jazz style and keeping it true to Bach's work. I loved that album. Bach is so brilliant when the notes are lived up to faithfully. The Swingle Singers… Listen to it. You'll be singing it to yourself for years after.

The Hi-Lo's,
Suddenly It's the Hi-Lo's
I'm a singer and I love harmony and this album really affected me. In college I was smitten by how adventurous some of these harmonies were. I'm not much of a jazzer but I got a couple of feet in the water with this one. Just listening and loving it. The high harmony really went wild. The chords were far out. Stretched harmonies.

Childhood friends, Simon and Garfunkel started singing together in sixth grade.
PHOTO BY HULTON ARCHIVE/GETTY IMAGES

SCOTT GORHAM
THIN LIZZY

The boys are back in town: Brian Robertson and Scott Gorham, the twin lead guitars of Thin Lizzy. PHOTO BY EBET ROBERTS/REDFERNS

Scott Gorham became part of rock 'n' roll history through his tenure as co-guitarist in the classic Thin Lizzy lineup. Formed in Dublin in 1969, Thin Lizzy scored a worldwide hit that remains a classic rock radio station mainstay with "The Boys Are Back in Town" from *Jailbreak* (1976). AllMusic critic Stephen Thomas Erelwine called the dual-guitar work by Gorham and Brian Robertson "one of the most distinctive sounds of '70s rock." While songwriter and vocalist Phil Lynott was the *de facto* leader of Thin Lizzy, it was Gorham who invented the idea of sinewy yet composed twin leads in a hard rock context along with his partner in crime Robertson. The lineup of Gorham, Robertson, Lynott and drummer Brian Downey released five studio albums and one live album. Once Robertson was out of the band Gorham continued his dual-guitar role with Gary Moore, Snowy White and finally John Sykes. Gorham has enjoyed a second rock 'n' roll life with his scrappy classic rock act Black Star Riders, recording multiple albums and embarking on many tours across North America and Europe.

The Beatles, Meet the Beatles!

I was 12 years old the first time I heard the Beatles. It was on the radio; my mom was driving me home from school and there they were. I think it was "I Want to Hold Your Hand' and so the album for me would have been **Meet the Beatles!**. I had never heard anything like that before. I liked music before that anyway, but now this is, wow man, it's a bunch of young dudes and it's four guys–pretty cool.

Now, going back three years, I used to pose in front of the mirror with brooms and maybe a tennis racket, I threw a few shapes in front of the mirror when the radio was on. And my dad, he noticed that, and when I was nine years old, there's this strange package under the Christmas tree. I couldn't really figure out what the hell that shape was. Well, he whips it open and there it was–a Sears Silvertone guitar. And I'm looking at this thing going, what am I supposed to do with this?! My dad took it from me and he played two really simple chords. And I went, oh my God, because I'm pretty sure my father couldn't play guitar. But all of a sudden he looked like this genius guy. What he did is the guy, whoever was at Sears, dad says, 'Can you just show me two really simple chords?' I'm sure it was just like a two-string thing. Anyway, to me as a nine-year-old, my dad looked like this genius musician. But you know something? I barely even picked up that guitar. I basically posed with it in front of the mirror for a couple more years. But after the Beatles I started plunking away on this thing, trying to make some sense of it. So because of that record, that became the real embryonic stages for me.

Cream, Disraeli Gears

I just loved the songwriting and what these guys were playing and how they played it. They just seemed to have this professional attitude. And the sound that Eric [Clapton] came up with was completely different from all these other guys who were just kind of plunking away. His whole sustain thing, I didn't even know that existed, that you could actually sustain a note on a guitar, of course at this time I'm 15 years old. And their psychedelic vibe, that was the times. These days it looks and sounds a little passé, a little old, but back then, you're 13, 14, 15 years old, and it was cutting edge.

The Jimi Hendrix Experience, Axis: Bold as Love

When Jimi came out with "Hey Joe," it was another step in what you can do with the guitar. I don't think Hendrix said it like this, but I'm sure it was a thing where, well, hey, Eric turned on to the guitar, but let me show you what else you can do. And that's what I think really captured everybody's thought process; it was, "Oh my God, I didn't know you could do that!" I was like, what's a wah-wah? I bought a wah-wah, and wow, he was great with that. And in a way, this is heavy metal getting invented but we weren't actually calling it heavy metal. It was just very guitar-dominated type of music, which I loved. I thought it was the greatest thing ever. The way he looked, the way he moved… they looked like rock gods. How can you not get inspired by that? But then a couple albums on we got **Axis: Bold as Love**, where now he shows everybody, yeah, I can actually turn the volume down and I'm going to do a little lead thing here, and that was single notes with double notes and it's going to be more like a chordy kind of element I'm going to throw in here, right? Which turned out really beautiful.

Fleetwood Mac, Mr. Wonderful

The Fleetwood Mac with Peter Green: here's a guy that unfortunately has kind of lost his edge these days with his illness and all that, but the way he approached things, his tone and the way he wrote songs was completely different from the other guys within that blues-based kind of deal. He had these really sort of meaningful lyrics and sometimes you had no idea what the lyrics even meant, but you didn't care. It was the way he sang them, the way he played, his style. It was just very cool. I ended up listening to a lot of Fleetwood Mac from that period.

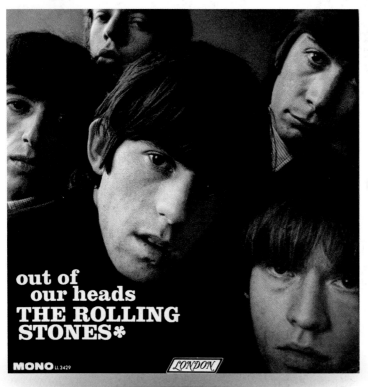

Led Zeppelin, I

First there was Yardbirds and then Jeff Beck, *Truth*. I thought Jeff Beck was just this killer guitar player and I loved that album. It had a lot of atmosphere to it. Probably that more than anything subliminally sunk in with me from that record. But at the same time, Jimmy forms Led Zeppelin, and I loved the whole Led Zeppelin thing because once again these guys were coming up with riffs along with Robert Plant who sang the hell out of 'em. And they had this rhythm section that was power-mad but then controlled at the same time. Jimmy Page, like Keith Richards, was consistently coming up with these amazingly emotional riffs that just stuck with you for… well, in my case, for the rest of my life. He was just one of those great players that could do that. I'd say Zeppelin more than any of these bands helped shape me; what I do today is shaped by what Jimmy did. You're always looking for that really great riff that everybody's going to remember, and those guys did that regularly.

The Rolling Stones, *Out of Our Heads*

There's always going to be the Rolling Stones. "Satisfaction," "Last Time," and also around then "19th Nervous Breakdown," although that was only a single. I never thought of Keith Richards as a real sort of rock god kinda guy because he never seemed to have that tone and he never really sustained a note. But it was the memorable riffs that he consistently came up with. Once again, it made you pick the guitar up and want to learn those songs. I wouldn't say the Rolling Stones were my favorite, favorite band, even at that point, but I absolutely recognize these guys as a band apart from most of the bands out there. I mean it was hit after hit after hit with these guys.

Deep Purple, *Shades of Deep Purple*

When you're talking about the heavy metal thing, you're going to go with Deep Purple. But I'll go back to *Shades of* and "Hush." I didn't know how Ritchie Blackmore was getting that sound. He was using the vibrato quite extensively and coming up with these really different sounds that set him apart from all the other guitar players, which was really cool. Back then everybody seemed to not want to sound like everybody else, as opposed to what's going on today. I have a hard time differentiating between one guitar player and another. Everybody seems to be homogenized, kind of blending in with each other. Back then it was a whole different ballgame, where you did not want to sound like the guy you were standing right next to.

Thin Lizzy's Phil Lynott, Brian Downey, Brian Robertson and Scott Gorham enjoy the fermented fruits of their rock 'n' roll labor.
PHOTO BY ERICA ECHENBERG/REDFERNS

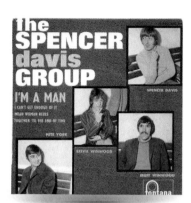

The Spencer Davis Group,
I'm a Man

Steve Winwood, Spencer Davis. "I'm a Man;" I still love that today. Whenever that song is on, my head starts bobbing, and when you hear it, you still can't understand it. Because it's this 17-year-old kid that's got this voice. It sounds like he's been smoking cigarettes and drinking bottles of whiskey and he's got this voice that could cut glass. It's just amazing.

The Allman Brothers,
Idlewild South

How could you not love that southern rock kind of thing? They did quite long passages, and played with such heart, even though they really thought these things through. They were really good at what they did and boy, did those guys cover a lot of ground. I'm not sure if they or Wishbone Ash influenced me to want to do the Thin Lizzy two-guitar, twin-lead thing, but I think subliminally they had to have been there.

Free, *Tons of Sobs*

You know, the band I really loved the most was probably Free. I just thought every one of those guys in the band was a great player. Their music was really simple, but it was really powerful at the same time. Paul Kossoff had the most wicked vibrato of all the guitar players. You know, if you're going to learn how to play guitar with vibrato, that's where you go. You want to go to the **Tons of Sobs** album and listen to Paul Kossoff and how he did it.

STEVE GORMAN
THE BLACK CROWES

The Black Crowes (from left): Jeff Cease, Chris Robinson, Rich Robinson, Steve Gorman and Johnny Colt. PHOTO BY MICK HUTSON/REDFERNS

For 15 years, Steve Gorman played drums for the Black Crowes, a classic-rock rooted band that sold more than 30 million albums. Combining Rolling Stones swagger and the boogie of the Faces, the Black Crowes exploded on the scene with their 1990 debut album *Shake Your Money Maker*, which peaked at No. 4 on the *Billboard 200* and featured two hit singles, "Hard to Handle," and "She Talks to Angels." Selling more than 5 million copies, *Shake Your Money Maker* paved the way for the band to be named "Best New American Band" by *Rolling Stone* magazine. The band's 1992 album, *The Southern Harmony and Musical Companion*, reached the top of the *Billboard 200*. And yet the Black Crowes were not wired for sustained success. Brash, hard-partying and led by two brothers, Chris and Rich Robinson, who were constantly at each others' throats, the Black Crowes disbanded in 2015.

Led Zeppelin, *I*

I bought by first drum kit in 1987, and at the same time, started listening to Led Zeppelin. I am not sure how I had missed them along the way, but discovering Bonham just as I began drumming was both a blessing and a curse–and an eternal source of inspiration and frustration. From the first listen, his playing made perfect sense to me. I remember thinking that those drums were what drums were supposed to sound like and his feel was how drums were supposed to feel. I felt a very deep and immediate connection to his drumming.

Devo, *Q: Are We Not Men? A: We Are Devo!*

I saw Devo on *Saturday Night Live* in 1978. I was confused and excited by whatever the hell they were doing. It didn't make sense, but I wanted in on whatever they were selling. I am happy to say that for a brief period of time, my two favorite bands were Devo and Earth, Wind & Fire.

R.E.M., *Murmur*

I love rock 'n' roll music because of The Bee Gees and The Beatles, but I initially became a musician because of R.E.M. What U2 started, R.E.M. finished. I saw them many times throughout the '80s, and I left every show with a burning desire to get a band together. This album, which has very few decipherable lyrics and is cloaked with such a mysterious and cloudy production, still makes me feel like a college freshman anytime I hear it. So interesting, and weird, and probably the album I have listened to straight through more than any other (suffice it to say that I had a lot of free time in 1983).

BARRY GOUDREAU
BOSTON

Boston in 1976 (from left): Brad Delp, Tom Scholz, Sib Hashian, Fran Sheehan and Barry Goudreau. PHOTO BY RON POWNALL/GETTY IMAGESGETTY IMAGES

Barry Goudreau counts himself lucky to be part of one of the biggest success stories in the music business when the band Boston shot like a rocket to the top of the *Billboard* charts with their self-titled debut in 1976. Now a a staple of classic rock radio stations, *Boston* sold approximately 17 million copies in the U.S. and spawned such hits as "More Than a Feeling," "Long Time" and "Peace of Mind." The band's 1978 follow-up, *Don't Look Back*, also featuring Goudreau on guitar, sold seven times platinum. Worldwide, Boston has sold approximately 75 million records, putting them in the upper echelon of sales, remarkable especially for an act with only a half dozen records. Leaving Boston in 1980, Goudreau went on to a solo career, recording with Orion the Hunter and RTZ, the latter featuring the soaring vocals of Boston great Brad Delp, with whom Goudreau also recorded post-RTZ. Delp also did some backups on *Orion the Hunter* album from 1984.

PHOTO BY ED PERLSTEIN/REDFERNS/GETTY IMAGES

The Jimi Hendrix Experience,
Are You Experienced

I had my first real stereo, and this record was a revelation. I remember turning the balance back and forth so I could hear instruments on one side and the other side, you know, pick out just what the guitar was playing or just what the bass was playing. And so that was huge. With Jimi, it was like, oh my God, how's he doing that and how do *I* do that?! He had some of the first use of the fuzz and wah-wah ever and was just taking it in a whole different direction from the blues that I had been listening to. The stuff before, you were either part of the poppy side or it was hardcore blues. And Jimi Hendrix kind of stepped in between that and had some of the most memorable lines as well.

The Paul Butterfield Blues Band,
East-West

A little later on I'd been playing for awhile and been in bands and so forth. I get into the blues and the Paul Butterfield **East-West** album. That was a big one for me because I actually learned a lot of my lead guitar playing, playing along with that record. Basically a friend in high school I was in a band with, he was a big blues fan and he introduced me to that record. He was a little more advanced than me at the time and was playing some lead guitar and started showing me some stuff and said, "Well here; take this record and play along with it." And that's really when I first became a lead guitarist.

Jeff Beck, *Truth*

There was a venue here in town called the Boston Tea Party that all the excellent bands went through back in the mid to late '60s. And I went to see Jeff Beck the first week they played in the country. I'd heard some of the cuts from **Truth** on WBCN radio—they were always way ahead of anybody else–but I don't think I had the album yet. And live, I was just taken aback by the sound. Jeff playing a Les Paul through a wah-wah pedal and Marshall stack was like, wow, that's the sound. With that mid-range tone, it cut through everything. So after Tom [Scholz] and I have been working together for awhile, I took him to some Jeff Beck shows and he'd gotten turned onto that kind of sound too. And you know, I think that had an influence on the Boston sound.

The Beatles, *Sgt. Pepper's Lonely Hearts Club Band*

I actually bought **Are you Experienced** the same time as **Sgt. Pepper**, brought both home from the record store at the same time. **Sgt. Pepper** took music a whole new direction with kind of the orchestral arrangements; it really gave you an idea of what you could do with music beyond just the strict rock format.

The Steve Miller Band, *Sailor*

One of his early ones, his second album, with "Living in the USA," which was one of my favorite songs. Loved that album back in the day and listened to it over and over and over again. This is before he really reached the popularity they got to later on; it wasn't that big a seller but I was a big fan. And again, Steve was a guy that was playing the blues but adding the rock, which is something I really, really liked.

The Beach Boys, *Surfin' Safari*

This was my first record. I was 12, 13 years old and just got my first white Fender Stratocaster. So the Beach Boys were huge, simply for the fact that they were playing guitar. Because basically back at that time, there wasn't a whole lot of music on TV. You know, Ricky Nelson would play guitar at the end of Ozzie and Harriet or something like that, but there wasn't really a whole lot of music around.

Queen, *A Night at the Opera*

We heard this as we were rehearsing for the Boston stuff. I really loved the layered vocals and the way guitar is very expressive–the guitar recordings were great. It's funny because I just saw the movie [**Bohemian Rhapsody**] and there's a scene where they're talking about what the single should be, and the record company wanted it to be "I'm in Love with My Car" and I must admit that was my favorite. You know, maybe he knew what he was talking about a little bit there. I'm sure we talked about Queen and there's an influence there. Brad Delp brought a lot to it in terms of knowing how to layer vocals. He was a huge Beatles fan. He knew every Beatles song inside and out and he could sing each Beatle part and sound like that particular Beatle. So he loved layered vocals and elaborate recordings. A lot of acts were getting into that at the time. It was a period when you could go in and make a record and not have to do one song a day and get it done in a week. You could kind of sit back and take some time.

Led Zeppelin, *I*

And so from that same venue, the Boston Tea Party, just a few weeks later I went to see Led Zeppelin, the first time they played in the country, and the **Led Zeppelin** album became a huge influence. Again, it was blues-based but rocked up with big, big guitars and big drum sounds. And I've got to admit, the first time I saw Led Zeppelin, I thought, oh my, this is the same thing as Jeff Beck–guitar, bass, drums, lead singer. Exactly. And he's doing blues songs. My God, they're copying Jeff Beck! At the time I didn't realize what the whole lineage was and actually how close they were. But to me it was the same frame of mind, lots of cross-pollination there.

As guitarists, they were also very similar but as time went on they went off in different directions. The further into it they got, I've got to admit I followed Jeff more than I follow Jimmy Page, although a lot of people compare me more to Jimmy Page than Jeff Beck, but hey. But **Led Zeppelin**, oh God, I loved all the songs. I really liked the reworks of the blues songs because I'd kind of come from the traditional Chicago blues and this kind of took that and put it on 11, so to speak.

Cream, *Wheels of Fire*

I remember seeing Cream when they came through Boston. That's the reason why I started playing an SG [Gibson]. Clapton was playing a red SG through Marshall stacks. And I thought, man, I gotta have that, and I had the SG guitar within months of that. But it took me a few more years before I could afford the amplifiers–pretty expensive. The first album was the one that really turned me onto them, but the live album, of course, was the ultimate. And again, as guitarists, these guys were pretty similar. They all had really good chops and they would take the blues and reinterpret it. I don't know if I could pick a favorite out of them now but at that point it was Jeff Beck. Of course Eric Clapton obviously had quite a career too.

Boston enjoying the bright lights of success in 1978. PHOTO BY RICHARD CREAMER/MICHAEL OCHS ARCHIVES/GETTY IMAGES

Boston, *Boston*

Of course the **Boston** album changed my life more than any of these records. What's funny, very early on, probably '69, '70, Tom and I went into a recording studio and did some recording. And I think at that point he realized to make it all work, he really had

to have his own equipment. And that's when he built his first multi-track recorder and things kind of took off from there. He started off with just four tracks, eight tracks, and I think he ended up building a 12-track recorder from scratch there. It was a whole different way of doing things. And I mean for that reason, the record company wasn't sure they wanted him producing the first record because they said, "My God, they did it in the basement. We can't let them make a record in the basement!" (laughs).

But yes, the success of that record was a combination of many things. It was the right music at the right time, the right people, the right label, you know, everything—the planets just aligned. So yes, oh God, absolutely, it changed my life. I was so lucky to have been involved. I can't say enough about it. Like I said, the stars just aligned with the right music at the right time, the right production and label and promotion, and you know, somehow people were ready to hear that music that we made.

BILL GOULD
FAITH NO MORE

Faith No More in 1990 (L-R): Bill Gould, Jim Martin, Mike Bordin, Roddy Bottum and Mike Patton. PHOTO BY MICK HUTSON/REDFERNS

Bill Gould is the bassist for the very bass-important and well-regarded Los Angeles band Faith No More. Gould also shows up on some pretty shocking and extremely metallic records by the likes of Brujeria. Faith No More became instantly loveable through the second version of their early anthem "We Care A Lot," from 1987's *Introduce Yourself* album. But it wasn't until the band emerged with new singer Mike Patton, that they hit gold, and then platinum, with 1989's *The Real Thing*, lead by single "Epic." The comparatively irascible and opaque *Angel Dust* went gold, but then the band found themselves at the fringes where the fans preferred them. 2015 saw the release of a reunion album called *Sol Invictus*, accompanied by concerts to packed houses. Then it was back to the bad news, when original singer Chuck Mosley was found dead in his Cleveland home in 2017 of a suspected heroin overdose.

PHOTO BY IAN DICKSON/REDFERNS

John Lennon, *Plastic Ono Band*

When I grew up, my father had a record collection and this was one of the records he never played. But it was in his pile. About 1971, eight years old, I would listen to it on my own, and it's actually a really radical record, I think, especially for an eight-year-old. And then I read the lyrics–I could read–and so I listened to it over and over. The music was really accessible but the content was intense. So that was a major influence.

Genesis, *Foxtrot*

I was in a band when I was 14 and I was at somebody's house, just playing in my friend's living room, and they put this record on. And it was just really interesting for me, because it was very lo-fi-recorded but extremely elaborately arranged. So it had this kind of homemade aspect to it. It has a real British feeling about it, with just an intense amount of work, but it was very lo-fi–it sounded fascinating.

Sex Pistols,
Never Mind the Bollocks, Here's the Sex Pistols

This was one of those cases where I wanted to hear it before I even knew what it sounded like, because of all the pictures and the imagery that went with it. I'd read about them in Time magazine (laughs). First time I heard it, I thought it was the worst thing I ever heard in my life. And by the end of the day that I'd heard it, the songs were still sticking in my head and that was it. This was in LA, actually the same place that I heard the Genesis record, at my friend's house, having rehearsal. And I remember taking it off the turntable and throwing it across the room, as a joke; like being very disrespectful about it because I thought it was so bad. But it's actually one of the greatest records of all time.

David Bowie, *Space Oddity*

Another album that my father had. He took me to see Bowie in concert when I was in fourth grade. I guess it was kind of a cultural mission of his or something. So I saw him around the **Ziggy Stardust** time when I was about fourth or fifth grade, That was another really dark record, actually (laughs), like **Plastic Ono Band**. I think it was a way darker record than any of Bowie's other records. There's a song called "Cygnet Committee" that was about ten minutes long, and it's kind of like his manifesto. It's pretty intense; it's kind of about the breakdown of social order. There's a song called "Unwashed and Somewhat Slightly Dazed," which is kind of about messed-up people. It's really punk rock, or proto-punk, I would say. Very, very dark stuff.

Kraftwerk, *Radio-Activity*

That was the first electronic record for me where it was very hooky and accessible but at the same time the tones and the colors were really lo-fi-ish and evocative. To me it was a kind of bridge. Like I'd heard experimental electronic music before, but this was the one that really first represented what they ended up accomplishing. They made a record that felt normal and natural but still had a lot of eclectic elements in it.

The thing about the Sex Pistols that was amazing was that the guitar was so aggressive, so driving. And then Johnny Rotten's vocals, they were kind of scary, threatening, kind of intimidating actually–this is first impressions. But by the time a couple days went by, I took the side of it, I took it on, I kind of absorbed it, incorporated it. But at the beginning it was pretty much somebody coming after me, it felt like, almost like a Stephen King character, like a villain, you know?

Public Image Ltd, *First Issue*

I'd listened to some dub and reggae and stuff, and this just blew it wide open. It kind of took the structure out of everything. It was a loose structure, like Sex Pistols without structure, like free jazz Sex Pistols. There was just nothing I could've compared it to. It was still extremely aggressive but it was hypnotic, one of those mind-blowing things, pointing to where you could take music. And bass was so fundamental there. Like I said, I was into some reggae and dub music already, but this was foreign to me. It had elements of that but without catering to it directly. And it made me think that there were things I liked about it that I could bring into what I did. Some of the other records I've picked, they have a lot of harmonic content and loud guitars, but this was different. These were my formative years, 18, 19 years old, and it was also a certain period of time when music was changing. If you want to go back, punk rock really came from pub rock and glam and it was still in a rock 'n' roll context. And then all of a sudden, with something like PiL, it shifts gears into this experimental world of weird possibilities.

Killing Joke, *Killing Joke*

First song, "Requiem," I thought it sounded like Rush and I hated it. It took me a while. I had to get past that first guitar tone, but whatever it was—"Change," "Wardance"—these guys somehow managed to get it to groove but still keep it really heavy and aggressive. And that to me was real mind-blowing. It had a funk element which was such a weird thing to bring that into this heavy atmospheric kind of noise. I thought that was just fascinating.

Metallica, *Ride the Lightning*

I'd heard the first album, **Kill 'Em All**. The drummer and I had a mutual friend, Cliff Burton, and it was Cliff's band, so there was no problem knowing who Metallica was. It's just weird that these long-haired kids with bell-bottoms were playing this kind of music. **Kill 'Em All** was a little primitive for me, but with **Ride the Lightning**, they really found their spot. They were really defining where heavy music could go. And for somebody like me who is not a heavy metal guy, it was kind of my gateway drug.

Faith No More hit the right chord by fusing heavy metal, funk, hip-hop and progressive rock. PHOTO BY MICK HUTSON/REDFERNS

Billy Gould and Mike Patton of Faith No More in 1991 PHOTO BY MICK HUTSON/REDFERNS

1965 – 1980

Basement 5,
1965 – 1980
Basement 5 were this British band with Don Letts in it, who ended up being in Big Audio Dynamite. It was kind of like pre-Bad Brains, where it was like a punk band, loud guitars, loud music, sort of Jamaican and dub music, but with super-over-driven guitars. And I would say that if ever there was a direct influence on Faith no More, that would be the biggest one out of all the ones I've listed, from the musical side, certainly. That was the first real bridge band that kind of fused those different worlds together in a way that I thought was really amazing. And it was a Martin Hannett production. In the late '70s, early '80s, he was the dude; he was doing all the Manchester stuff and coming up with a new sound.

Because if you look at our other influences, they are so diverse. Queen, Sparks, Black Flag… boy, I mean, we all listened to a lot of different music. Elton John was a big one. The first album I ever bought with my own money—I think Roddy, my keyboard player, too—was Elton John's **Greatest Hits**, when we were kids. If you think about the '70s and '80s and you listened to the radio, there was a real variation of what you could be listening to. When you'd go to somebody's house or you'd go to a party and look at their record collection, there was all kinds of different music and that was just normal. And now it doesn't seem like it as much. It's more demarcated, which is also because it's marketed to a specific crowd. You're this kind of person or you're this kind of person.

Laibach, *Opus Dei*
Laibach are from Slovenia, or before it became Slovenia, Yugoslavia. And Laibach was the German name for Ljubljana, during World War II. Extremely provocative. And usually music that was provocative I always found really fascinating. They would rearrange and re-engineer European pop songs that were horrible songs into sort of Wagnerian, traumatizing World War II-type stuff. I just thought it was amazing what they were doing with music. They were putting power back into music and not just making it a commercial product, but actually questioning and challenging people on a social level.

PAUL GRAY
THE DAMNED/
EDDIE AND THE HOT RODS

Eddie and the Hot Rods, 1979 (L-R): Paul Gray, Barrie Masters, Steve Nicol, Dave Higgs and Lew Lewis. PHOTO BY FIN COSTELLO/REDFERNS/GETTY IMAGES

Bass explorer Paul Gray is best known for his time with Eddie and the Hot Rods, The Damned and for five years in the '80s, UFO! Later, he returned to his rightful spot in The Damned, appearing on the Tony Visconti-produced album *Evil Spirits* from 2018. At the same time, he appeared as part of a rhythm section with his partner in punk grime drummer Rat Scabies. The Professor and the Madman was the name of the band, led by Alfie Agnew (Adolescents, D.I.) and Sean Elliott (Mind Over Four, D.I.), and their record was called *Disintegrate Me*, issued soon via Fullertone Records. Says Gray on the project, "They sent me across a track and I thought it was phenomenal. It was instantly connecting with me, because it's got all the things that I like. It's got energy, it's got spirit, and it's got great harmonies as well, great melodies. But it's also got all the right elements for me to go completely nuts on the bass." A consummate musician with an encyclopaedic musical knowledge, Gray has also played alongside Johnny Thunders, Rob Tyner and even Wham!'s Andrew Ridgley. But it is his appearance on *The Black Album* and *Strawberries* by The Damned that will stand as his most lasting legacy.

Paul Gray and Barrie Masters of Eddie and the Hot Rods. PHOTO BY EBET ROBERTS/REDFERNS

Slade, *Play It Loud*

It's the first album they did as Slade, and they're on the cover dressed like bovver boy yobbos, but the songs inside, they've got violins on them and it's just absolutely gorgeous. Fantastic songwriters. And the bass player, Jim Lea, has always been hugely underrated. He's a bit Jack Bruce-ish but with more melody. And he wrote nearly all the songs and he played the bass like a lead. And I love that. I thought, you know, this is really exciting, some fabulous songs in there. So that's the first one, 1970.

Alice Cooper, *School's Out*

Either that or *Killer*. But *School's Out*, that's the first album I probably learned to mime bass to, before I learned how to play it (laughs). So obviously a cracking album.

Hawkwind, *Space Ritual*

I saw Hawkwind live on that **Space Ritual** tour and that just changed my life. I thought that's what I want to do. You know, standing in front of Lemmy and his Rickenbacker and his Marshall cabinet painted all these weird colors, and Stacia dancing under the psychedelic lights, just sort of this incessant drive–brilliant. Hawkwind really did change my life. That's really what I aspired to be.

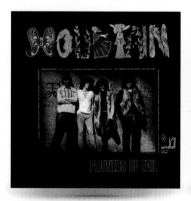

Mountain,
Flowers of Evil

Simply because there's a track on it called "Dream Sequence." It's pretty much the whole second side, and again, Felix Pappalardi, fabulous bass player, and playing between Corky Laing and Leslie West, just fabulous. So I love Mountain, and that particular track, brilliant.

Johann Sebastian Bach,
"St. Matthew Passion"

Gotta chuck that in. Yeah, it's the nearest I ever get to believing in God (laughs). Bach, you know, I could've given you the whole 168-CD set as one album, because I listen to Bach constantly. But that particular, "St. Matthew Passion," it just takes you to another place. So there you go, a list of records from the late '60s/early '70s, and one that's sort of the 1640s or whatever (laughs).

Various Artists: *Nuggets: Original Artyfacts from the First Psychedelic Era 1965 - 1968*

Every track on it. I mean, I could include any of those **Pebbles** albums too; I could include any Seeds albums. But to me, that is four sides of vinyl of perfect, you know, two-and-a-half, three-minute pop songs with a bit of fantastic psychedelia down the front. You look at "Liar, Liar" by The Castaways, perfect pop song, "Night Time" by The Strangeloves, you know, "I Had Too Much to Dream," every track, a winner. "Let's Talk about Girls"–what a great song for teenagers; yeah, let's talk about girls. It was all about what you go through as a teenager, those songs. Love it.

Eddie and the Hot Rods,
Teenage Depression

Specifically because that's the album, without that album, I wouldn't be here today, doing what I do. That set me off, and everything happened after that album, so I have to chuck that in. Punk hadn't started when the Hot Rods did the first album. You know, punk happened a bit later. Stranglers, they weren't a punk band; they were a pop band. The Clash hadn't formed. Joe Strummer was in the 101ers and they used to support the Hot Rods. They were a blues band. Punk hadn't started. Punk to us was **Nuggets**, which is my next favorite album. That, to us, was punk, and then we got introduced to the Stooges—that's punk.

But the first album, *Teenage Depression*, was really a rhythm and blues pop record as far as we're concerned. We didn't have any idea of punk, really. Billy Bragg said Eddie and the Hot Rods were the first punk band, and if anybody tells you otherwise, they're lying. That's on YouTube somewhere. But we were a rhythm and blues pop band. I mean, to me, The Seeds and The 13th Floor Elevators and The Kingsmen were punk bands. Punk started back in the mid-'60s with all those fantastic garage bands—that was punk. To be honest, we were four kind of kids under 20 in a room, just bashing it out, without a clear thought in the world. There was no plan, there was no, "How about this?" or, "We should play this." I'd grown up listening to kind of Hawkwind and The Who and Stackridge and Lindisfarne, and the guitar player listened to J. Geils and Sonny Boy Williamson and the singer would listen to The Doors. So we came from different musical backgrounds. But, you know, again, it's one of those situations where you all started working together and it just exploded. You just knew that you had something that was different. And apart from Feelgood, there was no band like the Hot Rods about then.

Barrie Masters, Dave Higgs, Steve Nicol and Paul Gray of Eddie and the Hot Rods fame. PHOTO BY ESTATE OF KEITH MORRIS/REDFERNS

Eddie & The Hot Rods (from left): Paul Gray, Steve Nicols, Barrie Masters, Lew Lewis and Dave Higgs. PHOTO BY CHARLIE GILLETT COLLECTION/REDFERNS

The Who, *Live at Leeds*

For obvious reasons. Just phenomenal. That, and the MC5's **Kick Out the Jams** are the two probably most exciting and edgy and dangerous albums ever done. **Live at Leeds**, John Entwistle, I mean, enough said–what can you say? And I just love the interplay between him and Townshend.

MC5, *Back in the USA*

I was lucky enough to work with Rob Tyner in sort of '77, do a single with him. And, you know, that voice, but that particular album, again, three-minute, perfect high-energy pop songs. Chock full of melody, but chock-full of kind of danger and spirit and fun and excitement and *joie de vivre*.

Deep Purple, *Machine Head*

That's an album that I grew up with at school– we all had it at school. I just fell in love with that bass sound, and then I found it was a Rickenbacker, and I thought, yeah (laughs), one day I'm gonna own one of them. Roger Glover, I think is an extraordinary bass player. I love bass players that take chances, and all these guys–Felix Pappalardi, Mountain, Entwistle and Dennis Dunaway–yeah, brilliant bass players. They're the ones who kind of set me on the path.

158

IAN HILL
JUDAS PRIEST

In 1970, Ian Hill and English school classmate K.K. Downing formed Judas Priest. Hill has been playing bass with the heavy metal band ever since. Decked out in leather, studs and chains, and combining the gothic doom or Black Sabbath with the riffs and speed of Led Zeppelin, Judas Priest helped form one of most enduring and pervasive musical forms on the planet. Judas Priest are frequently ranked as one of the greatest metal bands of all time, with their 1980 album **British Steel** often referred to as the record that defines heavy metal. The band has sold more than 50 albums. Judas Priest is so influential that director Rob Reiner went to see the band in concert as part of his preparation for making the film classic **This Is Spinal Tap** (1984), which spoofs British heavy metal bands.

Judas Priest (from left): K.K. Downing, Glenn Tipton, Rob Halford and Ian Hill. PHOTO BY FIN COSTELLO/REDFERNS

The Beatles, *Sgt. Pepper's Lonely Hearts Club Band*
And of course The Beatles. You've got to look at *Sgt. Pepper's*. The early stuff… they were a pop band, and then *Sgt. Pepper's* came out, and it's this big psychedelic album. That was way ahead of its time. And the amount of sound they got out of a little four-track recording machine is unbelievable.

Colosseum, *Live*
No one remembers Colosseum. Jon Hiseman… he's one drummer that every single up-and-coming drummer should listen to. He was a phenomenal drummer. They were sort of a jazz/rock band. The best lineup, I think, was Jon Hiseman on drums, "Clem" Clempson on guitar, Chris Farlowe on vocals and Dick Heckstall-Smith on saxophone, Mark Clarke on bass and Dave Greenslade on keyboards. And it was a great band. They did the live album in 1971. It's absolutely great. Check it out.

John Mayall, *Blues Breakers with Eric Clapton*
Mayall had been going since the late '50s. The amount of musicians that came through the Bluesbreakers was unbelievable. I mean, you've got all of Cream–Clapton, Bruce and Baker all played with him at one time or another. Then Fleetwood Mac… Pete Green, Mick Fleetwood and John McVie all went through there. Mick Taylor went through before he ended up playing with the Stones. It was a great breeding ground for talent.

GREG KIHN
THE GREG KIHN BAND

In the be-Kihn-ing, Greg Kihn (far right) with his band in 1970. PHOTO BY RICHARD MCCAFFREY/MICHAEL OCHS ARCHIVES/GETTY IMAGES

After building a cult following in the 1970s, Greg Kihn, fronting the Greg Kihn Band, earned his first hit in 1981 with the Top 20 single "The Breakup Song (They Don't Write 'Em)" from the ***Rockihnroll*** album. Kihn continued in a commercial pop vein through the 1980s with a series of pun-titled albums: ***Kihntinued*** (1982), ***Kihnspiracy*** (1983), ***Kihntagious*** (1984), and ***Citizen Kihn*** (1985). He scored his biggest hit with 1983's "Jeopardy." One more single broke the Top 40, 1985's "Lucky." The Greg Kihn Band remains active, playing shows mainly in California. In addition to music, Kihn is very involved with his favorite charities, including Operation Care and Comfort, which sends care packages to our men and women in uniform, and Children's Hospital in Oakland, California, to help fight cancer. His recent ***Best of Beserkley, '75-'84*** features 21 remastered songs from his career on the legendary Beserkley Records in San Francisco. While famous for his pop hits, Kihn's musical influences, as you shall see, range from folk to psychedelia to punk.

Greg Kihn in 2018. PHOTO BY GARY MILLER/GETTY IMAGES

Bob Dylan,
The Freewheelin' Bob Dylan

From the front cover to the incredible selection of original songs, I learned this album backward and forward. I was a folkie at the time, so I basically inhaled most of these songs. Bob set the standard with the definitive singer-songwriter LP. The songs were genius: "Blowin' in the Wind," "Don't Think Twice, It's All Right," "Masters of War," "A Hard Rain's A-Gonna Fall." It made me want to write songs. And I did.

The Rolling Stones,
Out of Our Heads

Another cover that you couldn't forget, complete with Keith Richards' acne scars. This is the album that made the Stones what they are today: the true bad boys of rock. I loved it from top to bottom. "(I Can't Get No) Satisfaction" became my generation's anthem, but there were other gems as well. This was only their third album, but it established Mick and Keith as a songwriting team to rival Lennon and McCartney.

The Jimi Hendrix Experience,
Are You Experienced

I remember the day it came out. My buddy and I went to the record store and we both had just enough money for one album, and I was torn between ***Are Your Experienced*** and ***Sgt. Pepper***. So, I bought Jimi Hendrix and my buddy bought The Beatles. We went back to his house to smoke a joint and listened to both records; we played them both over and over. That day lasted forever and blew my mind. Jimi Hendrix made the electric guitar sound completely new. He was light-years ahead of his time.

The Beatles, *Sgt. Pepper's Lonely Hearts Club Band*

The greatest record ever made. Consider this: the first two songs recorded for ***Sgt. Pepper*** never even made the album; they were pulled by EMI for a double-sided single, so two of The Beatles' greatest songs were left off. Imagine how strong it would have been with the inclusion of those first two songs: "Strawberry Fields Forever" and "Penny Lane."

Sex Pistols, *Never Mind the Bollocks, Here's the Sex Pistols*

What a great band these guys were, full of piss and vinegar. I witnessed the rise of punk in London in the mid '70s. The Damned beat everybody to the punch with the first punk hit single, "New Rose," but it paved the way for the Sex Pistols. I go back and listen to it now and then just to hear what raw primitive rock 'n' roll sounds like. You can almost smell their bad breath through the speakers.

The Wailers, *Burnin'*

I listened to this album a thousand times when it came out. The songs were from another planet, and I couldn't get them out of my head. I was already into reggae and I loved Toots, but this was the best-produced reggae at the time and the songs were classics like "I Shot the Sheriff," "Get Up, Stand Up" and "Small Axe." I saw them live in San Francisco on their first tour in a small club and it was hypnotic and mesmerizing.

GREG KIHN // **THE GREG KIHN BAND**

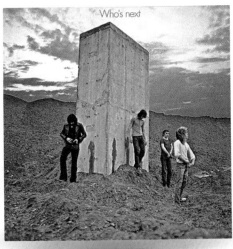

The Who, *Who's Next*

Back in 1978, The Greg Kihn Band got to record at Rampart Studios, owned by The Who, and let me tell you, those guys were passionate about their music. They would have fistfights about it. Nobody in that band took any shit. Pete is the father of the power chord and we owe him a lot. Let us now praise one of rock's best songwriters, and this classic album which has some of his best stuff. Still the gold standard for rock albums.

Van Morrison, *Astral Weeks*

This was a real life-changer when I was a young hippie. Van's long, jazzy, stream-of-consciousness lyrics were beyond anything I'd ever heard before. I used to lay there in the dark in my room and play it over and over again. And, God, could that man sing! Long before "Moondance," he was making incredible music. Every cut is great. There's never been anything like it before or since.

Greg Kihn performing in Chicago in 1980.
PHOTO BY PAUL NATKIN/GETTY IMAGES

In 1983 Greg Kihn had his only Top 10 hit with "Jeopardy" off the *Kihnspiracy* album. PHOTO BY PAUL NATKIN/GETTY IMAGES

Dave Van Ronk, *Folksinger*

The first real folk album I ever bought, when I was 14 years old, and it was a revelation. Dave Van Ronk was the big daddy of the Greenwich Village folk scene. Mentor to a young Bob Dylan, Bob actually stole Dave's version of "House of the Rising Sun" note for note on his first album. This album is a primer for all wannabe folkies. Every track is a stone classic. This is the good stuff.

The Beach Boys, *Pet Sounds*

The genius of Brian Wilson shows through every note of every song. This album is lush, emotional, passionate and brutally honest. It can bring you to tears. I cut my teeth on songs like "Wouldn't It Be Nice," "Caroline, No," "Sloop John B" and "God Only Knows." Hal Blaine wrote about the making of this amazing album in **The Wrecking Crew**. Still sounds as bright and shiny today as it did back in the day.

SAM KISZKA
GRETA VAN FLEET

Greta Van Fleet in 2018 (from left): Danny Wagner, Sam Kiszka, Josh Kiszka and Jake Kiszka. PHOTO BY GARY GERSHOFF/GETTY IMAGES

Greta Van Fleet have a rock sound that is strongly influenced by all the rock gods in the classic rock pantheon, from The Beatles to Led Zeppelin. That's a big mountain to climb in order to reach the summit. However, Greta Van Fleet do have the skill set, and in an era dominated by manufactured dance-pop, there is a void to fill. The band's name is a play on the name of Gretna Van Fleet, an elderly resident from Frankenmuth, Michigan, the band's hometown. The quirky choice did not alter the fate of becoming overnight sensations within the rock community. After releasing a couple electric EPs that quickly whet the appetite of many a rocker, Greta Van Fleet released their debut full-length studio album, *Anthem of the Peaceful Army*, in October 2018. Sam Kiszka, GVF's bassist and keyboardist, is one of three brothers: Josh is the vocalist and Jake is the guitarist. Drummer Danny Wagner grew up as a friend of the crew. Judging by Sam's remarks on his favorite ten albums, Danny also had a hand in turning Sam onto some classics.

PHOTO BY MARK HORTON/GETTY IMAGES

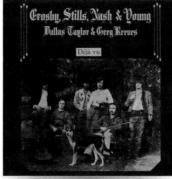

Crosby, Stills & Nash,
Crosby, Stills & Nash

This is my favorite album of all time. The reason it's so special for me is that I was listening to it during the time I started getting into music and playing music with my brothers. At the time, I played bass and keys only. When we were growing up, we'd sit out around a campfire and play music. I had nothing to play. No acoustic bass was loud enough and you couldn't bring a piano or a keyboard instrument out to a campfire, so I was pretty much left out. That's when I decided to play guitar and at the same time, this album was creeping into my life. This album changed my life; it brought me into songwriting. There is something so special about this album. The songs have this way of reaching through your chest and playing with your heart. You'll cry, you'll laugh, so many emotional moments. Three of the best musicians/songwriters had a hand in it. I learned how to play guitar from that record and became very obsessed with it very quickly. And I was able to sit around a campfire and play music.

Crosby, Stills, Nash & Young,
Déjà Vu

Steven Stills played all of the bass on the "couch" record; he played keyboards, most of the guitar, sang and wrote the songs. Nash and Crosby played acoustic on some songs and sang. I think they figured they couldn't perform live without another member so why not get another singer/songwriter? Neil Young had just left Buffalo Springfield and it was a magical occurrence that they would bring Neil into the band. Now, he's an enigmatic figure–he's Neil Young. The ***Déjà Vu*** record was as spectacular as CS&N and it followed the same outline. I learned all of those songs and that album taught me how to play my instruments. Most of what I know and my style was from that album.

The Beatles, *The Beatles*

There can be lots of filler material on double albums. They have the songs that are just okay, the songs that are great and then there are the true art pieces. But songs on the white album like "Revolution 9" and "Wild Honey Pie," are insane songs; they embody what was going on in the late 1960s. The Beatles were experimental trailblazers, and without them music wouldn't sound the way it does today. It's an important album historically, but it's an amazing piece of art. There's something for everyone on that album, you can appreciate all of the 23 songs, the album touches all genres and I think it embodies The Beatles more than ***Sgt. Pepper***. It's a very special album for all of us in the band as far as the production goes, very experimental. We've taken a few hints from The Beatles.

Joni Mitchell, *Blue*

This was a fairly recent discovery for me. I was not always a fan of Joni Mitchell, but funnily enough, while I was putting together a Christmas song playlist, I came across her "River" song. I thought this is not a Christmas song; it's a tale of lost love, getting away, a very emotional song with nothing to do with Christmas. And I was touched, a bit shocked, and I had had no idea what Joni Mitchell really was and did. I listened to the rest of the album and felt so strong about her music. She's an angel. If an angel came out of a cloud, she would sound like Joni Mitchell. Her lyrical songwriting… I don't think I've ever come so close to anything that touched me in such a soft way–so beautiful. I came to know her as the Bob Dylan of personal emotion. Dylan talks about the world, the condition of man, but Joni is the spokesperson of the heart, and *Blue* is one of the best albums ever.

SAM KISZKA // **GRETA VAN FLEET**

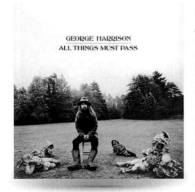

George Harrison, *All Things Must Pass*

George Harrison is someone who history will remember forever. He was not just a pop star but a figure of culture and of accepting others, kind of like the Gandhi of pop music. I don't think that Western civilization would fully have delved into Indian culture and classical Indian music without him. He was an important figure historically, and he'll end up in school iPad databases. And he was such an underdog; for the 10-year span of the Beatles, he was primarily in the background. Then the next to the last studio album they recorded, "Here Comes the Sun" and "While My Guitar Gently Weeps" came to fruition and George Harrison comes out of the gate... such an underdog story. Who knew he was capable of such an in-depth analysis of life and death and love? His songs take you on a mystical journey; you experience all things. And at the end, you're left a little bit crippled as to what just happened. An amazing record.

Miles Davis, *Kind of Blue*

This was the album that made me realize what music really is. It's kind of a philosophical album that doesn't say one word at all; it just grabs you, demands your attention. The thing about it that absolutely shocked me was that I didn't realize you could do that in music. When you're growing up, you think things are perfect; if someone makes a mistake, it gets fixed. But listen to Miles Davis, you'll hear something go flat on horn. It's emotion, it's a stream of consciousness, it's where he was at that exact moment. It may have been an absolutely sour note, but it's powered by the emotion of the player. That made me realize music isn't perfect, music shouldn't be perfect, it's about performances, being a musician, a songwriter.

And that's what we did on our new album–we captured the performances. We kept parts that weren't perfect, and the musicians in the room were working together, whatever came out was a result of the energy in the room and the mental connection of the musicians. Completely unmolested, untouched, it's a gemstone of the moment. Sometimes you capture gold, sometimes you don't. *Kind of Blue* is a very next-level album. Miles Davis changed that for pop music. Lots of people took notice of what he was doing. We all learned from that.

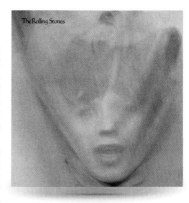

Rolling Stones, *Goats Head Soup*

As far as Rolling Stones songs go, this one has a lovely continuity for the reason that no one wanted the Stones, no country would let them in, so the record was recorded in Jamaica and the Netherlands. The musicians they used, like Billy Preston, were amazing, as was Mick Taylor on that album. "Doo Doo Doo Doo Doo (Heartbreaker)" is one of the best rock songs of all time; it embodies all the characteristics of rock 'n' roll, it has an unharnessed rock 'n' roll energy, it's a bit of a plea for change–the whole record is. And a couple of songs later, there's the beautiful, soft "Angie," which shows the band's dexterity. It was the band's 13th album and it shows the flexibility they had. They may not be the best band in the world, but when they came together, something special happened. It was the quintessential Rolling Stones album.

Paul Simon, *Paul Simon*

Early on, Simon & Garfunkel was really big for us, especially Daniel Wagner, our drummer, and I. We would sit outside of the Frankenmuth coffeehouse and play these acoustic songs–half that we knew were Simon & Garfunkel–and try to sing the harmonies. It just was such beautiful songwriting. It took me a long time to figure out who Paul Simon was. I knew the hits–"Me and Julio," "Duncan"– but it wasn't until very recently that I really sat down and listened to that whole album.

And I was very pleasantly surprised. I think those two songs are the kind that steal the spotlight; they're more pop-oriented. The production is unobtrusive, and it lets this soft-spoken man speak his mind. And he starts singing and you realize this guy has a lot to say, and very poetically. He's written some of the best lyrics of all time, he has very unique ways of putting things delicately and he's very powerful in a non-confrontational way. When someone starts yelling, all things shut down. When you say something politely, poetically, calmly with a level head, it travels so much further than anger or aggressiveness. And that's what is so special about this album.

Jimmy Smith, *The Sermon!*

This one is particularly special to me, and while no one will say it's one of the best albums of all time, they'd be a fool and an idiot to say it if I'm in a bad mood! *The Sermon!* opened me up to the world of jazz and spoke a language I could understand. I was getting into keyboards and I found my great grandfather's Hammond M103 in the garage. I was trying to figure out what the instrument was when I came across its application, where it was used, and realized it was used on everything–everyone used it! It has such a warm tonality, it speaks volumes, and that's the reason it's used so often in gospel and religious music. It's so powerful and uses electronics to

Elton John, *Elton John*

This is another record that Daniel came in high school. I remember he was taking me home from school one day and he said, "Have you heard this?" He put on "Sixty Years On" and I was absolutely floored, taken into some kind of ethereal realm of untouchable things. It was so experimental, so crisp and clean and in your face, beautiful and haunting at the same time. Still is. I think we all learned a lot from that album. When we were writing our album, we listened to that album a lot. It's very special, it shows what Elton John is, the soul, gospel, ballads, rock 'n' roll. It's very special to my heart and takes me to a different place.

stimulate the human heart in this amazing way.

And Jimmy Smith invented a whole style of playing organ, like an organized trio, playing the bass, rhythm and lead. At the time, I played bass and was getting into keyboards. It was the four of us in Greta Van Fleet and we didn't really know any bass players, so I would play bass with my left hand if I was also playing keyboards. This "organized trio" concept completely turned my world upside down, knowing that the bass lines you hear on *The Sermon!* were the result of his left hand and his feet. It was so incredible for me as it got me into learning how to do that.

I will never be a Jimmy Smith, but I learned to play bass with my feet from that record. It was a monumental "in my life" as it showed what you can do if you put your mind to it. Playing bass with my feet has become a part of Greta Van Fleet's sound. It's a flat instrument but can offer so much expression when you pair it with a drummer like Daniel who has so much feel and control. The expression of that album, his songs, even without words, you know exactly what the song is about. That's the beautiful thing about jazz music. The songs are yours, completely yours to interpret.

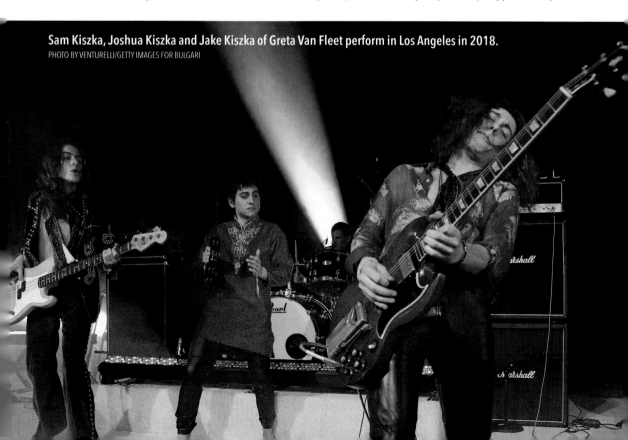

Sam Kiszka, Joshua Kiszka and Jake Kiszka of Greta Van Fleet perform in Los Angeles in 2018.
PHOTO BY VENTURELLI/GETTY IMAGES FOR BULGARI

PETER KOPPES
THE CHURCH

Peter Koppes (left) and The Church perform at The Royal Festival Hall in London in 2018. PHOTO BY LORNE THOMSON/REDFERNS

The Church are one of the most prolific and longstanding Australian pop bands of all time, but are known best in the States for their masterpiece *Starfish* album of 1986, which was certified gold in the U.S. on the strength of "Under the Milky Way," which reached #24 on the Billboard charts. Follow-up album ***Gold Afternoon Fix*** almost achieved gold, peaking at about 400,000 copies in the U.S. driven by the song "Metropolis." Beloved the world over and legendary for their long and varied live shows, The Church are still recording and touring, with approximately 25 albums to their name, depending on how you count. The band is lead by original bassist/vocalist Steven Kilbey and original guitarist Peter Koppes, who offers the following wide-ranging top ten.

Peter Koppes performs onstage in Austin, Texas, in 2015.

PHOTO BY TRAVIS P BALL/GETTY IMAGES FOR SXSW

Deep Purple, *In Rock*

I'm writing a music theory book on guitar scales, and what's interesting is the fact that Ritchie Blackmore was a session guitarist, along with Jimmy Page, because most of the guitarists couldn't harmonize the songs the way the Beatles did, couldn't finish the songs by providing harmonies. And George Martin had a degree in music, helped them to harmonize, which made them stand out. So what was special about *In Rock*, it was plainly obvious that Ritchie Blackmore was the finest guitarist of all of them, and he had the theory through his influence from Bach, which is also in the music we do with The Church, although it isn't overt or particularly deliberate. Plus Ritchie was inventing sweep picking and all sorts of things and he worked with arpeggios rather than just strum a bunch of chords.

The Jimi Hendrix Experience, *Smash Hits*

I was a drummer at the time, so Mitch Mitchell was a great influence. My father had a band, so actually I bought the Smash Hits album for his birthday, thinking that I would get to listen to it. And he was in a cabaret band, a singer. So I thought I was pretty sneaky about that. He didn't give me much pocket money, so I deserved that. And we used to play our records through a portable record player into one of these guitar amps, like an electronic kit amplifier. I suppose in some ways we were pretty upmarket because some people didn't even have stereo. But I've since realized Jimi is more like a bass player playing a lead guitar, because he never plays the same chords twice. He's actually playing chords and shapes and scales that a bass player would play, rather than kind of go through the same chord sequence in the song. And I've had to teach bass to people before they could understand the turnarounds and the details of what his music is.

The Beatles, *Rubber Soul*

My sister's boyfriend had left it in the house, and I didn't really like Rubber Soul very much, but there was a song on there, "Michelle," where the vinyl was all scratched out, so I became very curious about that and I was drawn in. But I first got into music through drumming, and the interesting thing about Ringo is he was left-handed, so he would lead all the fills with his left hand. Three of the Beatles were left-handed. George Harrison was left-handed, and Paul, of course, and Ringo. But John was twice the musician as the others, if you study the science of what he did.

Pink Floyd, *The Dark Side of the Moon*

Tough to pick a Pink Floyd, but this one is just such a part of pop consciousness. Jon Lord is one of my favorite keyboard players and so is Richard Wright, and the question I would want to ask David Gilmour is how much theoretical knowledge did you learn from your keyboard player? Because only bands with keyboard players can understand harmonization as good as this. But I loved the prog stuff, and the bands with keyboards, so also Yes, with **The Yes Album** and **Fragile**. But you've got my perspective on music, where it's not just a technical thing; it's also intuitive. But I'm definitely aware of how the technique thing affected me.

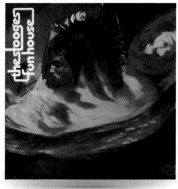

The Rolling Stones,
Get Yer Ya-Ya's Out!

Live albums had a significant effect on me, and I was turned more towards the Stones by this one than I was by their earlier, poppy stuff like "Satisfaction." They became more of a rock 'n' roll band when Keith discovered open tuning. They became the world's greatest rock 'n' roll band, or they deserved that title, when Keith started using those open tunings on the five-string Telecaster that he used. I love the Stones. A desert island album for me is **Sticky Fingers** but I wouldn't call it like an influencing album–I'd pick that one more from a complete and pure listening standpoint.

The Stooges, *Fun House*

I'd want to put all three of them there, as an identity–fantastic. But sometimes it goes in and out of fashion too. Sometimes it just seemed like a silly extreme adolescent kind of band, but then you get the cleverness of Iggy Pop and having sax solos in there and these John Coltrane-styled sax songs like "LA Blues." They call this the roots of punk, but the later punk… punk was a misnomer. I don't really believe in punk as far as like, the bands that were called punk. Like The Clash were not punk. And a lot of the songs were too simplistic or too fashionable. I was in London and Berlin during the punk era and I didn't enjoy it.

The Beatles,
Magical Mystery Tour

I'm supposed to pick Sgt. Pepper but I'll pick Magical Mystery Tour, only because it should be advertised as an album, although it wasn't an album until later. It's like the transition period where they released the best songs as singles and the album was apparently just what was left over? So is that allowed? Because that's the best Beatles album by far! The John Lennon side of Abbey Road is okay, but I really don't like Paul's at all. But no, a lot of great music. I feel very, very blessed that I got to be a teenager in the '60s.

The Average White Band, *AWB*

I joined a record club and got a few things that I didn't like, from the record club. But interestingly, I never liked funk music, but Average White Band, **AWB**, was quite an interesting album I liked. I like to think that I had a broad taste of music, especially coming from the '60s, when you had comedy and dance and these kinds of distractions. But I was pretty myopic when it came to the instrument I was interested in, which at first was the drums.

Santana, *Santana*

The third Santana album had a lead guitarist on it named Neal Schon who joined Journey, and most people didn't realize that the more exciting leads on that album were actually Neal Schon, but Carlos always held his own against him, because he such a consummate, beautiful, pure musician. I'd almost want to include Abraxas as well.

Joy Division, *Unknown Pleasures*

I like the debut, but my favorites from them are really "Atmosphere" and "Love Will Tear Us Apart," sublime songs. Another problem with picking albums is sometimes it's the live versions that matter more or even the live experience. I think you can hear the influence of a song like "Atmosphere" on The Church.

ALEXI LAIHO
CHILDREN OF BODOM

Alexi Laiho of the Finnish band Children of Bodom performs in Berlin in 2017. PHOTO BY FRANK HOENSCH/REDFERNS

Alexi Laiho is the chief writer, vocalist and guitarist for Finnish heavy metal act, Children of Bodom, who have the distinction of being one of Finland's biggest selling artists of all time, furthermore, a touring perennial in North America with over a dozen releases (studio albums, live albums, EPs and DVDs) since inception in 1993. The band's sound is a celebrated and unique gumbo of jumbled signals, touching down on power metal, death metal, black metal and thrash. The sound is tempered by the clarion-clean keyboards of Janne Wirman along with Laiho's disciplined and technical axe work. The band's hard-drinking ways on the road are the stuff of legend, but the toll of the band's exhaustive touring schedule over decades now has had the band somewhat mending their ways in recent years. Still, don't ever challenge the Bodoms—or any Finnish metal band—to a drinking contest.

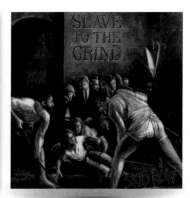

Dire Straits, *Brothers in Arms*

The first time I recall hearing guitar was when I heard my dad playing Dire Straits, the ***Brothers in Arms*** record, and it was "Money for Nothing." He also taught me about The Eagles, The Beatles and Creedence Clearwater Revival—we actually covered "Lookin' Out My Back Door." And The Beatles taught me a lot just about being creative. But I was like six when I heard Brothers in Arms and believe it or not, I still listen to Dire Straits; I absolutely love it. And I love "Sultans of Swing" also. Mark Knopfler's guitar playing is essentially the reason why I wanted to start playing guitar.

Guns N' Roses,
Appetite for Destruction

So bad-ass. It just seemed so angry because at that point I was still young, eight years old. I hadn't heard any music that angry before. That was before I heard like death metal and black metal. That album still kicks a lot of black metal bands' asses as far as being angry. It's so cool.

Skid Row,
Slave to the Grind

I love the first album, but ***Slave to the Grind*** is just so heavy. They sort of combined two cool things that I was into back in the day and I still am; it's like, the band looks great, but the album sounded super-heavy. I mean, it is pretty heavy, that album.

W.A.S.P., *W.A.S.P.*

First W.A.S.P. album for sure. I loved Blackie's voice, for one, and also, there's not one bad song on that album; every single one is just killer. They also looked bad-ass, and in a similar but darker way than Mötley Crüe. We covered "Hellion" from that album on ***Skeletons in the Closet***, 2009, which is a compilation album of all our many covers that were bonus tracks and stuff.

Mötley Crüe, *Dr. Feelgood*

I was ten when that came out and then I went back and got into the older stuff. I love Mick Mars. I know a lot of people talk crap about him, but I think he's one of the main reasons they stuck out from that whole scene. His guitar playing was more like old school and bluesy as opposed to showing off and trying to play like Eddie Van Halen. There's nothing wrong with that–I was into Steve Vai and Malmsteen the shredders–but I'm just saying that Mick Mars' playing was very different.

Ozzy Osbourne, *Tribute*

The tribute to Randy Rhoads live album was the first Ozzy album I ever heard and to this date it's my favorite. Randy Rhoads' style of playing was different. I learned that, you know, playing fast and playing technical stuff—that's cool—but the way he played, he played for the music, to serve the music, to serve the song, to make the song sound better and not for his own benefit, if that makes any sense.

Yngwie Malmsteen, *Fire & Ice*

The keyboards in Children of Bodom are inspired by just all the popular '80s music that was around everywhere. When those sort of fake and cheesy keyboards sounds first started getting used, I just loved them and that's why we use them in Children of Bodom, I guess. I'm an '80s kid—Accept, Maiden, AC/DC—and getting into all the '70s hard rock, that came later for me. The '80s stuff was what my sister was playing for me. As far as keyboard leads that we have, I know Jon Lord and Deep Purple did it first, but for me it was Yngwie Malmsteen and Jens Johansson and then later Mats Olausson—the first one I bought was either Odyssey or Fire & Ice–them dueling and doing all that stuff. It was–and still is–amazing. And obviously, that's a trademark thing that we do too.

Darkthrone, *A Blaze in the Northern Sky*

Black metal was important too, which you can hear in Children of Bodom. A big album for me is Ugra-Karma by Impaled Nazarene—we covered them too, but I would have to pick A Blaze in the Northern Sky, by Darkthrone, 1992. And why? Just that it really does sound like what pure evil would sound like–that's why (laughs).

Judas Priest, *Painkiller*

I remember when Painkiller came out, 1990 and I had heard of Judas Priest before but as a matter of fact, I didn't even know it was a band. I thought there was a guy whose name was that! But anyway, one of my friends had a cassette of Painkiller and I just thought it was insane, especially Halford's voice. I still have that CD in my car. I was listening to it the other day. It just never gets old.

Sepultura, *Arise*

For the heavier stuff, that maybe sounds like more where I took Children of Bodom, the first Metallica I heard was …**And Justice for All** and I must've been like nine or whatever. And then I heard **Kill 'em All** and that was like, holy, I just loved that album; I still do. And then there was Anthrax and Slayer and then all of sudden, here's one album that's very important for me: Arise by Sepultura. When I heard that I was like… well, I had never heard anybody sing like that for one. And the music was so fast and insane and, and as a ten-year-old or 11 or whatever the hell I was, you're thinking, in your head, those guys are evil. I mean they've got to be crazy and dangerous. It was just super-cool. And then from there I just got heavier and heavier—or not necessarily heavier, but more extreme.

JAKE E LEE
OZZY OSBOURNE

Ozzy Osbourne's band in 1986 (L-R) Phil Soussan, Osbourne, Randy Castillo (1950 - 2002) and Jake E Lee. PHOTO BY PAUL NATKIN/GETTY IMAGES

PHOTO BY PAUL NATKIN/GETTY IMAGES

Six-string gunslinger Jake E Lee had too much soul to be an '80s shred-der from L.A, and so it made sense that he stood out among the masses vying to replace the dearly departed Randy Rhoads in the Ozzy Os-bourne band back in 1983. Lee, of course, got the job, recording **Bark at the Moon** with the band that year and then **The Ultimate Sin** in 1986, the former scoring triple platinum and the latter sold nearly as well. Next for Lee was the revered Badlands supergroup, for which he crafted a clas-sic self-titled in 1989, followed by Voodoo Highway in 1991. What followed were the quiet—almost reclusive—years, Lee issuing a few low-key solo albums, after which he returned with a band called Red Dragon Cartel. Bluesy, highly electric with tone for miles, psychedelic and perfectly balanced between the traditional and the inventive, Jake E Lee is the consummate guitarist's guitarist, known, as alluded to, for tasty licks as opposed to the tiringly technical.

174

Iron Butterfly,
In-a-Gadda-da-Vida

This was in fact the first rock record that I bought. Before that I'd always buy James Bond soundtracks. I love James Bond movies, and back then, once the movie was out of the theatre, you're never going to see it again. The only way you could really kind of relive it was by buying the soundtrack album. But Iron Butterfly, I loved the heaviness. This would be before Sabbath and it was maybe as heavy as you could get back then before Sabbath showed the world how to really do it. And the guitar player was good and I really loved psychedelia, although with psychedelia, it was more of a single thing back then. The Electric Prunes, Strawberry Alarm Clock… I really loved that era of rock 'n' roll and I try to incorporate that into my sound.

Black Sabbath, *Black Sabbath*

Black Sabbath's first record was huge because as a kid I remember listening to it and thinking nobody else sounded like that. Nobody was that heavy—it was just so damn cool. Although I will say that their second record, Paranoid, is the one I played more than any other Sabbath.

Jimi Hendrix Experience,
Band of Gypsies

Are You Experienced would be the reason I picked a guitar up in the first place, and although I know that's the reason I picked up the guitar, I would have to say Band of Gypsies is the one album from Jimi that I can never get enough of and have listened to more often than any of his other ones. As far as guitar playing, he was so much harder to learn from than the other guys. And I love the other guys, [Jimmy] Page, [Eric] Clapton, the standard guys. They would work around standard licks, licks that all guitar players knew and shapes that all guitar players knew and then they would work around that, those parameters. And it made it easier as a young guitar player to figure out. But Jimi just came out of nowhere. I mean, he would play things and I'd go wait a minute, I don't know that lick. I don't know this pattern. I don't. Where did he come up with this? It was almost jazz-like, that. I don't have a deep understanding of jazz, so I'm sure they do have their patterns and scales they stick to, but he was like a John Coltrane on guitar–where did he come from? And that's what really struck me with Jimi. And it was always so passionate and heartfelt and never sounded like he just phoned it in.

Ozzy Osbourne and Jake E Lee perfoming in Los Angeles, 1986. PHOTO BY SGRANITZ/WIREIMAGE

Led Zeppelin, *III*

My favorite album by Led Zepplin ended up being *III*, which is probably their most unlikely album. When I was kid, I'd save up my allowance and I could buy one album a month. So that album was always precious to me. And usually I'd buy something that I knew, something that I'd heard at a friend's house and I knew I was gonna like. But Led Zeppelin *III* had just come out. I was going to buy a Led Zeppelin record anyway, but it was going to be the second one. But I heard "Immigrant Song" on the radio and it was just such a nasty riff and a spooky song and I was like, great, this album's going to be bitchin'. And I took it home and that's the only song like it on the whole record. It pissed me off. I tried to take the record back and they wanted to know why. And I said, "Because I don't like it." "You can't bring a record back just because you don't like it." And so I was stuck with it for the next month until I could buy another new album. So it was the only new music I could listen to then. And it grew on me. After a month, it was—and still to this day is—my favorite Led Zeppelin record. And the reason I wanted to address that is I kind of feel like our Red Dragon Cartel record, Patina, is like that—most of the songs on there aren't immediately accessible.

Deep Purple, *Machine Head*

Machine Head I listened to a lot. I don't know how to actually put it into words, but with Ritchie Blackmore, the reason I liked him...a lot of it was his sound. It was because he had a Strat and I was never a Strat guy growing up. I was always a Gibson guy because they sounded heavier. But he made a Stratocaster sounds so thick and powerful. And Ritchie had a blues influence, which I always had. And he was so articulate. I've got to say though, his rhythm playing was a little lazy. I'm going to get in trouble now.

Montrose, *Montrose*

Yeah, that was big. Ronnie Montrose was such a... I wouldn't call him underrated but not as applauded as he should have been, because he was a monster guitar player and his tone was great and the songs are all solid. Sammy Hagar was singing at his best on that record. And just the production, it was so kind of bare-bones and yet so electric.

Aerosmith, *Rocks*

Here again, the first record that I got from them and made me an Aerosmith fan was *Get Your Wings* and that's a great record. But my favorite one was *Rocks*. And yeah, Joe Perry, I love his—well, everyone in the band is great—but Joe in particular, I loved his looseness. I don't want to say sloppy because that sounds insulting, but in a way it's sort of this loose sloppiness that just fits the songs so well. And I always enjoyed his playing and I blame him if people think I'm sloppy.

Van Halen, *Van Halen*

But then Van Halen came along, and yeah, they changed my life; they did (laughs). When that first Van Halen album came out, I said, oh, okay, yeah, that's how you do rock 'n' roll. And yeah, I quit the other bands I was in and I just stayed in the rock band and we did a lot of Van Halen covers and started trying to write songs in that vein because that first record was just so magnificent. Eddie's playing really turned everybody's thoughts on how to play guitar upside-down. Yeah, *Van Halen* was huge.

Ozzy Osbourne and Lee perform in New York in 1986.
PHOTO BY LARRY BUSACCA/WIREIMAGE

Scorpions, *Virgin Killer*

I was in bands by this point. I was going through a lot of different bands. I was in a funk band and we had a full horn section and I loved playing that stuff. I was also in a fusion band where we did a lot of Return to Forever and Mahavishnu Orchestra; it wasn't a popular band (laughs), but it was a fun one to play in. I was in a rock band and for me at that point Ted Nugent was big but he was not really my cup of tea. He sort of simplified everything and it was making it less interesting and I was getting a little bit tired of rock. So I think the only band I really enjoyed back then at that moment was Scorpions. Uli Jon Roth was a beast on guitar. But like I say, I was not 100% in rock. I was in other bands that interested me more.

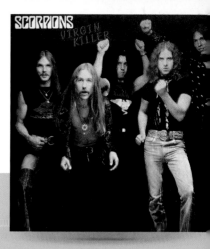

Ozzy Osbourne, *Bark at the Moon*

So this record changed my life in pretty much every way possible. Yeah. And it was a fun record to make. Well, maybe not fun. Exciting–let's put it that way, because it was the first time I got to work with say, pro musicians, musicians that I had looked up to when I was younger, like Bob Daisley and Tommy Aldridge and Ozzy. That was exciting. The fact that I was in a foreign country was exciting. The fact that I was in the middle of the country on a farm in a foreign country was exciting. And being able to make that first record was… I'm trying to think of another word but I'll go exciting. It was just exciting. Brand new and yeah, I have fond memories of that.

SHELBY LYNNE

Shelby Lynne's musical interests are vast, including her love for Willie Nelson who she joined in concert in New York. PHOTO BY STEPHEN LOVEKIN/FILMMAGIC

Singer-songwriter-guitarist-producer Shelby Lynne has traversed a long country-folk-pop-swing-rock-'n'-roll road since her startling 1989 *Sunrise* debut. Ten years into her career, she won a Grammy as Best New Artist for *I Am Shelby Lynne*. After her sublime 2008 Dusty Springfield tribute album, *Just A Little Lovin'*, she took matters into her own hands. For her 11th album, *Tears, Lies & Alibis*, she formed her own record label, issuing one more record, *Revelation Road*, that way before re-signing with a label. On this most personal of all her albums, Lynne sang, wrote, produced and played every instrument on every song. Long considered one of the most eclectic artists to emanate from Nashville—she once shocked even her own band by singing some James Brown while opening for Kenny Rogers on his annual Christmas tour—her Top Ten is as far-reaching as her artistry. "This was hard," she said, "and they're in no certain order."

PHOTO BY KEVIN WINTER/GETTY IMAGES

Frank Sinatra,
In the Wee Small Hours
I chose this album from The Chairman of the Board because of the drama effect. I'm a fool for the swinging stuff—have to have a shot of that every so often—but having to make a choice, I simply went with that voice. Those Jack Daniels-soaked, Camel-scorched vocal cords aching in the melody of those tearjerkers. It closes down the joint every time.

Marvin Gaye, *What's Going On*
If only we had someone today who could take charge as an artist, make a stand against what the record companies are so afraid of and just go with their gut about the world we live in to-day like this amazing man did with this record, we would have something special. *What's Going On* is important: political in content but compassionate for the universe in its delivery. And, of course, off-the-charts sexy as hell.

Edith Piaf, *Voice of the Sparrow: The Very Best of Edith Piaf*
When she sang, you can feel her crying from inside. No matter what the language, she draws you in with the passion and acting out the lyric. It's like hearing someone delivering their lines in the theater.

Willie Nelson,
Willie and Family Live
My childhood: I can remember daddy pulling up in the driveway in his pickup with this album on the front seat. He had been to a Mobile, Alabama, record store to buy it.

The Beatles, *The Beatles*
Well, since I have to limit my choices to only ten, I'm taking The Beatles album with the most tracks on it. I couldn't live without "Julia."

Joni Mitchell, *Court and Spark*
I was late to discover Joni, but when I listened to this vinyl, I was made aware of what female songwriting should be. Pure art. It's like looking at a Monet painting with your ear bone.

Miles Davis, *Kind of Blue*
When I hear it, I relax. Miles re-invented music every time he played.

John Lennon, *Plastic Ono Band*
It was my first introduction to John and his solo songwriting. "Mother" was unlike anything I had ever heard before.

Black Sabbath, *Paranoid*
Ozzy's singing is stellar. What a voice! The record is recorded so well … clean. Of course I love the original vinyl pressing best. Heavy metal had to scare people to death! No one had ever heard such a thing.

Django Reinhardt, *The Essential*
When I discovered Django, I was entering into my swing phase, early '90s. I fell in love with the music and the swing. The records he did with Stephane Grappelli were sublime. When I was doing the demos for my ***Temptation*** album, my fiddle player, Randy Howard, played so much like Stephane that I was in heaven. Randy died several years ago, and I can't hear Django and Stephane play together without a tear in my heart.

Lynne earned a Grammy in 2001 for Best New Artist.
PHOTO BY JOHN SHEARER/WIREIMAGE

DAVID MARKS
THE BEACH BOYS

The Beach Boys in 1962 (L-R): Brian Wilson, Mike Love, Dennis Wilson, Carl Wilson and David Marks PHOTO BY MICHAEL OCHS ARCHIVES/GETTY IMAGES

S inging songs of an idealized version of California where the summers were endless, the cars were fast and all the girls were pretty, The Beach Boys emerged in the early 1960s as the ultimate beach-blanket band. Such hits as "Surfin' USA," "California Girls," "Fun, Fun, Fun" and many, many more anointed the band surf-rock royalty. As an original founding member of The Beach Boys, guitarist David Marks took lessons with bandmate Carl Wilson from none other than John Maus (Walker Brothers). After appearing on the first four Beach Boys' albums—*Surfin' Safari*, *Surfin' USA*, *Surfer Girl* and *Little Deuce Coupe*—Marks ventured out on his own, first with Dave & The Marksmen and then with The Moon. He twice returned to the Beach Boys fold, in 1997 and 2011. Here he shares the influences that continue to shape his musical impulses.

B.B. King, *Live*

B.B. King introduced me to the blues and improvising guitar solos, which had a huge effect on me and changed the way I played. Since then, I have preferred improvisational playing.

J.S. Bach, *Harpsichord Music and Lute Suites*

This album got me totally into classical music, which in turn led me to jazz, because I found out he improvised everything and then wrote it down. Bach opened up that whole world of music theory to me.

The Paul Butterfield Blues Band, *The Paul Butterfield Blues Band*

After hearing that album, it made me realize that white guys could interpret that style of music, and I never looked back. Also, Mike Bloomfield, the guitar player in that band, had a profound influence on my guitar playing.

Aretha Franklin, *I Never Loved a Man the Way I Love You*

My introduction to keyboards. That Hammond B3, Wurlitzer electric piano and baby grand became my favorite combination of sounds. I immediately went out and bought a Wurlitzer, which vastly expanded my songwriting possibilities.

Chuck Berry, *Chuck Berry is on Top*

This is the album that really bonded Carl Wilson and I as guitar players. We'd been playing surf instrumentals together, but when that album came out, we decided to dedicate ourselves to becoming guitar players. We focused on coming up with our own sound, but you can really hear that Chuck Berry influence in our music.

The Ventures, *Walk Don't Run*

"Walk Don't Run" was the first song I played with a band, even before The Beach Boys. It was me and Carl Wilson on guitars and Kenny and John Poole on bass and drums. We were just kids in the neighborhood messing around, but playing with other musicians like that cemented the idea that playing in a band was what I wanted to do.

Dick Dale, *Surfer's Choice*

Dick Dale influenced our sound. We wanted to sound big like him. We didn't sound like him musically, although we tried. But we got our Fender equipment based on what he used to try to emulate with that Dick Dale wall of sound. In the early days of The Beach Boys, we didn't have that many original songs so we filled our sets with covers and we did just about all the songs on **Surfer's Choice**. We even recorded a few on the **Surfin' USA** album.

The Beatles, *Rubber Soul*
Rubber Soul was inspirational because it was totally innovative and off the beaten track, so to speak. *Rubber Soul* gave me the courage to be creative and inspired me to be original with my own compositions and write songs that were new and unique instead of trying to write generic songs that everyone else was putting out.

Ray Charles, *What'd I Say*
This album got me interested in singing. Just hearing his voice inspired me to want to sing. I can vividly remember Carl and I laying on our backs listening to that record with our eyes closed and being blown away.

Duane Eddy,
Have Twangy Guitar, Will Travel
This is the first album that got me serious about playing guitar when I was ten years old. The first songs I played I wrote myself, but "Ramrod" was the first song I learned to play by another artist.

The Beach Boys during a photo shoot for their 1962 debut studio album *Surfin Safari*.
PHOTO BY MICHAEL OCHS ARCHIVES/GETTY IMAGES

ERIC MARTIN
MR. BIG

Mr. Big in 1989 (L-R): Eric Martin, Pat Torpey, Paul Gilbert and Billy Sheehan PHOTO BY CHRIS WALTER/GETTY IMAGES

Soulful singing North Californian Eric Martin already had for himself a tidy solo career before he rose to fame as part of hotshot hair metal supergroup Mr. Big. Even without America, the band would have had for itself a solid career based on their Japanese fan base alone, with all of the first five records going gold or platinum in Japan. Still, Mr. Big—which included as part of their classic lineup, Paul Gilbert, Billy Sheehan and Pat Torpey (each "shredders" on their particular instrument)—found fame with 1991's *Lean into It*, which produced two hit singles, "Green-Tinted Sixties Mind" and the elegant ballad "To Be with You," sending the record platinum in America. Martin, a consummate singer's singer, has continued on with a plethora of solo albums amidst more records and worldwide tours with Mr. Big, his inventive Paul Rodgers-like phrasing engaging fans the world over now through a career spanning nearly 35 years.

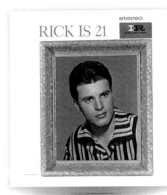

Rick Nelson, *Rick Is 21*

First album that I ever had, I didn't buy it. I found it in a field and it was chipped and it was, believe it or not, a Ricky Nelson record and it had "Travelin' Man' and 'Hello Mary Lou." My dad was in the army, so I lived in Italy and Germany and all over the United States. But mainly when I lived in Europe, that's when I started discovering music. I liked The Beatles and the Stones and all this pop stuff that was on the radio, like Shocking Blue and Paper Lace and Edison Lighthouse, but they were really formulaic stuff. But then I found that Ricky Nelson record and I'm not saying it changed my thing, but I loved the harmonies on that stuff and that's when I first started to sing harmony, learning from the lead singing on that record. So yeah, I would say Rick Nelson has to be my first pick.

Joe Cocker,
Mad Dogs & Englishmen

Great record. Super live and off the cuff. They didn't sound like they rehearsed very much, but it sounds like they didn't drink too much and just played this really great show. Had to be about 25 people. It was like a kind of Medicine Ball Caravan kind of gig, but it's a great sounding record that has so much soul and just kind of a hippie choir on top of bass, drums, guitar and Leon Russell's honky tonk piano. It just floors me how good it is and how it was kind of thrown together. I read about it recently. They were just lying around California going, "Hey what do you wanna do, huh?" "Let's play a show and record it." But it's not as sloppy as you would think. It's pretty... I don't know how they came together. It sounds like one big traffic jam, but everybody lived, you know?

Various Artists,
The Motown Story

I was into a lot of soul music as a teenager and I had **The Motown Story**, which was like a vinyl box set, all these vinyls on top of each other. I even changed the *Motown* to put *The Martin Story* on it. And I even have that record and I showed it to my kids the other day and my kids were like, "Why would you do that?!" "It's because this album was inspiring!" (laughs). So yeah, this was my first big huge influence, and I changed the Motown... I actually wrote it in ballpoint pen, grooved right into the cover.

Earth Quake, *Rocking the World*

Earth Quake. Another band that like nobody's ever heard of. This guy Gary Phillips was in a band called Copperhead, and he had a band with this guy, John Doukas who was lead singer, Stan Miller on bass. That first Earth Quake they did for Beserkley, actually their third, that album kicked my ass. I went to see Earth Quake. Okay, Queen and Y&T was my first big rock concert, but I saw Earth Quake a million times (laughs). Th ey played ice skating rinks like in my hometown, Sacramento, when I was a kid.

Gary Phillips is the guy that introduced me to the Bay area rock 'n' roll scene. He brought me in. Like, I met him, I dressed like him, I used to wear a football shirt with two O's on it, black football shirt, and I totally emulated the guy. And on this record, they did one of the coolest versions of the song "Friday on My Mind," Vanda and Young. It's way better than Gary Moore's; it's way better than David Bowie's. Man, I wish I still had that record.

Bad Company, *Bad Company*

Bad Company was like a hybrid of Motown, Stax/Volt kinda lead singer guy with a rock band. I want to say I was going to say Free as well. I had a Free album that had "Wishing Well" and all that stuff. And I liked that but Free and Humble Pie and Spooky Tooth, it's kind of cool but it sounded like live records. Meaning they were jammy and it was free-form. And it was fun to listen to that kind of music, but Bad Company… you know, I was a pop guy. I listened to pop radio as a kid and Bad Company just had this slick, rock and soul sound, that first album, and I love all of it. I played it to death and I listened to every song on it and in my first couple of bands when I was 16 years old, it was all Bad Company covers. You know, everybody went, "Let's do Skynyrd." "Nope, let's do Bad Company."

Montrose, *Montrose*

During the Bad Company years, I also loved those first couple of Montrose albums. Man, you could go see a concert for five bucks back in the day. I mean, I saw Montrose and Queen and Y&T when they were like 16 years old. But that first Montrose album kicked my ass. Like Bad Company, it was another great lead singer, Sammy Hagar. But Bad Company was a little more British with Mick Ralphs, who had a different style. But with Ronnie Montrose, it was like I was proud to be an American, because this was like our American Led Zeppelin.

AC/DC, *Let There Be Rock*

I moved by myself to San Francisco and I joined a band called Kid Courage and Kid Courage opened for all these national and international acts that came to town. And AC/DC came into town and they sounded like they were a punk band, kind of punk pop. '77 is when they toured America, and they only did a little bit but then 1978 they came to San Francisco and that's actually the first time I'd heard of them. I remember going, you know, "Oh, who's this band?" and we were kind of a popular band in San Francisco and they came through town and it was a good 600-seater club called the Old Waldorf. And I remember playing pool with Bon Scott in the dressing room, looking at Angus Young and then looking back at Bon Scott going, "Who's this dude?" You know, kinda like, "What's he wearing?" And he goes, "Well, it's kind of a gimmick that he's got going on." I go, "That'll never work." I've put my foot in my mouth many times, but that time… and then I went out to Rasputin's in Berkeley, California, and I got *Let There Be Rock*.

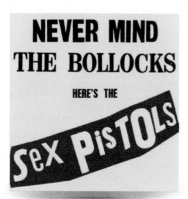

Sex Pistols, *Never Mind the Bollocks, Here's the Sex Pistols*

I love the energy of that album. I saw them play at Winterland and that's one of those things where they didn't play it on the radio. Somebody had it at a party and it was, you know, "Anarchy in the UK." So you're hanging out at a party, listening to this cool, thrashy, almost easy-to-play kind of music. Not a lot of notes, you know; really kind of bashing out the A chords. I loved that, and I went to see them play and then I had to have the album. That's how it was through my whole musical history.

As for the singing, Joe Strummer and Johnny Rotten, I didn't think of them as bad singers. Instead, they kinda gave me a broader perspective. It opened my mind a little bit listening to these other lead singers. We always listened to people like Paul Rodgers and Otis Redding and like Daryl Hall over the years, but these guys are just shouting at you and screaming and stuff. But I love Bob Dylan as well and he's not the greatest singer. And nothing to do with screaming and shouting, but lyrically and angst-wise and with the deep lyrical content, there's a similarity. All the girlfriends that I loved back in the day were Gothic kind of chicks, and they loved The Clash and the Sex Pistols.

Pearl Harbor & the Explosions,
Pearl Harbor and the Explosions
It was a girl, Pearl E. Gates, really hot, and again, one of those Betty Page gothic chicks that I just absolutely adored. She married Paul Simonon from The Clash later on in life. That record was right up there with *Never Mind the Bollocks*. It was punk, but it was dancy punk. I really love that record.

Bryan Adams,
You Want It You Got It
Well that album kind of did it for me, particularly "Fits Ya Good." I liked Bryan Adams. I liked his voice. He was soulful but his voice had this really guttural edge to it. Great songwriter; you know, like every song that he did kinda had this big, huge, epic, grandiose, anthemic kind of sound. That album introduced me to him but I love all that stuff, "Summer of '69." And actually there was one album later, *Into the Fire*, that I listened to a lot mainly for songwriting vibe. I don't know if it was a great album, but it was by far my favorite songwriting kind of influenced record of his. But it wasn't like a biggie–there weren't any big hit songs on it.

Mr. Big hit it big with the ballad "To Be With You," released late in 1991.
PHOTO BY PAUL NATKIN/WIREIMAGE

JOHN MAYALL
BLUESBREAKERS

Larry Taylor (bass) and John Mayall in 1971 in Copenhagen. PHOTO BY JORGEN ANGEL/REDFERNS

John Mayall is the elder statesman of British blues, better known by many as a mentor and bandleader than as a performer. It's difficult to argue with that perception. After all, throughout the 1960s his band, the Bluesbreakers, served as a finishing school of sorts for some of the finest British blues-rock musicians of the era. Guitarists Eric Clapton, Peter Green and Mick Taylor joined his band in a remarkable succession in the mid-'60s, honing their skills with Mayall before going on to join Cream, Fleetwood Mac and the Rolling Stones, respectively. John McVie and Mick Fleetwood, Jack Bruce, Aynsley Dunbar, Dick Heckstall-Smith, Andy Fraser (of Free), John Almond and Jon Mark also played and recorded with Mayall for varying lengths of time in the '60s. "If I hire somebody to play with me, I'm hiring them because I love their playing," Mayall says. "I gave them the freedom to help them develop their own style."

J.B. Lenoir, *Martin Scorsese Presents the Blues*
The blues-loving Mr. Scorsese was obviously as thrilled as I was when I first heard the unique J.B. on this gem.

Big Maceo, *The Best of*
This guy was of the most powerful of all boogie-woogie pianists and he remains one of my major influences as far as the blues goes.

Albert Ammons, *Boogie Woogie Stomp*
When I first heard Albert Ammons on record, it turned me on to the art of playing piano. No one will ever match him or his ability.

DAN MCCAFFERTY
NAZARETH

Dan McCafferty is the gritty-voiced vocalist of the Scottish hard-rock quartet Nazareth, who had a handful of hits in the late '70s, including the power ballad "Love Hurts, a revamped version of the Everly Brothers' tune. Formed in 1968, the band featured McCafferty, guitarist Manny Charlton, bassist Pete Agnew and drummer Darrell Sweet. Nazareth hit it big in 1974 with the album *Hair of the Dog*, establishing Nazareth as rockers to be reckoned with. The title track sets the mood for this hard driving album with its combination of relentless guitar riffs, a throbbing, cowbell-driven beat and an angry vocal from McCafferty, who growls at his girl, calling her a "heart-breaker, soul-shaker." The album sold over a million copies in the U.S. Until the end of the '70s, the band continued successfully as a quartet, releasing a series of Top 100 albums. McCafferty grew up in a time when, he says, "You got some money in your pocket, you went and got music or you went to the movies because there was nothing else you could do." With some cash in hand, this is the music McCafferty sought out.

Classic Nazareth lineup (L-R): Manny Charlton, Pete Agnew, Dan McCafferty and Darrell Sweet. PHOTO BY IAN DICKSON/REDFERNS

The Beatles, *Sgt. Pepper's Lonely Hearts Club Band*
I mean, when **Sgt. Pepper** came out, I thought I should become an interior decorator or something, because this is way beyond what I know (laughs).

Led Zeppelin, *IV*
The thing is, we all loved Led Zeppelin anyway. And after **III**, we thought it was great. And then they put out **IV**, and it was like, wow. They just lifted the bar even higher, which was really appreciated by us, the fans.

The Who, *Tommy*
The first time The Who did **Tommy**, they used to leave London and do Glasgow University, the Kinema Ballroom in Dunfermline, and that's where they used to practice their new set, to play it in front of people and see how it went. I saw the second ever live version of **Tommy**. Oh yeah, I love The Who.

JIM McCARTY
THE YARDBIRDS

The Yardbirds in 1965 (L-R): Jeff Beck, Paul Samwell-Smith, Keith Relf, Chris Dreja and Jim McCarty. Photo by Michael Ochs Archives/Getty Images

Jim McCarty is the drummer and original member of The Yardbirds, the seminal '60s band that featured at one time the likes of Eric Clapton, Jeff Beck and Jimmy Page. Still touring, McCarty and his band keep delivering the sermon of original rock 'n' roll and where it came from. Inducted into the Rock and Roll Hall of Fame in 1992, The Yardbirds started out a blues cover band in London in 1963, but their innovative use of feedback and distortion shaped such diverse genres as psychedelic rock, prog and punk. You'll note the band's influence mentioned throughout this book. Before reforming The Yardbirds, McCarty was a member of light prog bands Renaissance and Illusion. In the '80s, he and his fellow original Yardbirds' bassist Chris Dreja made waves with a collaborative band concept called Box of Frogs, which also featured The Yardbirds Paul Samwell-Smith. That band made two well-received major label albums featuring an impressive list of guest stars.

Photo by Phil Bourne/Redferns

The Everly Brothers, *The Very Best of The Everly Brothers*

Well, we were at school when we heard that. We had a school band. We used to play like at the school dances in the intervals. We'd play rock 'n' roll. And Paul Samwell-Smith, the Yardbirds bass player, he was at my school and Paul and I used to sing a lot of harmonies, Everly Brothers, for a laugh. But we loved The Everly Brothers; they were great at that time. I was about 16, 17, you know?

The Crickets, *The Chirping Crickets*

Well, the Chirping Crickets, that was about the same era, Buddy Holly of course. And we would play some Buddy Holly songs in our repertoire in the school band. It was great hearing that great Strat sound he had, which was very unusual at that time. And the stuff they did was fantastic, great harmonies, very nice songs.

Jimmy Reed, *Live at Carnegie Hall*

That was also to do with Paul Samwell-Smith, because after we'd left school I bumped into him one day and we always loved music, you know, as we were in the band and we'd been in school groups and all that and he said, "Oh, you've gotta come round and hear this album, Jimmy Reed, *Live at Carnegie Hall*. And it was the sort of music I'd never quite heard before because it was like sorta rock but not. It was bluesy rock and I was really taken with it. We adopted that sort of a type of music for the first incarnation of The Yardbirds.

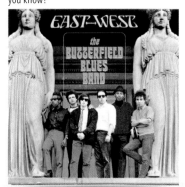

The Paul Butterfield Blues Band, *East-West*

Well, that was an album we used to play, Keith Relf and I, when we were on the road. We used to share hotel rooms. We used to have one of those funny little portable record players where you could take the speakers off, make it stereo. And Butterfield was one of the things we played and we, we sort of put those Buddhist candles on and create an atmosphere with incense, maybe have a couple of joints. That was such good music. It's actually the same as the same story with The Mothers of Invention because we used to play that way too, but they were both in our hippie days.

The Yardbirds with Jimmy Page, Jim McCarty, Keith Relf and Chris Dreja.
PHOTO BY GAB ARCHIVE/REDFERNS

The Mothers of Invention,
Freak Out!

Wow, *Freak Out!* was very funny and very un-usual. I did go and see them live and he was a tremendous player, Frank [Zappa]. But they just pissed about; it was very over the top (laughs). The way they all jumped in the air, you know, when, when he told them to. But they were very, very clever musicians at the same time. It was like you thought it was going to be a joke, but they were actually very, very good, very tight.

The Beach Boys, *Pet Sounds*

Well I just thought that was a one-off. I thought it was absolutely beautiful, wonderful music to hear. And of course, you know, the fact they did it with an orchestra. They didn't have the regular bass and drum lineup. So it was very deep and full and exotic and made a big impression on me. Exotically beautiful, you might say. It was a beautiful thing to hear, the harmonies and the songs and everything. It was such a wonderful collection of music.

Jimmy Smith, *Bashin' - The Unpredictable Jimmy Smith*

"Walk on the Wild Side." Also a wonderful, at-mospheric thing, with a fantastic drum sound, really ambient. It must have been recorded in New York because it had such a big ambient sound. And great playing on the organ and the bass. And (laughs) it was sort of another record that you heard when you walked around Lon-don in the '60s. You heard it coming out of the windows all the time.

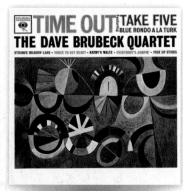

The Beatles, *Sgt. Pepper's Lonely Hearts Club Band*

Well, I thought that was really a one-off, and some of it was quite proggy. "A Day in the Life" was a real prog song, one of the first that I'd heard. That was in the days when I was living in London in a sort of basement flat and people would come around and we'd smoke joints and stuff, get high. That was in those days, sort of exciting '60s when you'd go out and walk down the King's Road and get that vibe and even sort of caught that vibe, somehow. And everyone was listening to it. Every-where you went, you'd hear it. And I would sit in my flat and play the whole thing every night. It was psychedelic, as was **Pet Sounds** I suppose, and these records created an atmosphere.

The Doors, *Strange Days*

It was so evocative. It created pictures in your mind. It created an atmosphere and I always loved that sort of atmospheric music, which I suppose all of these records fall into that sort of category. The carnival music side of The Doors, maybe that side of them I wasn't so keen on; I found it a bit odd. I liked the straighter songs, and the keeping of the riff steady with the keyboards and the guitars, with Jim [Morrison] doing his thing over the top. I never met them at the time, unfortunately. I have more recently because we've played ever since and we did a tour with them about ten years ago. They did a reformation and we did a few gigs. They were lovely guys. No Jim unfortunately but they still had those great songs.

The Dave Brubeck Quartet,
Time Out

Well, we were always into jazz, particularly Keith Relf and myself. I loved Joe Morello and I loved the main song on there, "Blue Rondo"; it was very hypnotic music. And one of the songs we sort of vaguely lifted for "Shapes of Things." We lifted one of the bass riffs in one of those songs; sort of done, anyway. But Joe, in this band, he was a great influ-ence, as was, also from the jazz realm, Art Blakey, Gene Krupa and the guy from the MJQ, Connie Kay—because I just loved drumming, all the solo stuff, the swing stuff, even African drumming. I also loved Keith Moon. I played with him a few times and I thought he had a very good technique and a lot of energy and he was a funny guy.

IAN McCULLOCH
ECHO & THE BUNNYMEN

Echo & the Bunnymen in 1981 (from left): Les Pattinson, Will Sergeant, Ian McCulloch and Pete de Freitas (1961-1989). PHOTO BY PAUL NATKIN/GETTY IMAGES

With the outsized persona of singer Ian McCulloch and the frequently brilliant guitar work of Will Sergeant, Echo & the Bunnymen became a post-punk institution that still stands some 40 years later. Echo & the Bunnymen had a handful of British hits in the early '80s, while attracting a cult following in the United States. To be sure, the band's success never translated in North America, but their presence has been bold, fueled by their artful and exotic song skills and daring creative manoeuvres record to record. Through records like the instantly successful debut *Crocodiles* from 1980 and 1983's forever classic *Ocean Rain*, featuring the dramatic and majestic "The Killing Moon," Echo & the Bunnymen bound past the constraints of punk. "'The Killing Moon' is more than a song, it's about everything," McCulloch told *Rolling Stone*. "It's up there with 'Suzanne,' by Leonard Cohen, 'Blowin' in the Wind,' 'In My Life.' Every time I sing it I feel like, 'Whoa, something just happened there!'"

PHOTO BY DAVE HOGAN/GETTY IMAGES

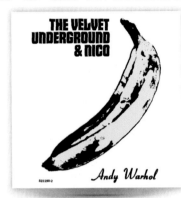

The Velvet Underground,
The Velvet Underground & Nico
Plus the Velvet Underground's third album, the self-titled, and Lou Reed's **Transformer**. It was Lou Reed—and it's the trousers again (laughs). Echo & the Bunnymen got more inspiration and energy from the Velvet Underground and Lou Reed than we got from punk. He was just cool. I got into the Velvets and Iggy through Bowie, because he would mention them once in a while. I think when you like something early you kind of go back and then continue forward with it as well; it's in your blood. And I just liked, as much as anything, just the image.

The Doors, *The Doors*
It's the trousers. Well, everything about Jim [Morrison], but no more than Mick [Jagger], well, probably a lot less than Mick. I thought they were the perfect four-piece. All the songs were just the perfect kind of slightly sweaty but relaxed, kind of thing. Fantastic. Just the atmospheres and stuff. I liked his pop things like "Light My Fire" and things like, "Hello, I love you won't you tell me your name." I like those sorts of things. The long ones, I think you just end up falling into an abyss, which it kind of sounds like on "The End," and it's probably meant to. Come on, are you going to listen to this again in ten years time?

The Clash, *The Clash*
First album, definitely. The Clash verged on cartoon later, but you don't remember The Clash with the other members. It's the original Clash, which was fantastic. And I suppose I wasn't… well, I was left wing, but I still don't know what the hell that means. I don't think the Labour Party do either. But the hint of political knowledge that Joe Strummer seemed to have was cool, kind of where it wasn't over the top. Whereas "God Save the Queen" was over the top. Boy, I loved that; I thought that was the best song ever. "God save the Queen, she ain't no human being."

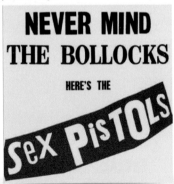

Sex Pistols,
Never Mind the Bollocks,
Here's the Sex Pistols
The Pistols, the original single and the second and third one as well. I'd wished they hadn't made the album because I thought those four A-sides were fantastic. Powerful, but then it became a cartoon.

The Fall, *Dragnet*
I was into them then more than the later albums. I saw them, and it was like, "Wow." And then he went on and made three million albums, you know, The Fall with Mark E. Smith.

Rolling Stones, *Big Hits*
(High Tide and Green Grass)
Bloody 'ell, Stones, **Big Hits**, all the way around. Or **Some Girls**; I like **Some Girls**. But I do love me old compilations of the Stones stuff.

David Bowie,

The Rise and Fall of Ziggy Stardust and the Spiders from Mars

Ziggy Stardust, *Station to Station*… I mean, these albums were important to me, but I'm not saying they're the greatest albums ever made. But Bowie's face; it's just the best face of all time, or head, even. It just went all the way 'round. I also like **Hunky Dory**.

REM, *Automatic for the People*

It's just obviously a fantastic album. It was one of the first albums that I thought I had to go out and actually buy. You know, from start to finish, more or less, it's brilliant, perfect. And "Find the River;" I remember hearing that and playing it over and over again. I remember thinking, I'm obsessed—I don't think I can write a song as good as that one. And now I think it was a phase where I just thought they were probably the best band in the world. I've never really said much about REM. They were great, and they did their own thing, fantastic stage presence, just great songs. "Everybody Hurts" was another one I wished I'd written.

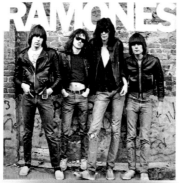

Ramones, *Ramones*

We were called post-punk, which… it was after it (laughs). That's it in a nutshell. But it was more the indie thing that punk kind of kicked off. So there was punk, but post-punk was something that sounds like it was made up by journalists. And it made punk already dated. For me, punk was like '76, '77, and mind you we formed in '78, I suppose. By that point, people found that they could get on the bandwagon. It was an opportunity to come and form a band and be what you wanted to be and then disappear probably. But punk in Britain was different from the American punk, obviously. And I thought the Ramones *were* punk (laughs), with their three-and-a-half second songs. I was the first person in Liverpool to get the Ramones album, and Patti Smith *Horses*, which were just in on import, and I was chuffed. Kept it to myself too, although I mentioned it in interviews a few times. But in Britain, I suppose the punk rock thing was kind of the northern towns more, with loads of bands coming out of there—Leeds, Sheffield, Manchester, Liverpool; Glasgow had a load. And I just think there was a sense of "We can do this now" because of the punk thing.

Echo & the Bunnymen, *Ocean Rain*

In my opinion, with **Ocean Rain**, we took it into some areas where… we'd gone from like, I suppose people would think we were a doomy, Northern band, very atmospheric. With **Ocean Rain**, it was like, I just wanted to go, well, we're not any of the things you think we are. I mean, if you listen to the first three albums, there's such a variety of song style. But I think on that one we didn't jump from one style to another. Best produced too, although I really like **Siberia** as well.

PHOTO BY ROSS GILMORE/REDFERNS

JOHN MCEUEN
NITTY GRITTY DIRT BAND

John McEuen (left) and the Nitty Gritty Dirt Band broke through in 1970 with the Top 10 hit "Mr. Bojangles." PHOTO BY MICHAEL OCHS ARCHIVES/GETTY IMAGES

A founding member of the Nitty Gritty Dirt Band, John McEuen's 50-plus year career has earned him a stellar reputation for sharing his varied and versatile skills on a multitude of stringed instruments. With the Nitty Gritty Dirt Band, he made 34 albums, including the platinum-selling *Will the Circle Be Unbroken*, initiated by McEuen asking Earl Scruggs and Doc Watson to record with his bandmates (produced by the band's manager Bill McEuen, John's brother,) in 1971. Indisputably "one of the most important recordings ever come out of Nashville" (*Rolling Stone*, 1972), the album is recognized today as a music milestone and integral part of Americana history. *Will the Circle Be Unbroken* has been inducted in to the Library of Congress and the Grammy Hall of Fame as "one of America's most important historic recordings." Through the course of his career, McEuen has performed with or recorded Dolly Parton, Willie Nelson, Bill Wyman, Johnny Cash, Tom Petty, Bill Monroe, Leon Russell and the Doobie Brothers, among a long, long list of star performers.

PHOTO BY JOHN SHEARER/WIREIMAGE

196

The Dillards,
Back Porch Bluegrass

When I first saw The Dillards in 1963 I knew my life was about to change. Doug Dillard took the stage and made me catatonic, and provided the perfect tonic for my future: be a musician and travel the world. Their first album, *Back Porch Bluegrass*, was a perfect set of originals and traditionals executed masterfully, and influenced thousands. I am one of them.

Lightnin' Hopkins,
Last Night Blues

Houston's Lightnin' Hopkins became my favorite bluesman. Fortunate to see him in the mid-'60s. He was captivating, a window into America that showed things not found in Garden Grove, where I lived through my college years. As one of **Rolling Stone's** top 100 guitarists, it is safe to assume he influenced more on that list than most of the others.

Lester Flatt & Earl Scruggs,
The Original Sound

This 1949 recording set the benchmark for what bluegrass should–or could–be. Recorded in a three-hour Florida session as a hurricane was headed their way, it took me to a place I'd never been, but wanted to be. I knew I would play with them someday, but had no idea how. Recorded with one mic, their original sound became the pathway to bluegrass for many.

PHOTO BY MICHAEL OCHS ARCHIVES/GETTY IMAGES

Lester Flatt & Earl Scruggs, *Songs of the Famous Carter Family*

In the mid-'60s I fell in love with the Carter Family music and set to playing these songs as much like Earl Scruggs as I could. Earl played a lot of guitar. Maybelle Carter was a big influence on his overall music. Carter-style guitar became the second love of mine. I've often used it over the years. Carter melodies captured me first, then the words of genuine Appalachian heritage.

Bill Keith and Jim Rooney, *Livin' on the Mountain*

Second generation of pickers in a Boston library did some original songs and a *lot* of original picking on one mic. In Bill Keith's hands the banjo went to new frontiers and he conquered them. Their songs spoke of moonshiners, oceans of diamonds, and log cabins in the lane. English balladry with a different inflection than the other bluegrass I was into at the time.

The Beatles, *Sgt. Pepper's Lonely Hearts Club Band*

It was great to hear just how much one can do recording! Sounds and lyrics that create whole stories, rock with orchestra… all of it. This album gave me great relief and time away from the other music I was into, but then I kept hearing licks that sounded familiar! I found that "When I'm Sixty-Four" was a ragtime piano song from around 1915. It showed me that influences come from many directions.

The Band, *Music from Big Pink*

During the second month of filming on Paramount Pictures' **Paint Your Wagon** in 1968, *Big Pink* came out. The remote Oregon forest where filming was taking place was 90 minutes from where we stayed during that four months, and every long set day was spent anticipating hearing the album again that night. When Levon Helm asked me to sit in on his 70th birthday show it was a high point.

Various Artists, *The Music Man: Original Soundtrack*

In my teenage years working in Disneyland's Magic Shop I somehow came across this album after seeing the film. Masterful writing and execution that took me away, I learned early from Robert Preston's "Trouble" and found it a great way to warm up vocally in later years. It also had a song that would become one of The Beatles' early hits, "Till There Was You," sung by Paul.

Don Reno & Red Smiley, *Another Day with Reno & Smiley*

A bit more "raw" than Flat & Scruggs, Reno & Smiley had killer harmonies and new style picking, thanks mainly to Don Reno's multi-layered, innovative approaches to banjo: single string, many strings at once, unusual phrases that hearkened back to early rock 'n' roll, bluegrass rolls and Merle Travis-style banjo breaks.

John McEuen and Special Guests, *Made in Brooklyn*

Not to be self-serving here, I list this as one of my favorites because of what all the great performers did here in two magic days of recording in an old Brooklyn Church–14 cuts by acoustic and vocal masters was an idea formulating for years, and then I ran into Norman Chesky. His label records audio the best, and their one mic process quality was what I'd been looking for.

McEuen produced and played on longtime friend Steve Martin's **The Crow: New Songs for the Five-String Banjo**, which won a Grammy as Best Bluegrass Album in 2009.

PHOTO BY RICK DIAMOND/GETTY IMAGES FOR COUNTRY THUNDER USA

IAN McLAGAN
SMALL FACES/FACES

The Small Faces in 1966 (L-R): Ronnie Lane, Steve Marriott, Ian McLagan and Kenney Jones. PHOTO BY GAB ARCHIVE/REDFERNS

Ian McLagan was best known as keyboardist with the British rock bands the Small Faces and later the Faces, but he also traveled widely in top-tier rock circles, touring or recording with Bob Dylan, the Rolling Stones and Bruce Springsteen, among others. McLagan, who was born in London in 1945, joined the Small Faces as an organist in the mid-1960s, bringing a rollicking flair to a band that provided some of the signature sounds of the fashion-flashy Carnaby Street era of British rock. The Small Faces morphed into the more popular Faces when lead singer Steve Marriott left to form Humble Pie, and guitarist Ronnie Wood and singer Rod Stewart joined the three remaining members: McLagan, bassist Ronnie Lane and drummer Kenney Jones. The band's 1971 album, *A Nod Is as Good as a Wink ... to a Blind Horse*, which included the hit single "Stay With Me," made the *Billboard Top 10,* propelled by Stewart's popularity. McLagan was also featured on several of Stewart's albums, including *Gasoline Alley* and *Every Picture Tells a Story*. The Small Faces and the Faces were inducted into the Rock and Roll Hall of Fame in 2012. McLagan shared his list before his death in 2014 at the age of 69.

Bob Dylan, *Blonde on Blonde*
Bob was opening doors and windows on this great album. I was in Sweden soon after it came out and found an identical suede coat to the one he's wearing on the cover. It was stolen a few days later.

Booker T. and the M.G.s,
Green Onions
You can add their Soul Dressing album, too. In fact, you can add all their albums. When I first heard **Green Onions**, I just had to get a Hammond to try and make that sound. Booker is the greatest organist, and his new album is a winner, too, as is guitarist Steve Cropper's latest. Bassist Duck Dunn is sadly missed.

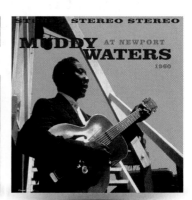

Muddy Waters, *At Newport 1960*
This album was the glue between me, Steve Marriott, Ronnie Wood and Rod Stewart. It was the album that first gave us something to play when The Faces were just starting, and it has the great Otis Spann on piano, my main influence.

STEVE MORSE
DIXIE DREGS/DEEP PURPLE

The Dixie Dregs (from left): Allen Sloan, Tee Lavitz, Rod Morgenstein, Steve Morse and Andy West. PHOTO BY MICHAEL OCHS ARCHIVES/GETTY IMAGES

Guitarist Steve Morse's resume reads part Renaissance man, part hired gun. Rock, country, funk, jazz, classical and fusion music—those styles are all in there, somewhere, on the 50-plus albums he's been part of so far. In 1970 Morse put together his first band called Dixie Grit which would evolve into the Dixie Dregs (later simply known as the Dregs), which would go on to become one of the defining groups in the fusion genre. Morse fronted the Dregs on some 14 albums. He's had with The Steve Morse Band, Kansas, Deep Purple, Angelfire and Living Loud, as well as tons of solo work. Morse took a break from the music industry to become a commercial pilot. But it wasn't that long before he returned to music to perform on a live recording with Lynyrd Skynyrd, a move that reminded him where his passion lay. These days, Morse keeps busy with his solo work, collaborative projects and is back touring with the Dixie Dregs. So exactly what kind of albums could be notable enough to influence Morse? If you guessed it would be an eclectic bunch, you're right.

PHOTO BY TIM MOSENFELDER/GETTY IMAGES

The Rolling Stones,
Beggars Banquet

This was typical of their albums for me, several songs that I just loved, and many others that were pretty good. I loved the guitar work and the feel of their music. I didn't have a very long attention span at that time in my life, but it suited me fine.

The Beach Boys, *Surfin' Safari*

Yes, I know some of their sound was straight Chuck Berry style, but most of it was a new kind of pop rock called surf music. I didn't really care about surfing, but to my young ears, they sounded great, and still do.

The Jimi Hendrix Experience,
Are You Experienced

Every song pretty much spoke to me and still does. Jimi could play with such melodic fury and always played such great rhythmic parts too.

The Beatles, *Meet The Beatles!*

I saw them on TV and they sounded incredible. I had just gotten a small reel-to-reel tape recorder. I put the microphone up to the TV speakers and made my first bootleg. I listened to it and loved the sound that they got. Then, one of my school friends invited me over to listen to The Beatles album they had bought. It was the best-sounding music I had ever heard. I never got the money together to buy that album, but my brother and I did buy a four-song EP that included "I Saw Her Standing There."

Morse performing in Atlanta in the 1980s.
PHOTO BY MICHAEL OCHS ARCHIVES/GETTY IMAGES

PPENS

Crosby, Stills and Nash, *Crosby, Stills and Nash*

I was in a band at the time, and I remember the bass player saying, "It seems like there's no way anybody can do a better record than this; they are such geniuses." I wasn't such a big fan until I heard this; then I had to agree. The vocal harmony made me think of a much hipper Beach Boys; then I heard so many more influences that appealed to me. Actually, I really liked when Neil Young came aboard, too, later on.

Led Zeppelin, *II*

I loved their first one too. This album, however, had every single song sounding perfect to me. Jimmy Page was one of my many guitar heroes, partially because he was so great at coming up with riffs that sounded and felt fantastic.

Tallis Scholars, *Stabat Mater*

Yes, this one is highly unlikely for somebody who still plays in Deep Purple. But it's awe-inspiring to hear such a perfect performance of an *a cappella* vocal group performing weaving, carefully written music from long ago. It's one of those albums that I can only listen to with complete attention and quiet.

The Mahavishnu Orchestra, *The Inner Mounting Flame*

John McLaughlin will always be one of my heroes because of his superlative playing and writing. He literally charges forward with whatever he believes in, regardless of what is in fashion. He created the blend of jazz and rock that I modeled for Dixie Dregs shortly after that album came out, before we began to infuse our own country influences. I still tour occasionally with one of the original Mahavishnu members, Jerry Goodman. This album is raw, energetic, and the style was so new and inspiring to me.

Enya, *Watermark*

I came late to the party of appreciating beautiful sounding female vocalists. But this album became one of my favorites because of the haunting, immaculate vocals plus the lush synth arrangements. It's the kind of album I would play to relax. Yes, it was later in my life that I ever did want to relax, but this one was special; every track sounds appealing to me. It is one of the inspirations that led me to record my own discovery, Sarah Spencer, with a voice that can soothe anybody, any time, in our album called **Angelfire**.

Walter Carlos, *The Well-Tempered Synthesizer*

Here is possibly the most amazing album I've ever heard. Walter Carlos performed each note laboriously on separate tracks, carefully creating each sound with old Moog patch-cord synthesizers. He picked the pieces perfectly to make them come alive thousands more with his amazing arrangements. I don't even have a recording of it anymore, just the memory burned into my brain of the best classical pieces of all time.

CANDICE NIGHT
BLACKMORE'S NIGHT

Blackmore's Night features Ritchie Blackmore (right) and wife Candice Night. PHOTO BY DAGMAR SCHERF/ULLSTEIN BILD VIA GETTY IMAGES

L yricist, multi-instrumentalist, composer. Singer of Blackmore's Night, traditional folk rock group. Solo artist. Wife of guitar virtuoso and founding member of Deep Purple, Ritchie Blackmore. All of these things stand out on the musical resume of Candice Night. When you put down the resume and pick up a Blackmore's Night album it's her voice that grabs your attention. Night's remarkable, ethereal voice, can be heard across ten Blackmore's Night records of distinct and authentic revival renaissance music. And that's just the studio stuff. The band is as known for its joyous live celebrations in which a renaissance wardrobe is mandatory among the castle-bound faithful—for this reason, the band also has a spate of live albums and live DVDs. The band is a world unto itself, sweeping up within it the remarkable narrative of the Deep Purple and Rainbow legend that is Ritchie Blackmore and transforming his style far beyond the realm of his previous electric persona. The Following is Candice's colorful and surprising list.

Buckingham Nicks,
Buckingham Nicks

This was the first album that Stevie Nicks recorded with her then boyfriend Lindsey Buckingham. I loved the way that their harmonies were like one voice. The songs were folk/rock powerful. "Frozen Love" and "Long Distance Winner" were great. But I also loved Lindsey's guitar work on "Stephanie" and "Django." His fingerpicking, haunting instrumental melodies really captured the moment.

Rainbow, *Rising*

The best hard rock album to date, in my opinion. Ritchie's brilliant composing based on classical influences, Arabic tones and Arabic scales, melded together with classic rock instrumentation implemented with orchestral work and Ronnie Dio's brilliant visual lyrics and amazing power-rock voice can not be beat. Each member of this lineup was a master of what they did and this album shone brightly and continues to shine.

Sarah Brightman, *Eden*

I'm totally in love with Sarah Brightman's versatility in being able to sing pop opera-style with a touch of Kate Bush mixed with her own inimitable style. Her version of opera classics like "Nessun Dorma" mixed in ethnic sounds, as did "Deliver Me," while she's still being gentle enough to sing "Anytime, Anywhere" or "Only an Ocean Away." Sarah's voice is the sound of dreams. Her stage show was unparalleled.

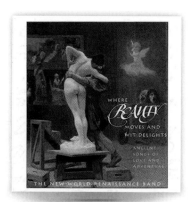  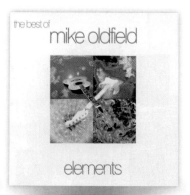

New World Renaissance Band,
Where Beauty Moves and Wit Delights

Stumbled across the great bard Owain Phyfe at the Arizona Renaissance Faire many years ago and was totally mesmerized by his voice and his true and pure connection with traditional songs. To hear Owain sing was truly to be transported back in time, and all who heard his voice instantly fell in love.

Fleetwood Mac, *Tusk*

It is impossible to sit still when you hear the tribal rhythms of the title track "Tusk," but I also loved the intimacy of the Stevie Nicks songs "Storms" and "Beautiful Child." Her "Sisters of the Moon" was all a rock 'n' roll gypsy should be—mystical, strong, dark, sexy, mysterious and magical all in one. I still find myself captivated by Stevie's lyrics and her presence.

Mike Oldfield, *Elements*

"Moonlight Shadow" introduced me to Maggie Reilly and her beautiful pure tones. My favorite song off of this album is "To France," though. Its melody and the way that Maggie Reilly sings it is just beautiful. "Five Miles Out" is another favorite.

Maggie Reilly, *Midnight Sun*

Again, Maggie Reilly's beautiful pure voice is just amazing. Although the songs aren't played in the US where I live, when I was touring they were often played on the radio overseas. That was how I learned about this CD and some of her other brilliant CDs like **Echoes**. Listening to Maggie Reilly's voice while being outside and feeling the wind through your hair and the sun on your face is just a beautiful place to be.

Rainbow, *Stranger in Us All*

Changed my life because they needed a lyricist and backing vocalist to complete some of the songs on this CD so I contributed the lyrics and vocals to "Wolf to the Moon," "Black Masquerade," "Hall of the Mountain King" and my favorite, "Ariel," while they were in the studio. "Ariel" wound up being played for the German soccer matches and "Black Masquerade" went to the top of the charts in Japan. This CD earned me my first gold album and was how I entered into the musical writing world.

Blackmore's Night, *Shadow of the Moon*

This was my first moment of writing lyrics, singing lead, playing an instrument and truly collaborating with Ritchie. We first started playing just for the two of us as an escape from the stress of the rock 'n' roll world for him, but the Japanese record company decided to release our songs on CD and we began touring. It was a whole new world for me. And I continue on this dream path to date over 20 years later.

Candice Night and Ritchie Blackmore of Blackmore's Night. PHOTO BY STEVE THORNE/REDFERNS

Candice Night, *Starlight Starbright*

This is my most recent release and it changed my life because the story behind the songs was that it was originally created while I was pregnant with my first child, Autumn, and continued in the studio with it with my second child, Rory. It is a true labor of love as every song sung was created while immersed in the total love for my individual children. And that translates to what you hear on the CD. Pure, innocent, beautiful moments.

Lead vocalist Candice Night of Blackmore's Night. PHOTO BY DAGMAR SCHERF/ULLSTEIN BILD VIA GETTY IMAGES

TED NUGENT

Ted Nugent lets his hair down while performing at Hammersmith Odeon, London, in 1980 PHOTO BY TERRY LOTT/SONY MUSIC ARCHIVE/GETTY IMAGES

Whether you love him for his guitar licks or love/hate him for his politics, Ted Nugent manages to make a lasting impression upon those he encounters. With the NRA spokesman work and the point-blank political pronouncements, people tend to forget the vast accomplishments Nugent has achieved in rock 'n' roll with his howling hollow-body as well as his deft song skills and underrated vocals (which get better with age, oddly). If one includes double live and hits packs, Nugent has five multi-platinum albums to his name. On top of that, there was his run with Damn Yankees as well as the dent he put in heads as a psych artist with The Amboy Dukes. So what, exactly, impressed the one-time boy wonder from Detroit Rock City to pursue music as a career, as opposed to oh, say, being an insurance salesman, a neurosurgeon, a flight attendant or a hairdresser? We can't speak to every single reason Uncle Ted might have had when he chose music (or music chose him), but we can shine a little light on the man behind the music with this list.

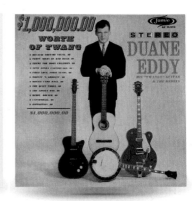

The Ventures, *Walk Don't Run*

All these albums certainly projected tone for this guitar freak. I mean, I was a guitar freak the minute I heard "Walk Don't Run" and "Perfidia."

Chuck Berry, *Greatest Hits*

I still live that garage band dream, trying to play Chuck Berry and Bo Diddley stuff with the spirit that those originators provided us. And I played bass for Bo Diddley and Chuck Berry for a couple of gigs, so I've been in the belly of the beast. I've ridden that angry stallion onto the mountaintop. A very happy, angry stallion (laughs).

Duane Eddy,
$1,000,000 Worth of Twang

This was the opening volley of Les Paul's new creation. There was a bunch of what I call opening-day enthusiasts for the electric guitar. You can't fail to mention Duane Eddy, *$1,000,000 Worth of Twang*. Just listen to the richness of these tones. Here was a guy who took a brand-new invention, figured it out immediately and took the adventure. Lonnie Mack, Duane Eddy, certainly Chuck Berry, Bo Diddley: Those guys were the Lewis and Clark of guitar tone.

The Jimi Hendrix Experience,
Are You Experienced

Jimi, obviously, was an explosion of unprecedented creativity, the next outrageous, defiance of the electric guitar via Les Paul. The bending of the strings and the noises and the feedback, the experiment with sound, distortion pedals... he was what I would call the front man for Lewis and Clark. He was days ahead of the expedition (laughs). He was the first guy to see an antelope. He's the first guy to see this black and white, prong-horned antelope and was taking notes on the newly discovered species. And in the world of Jimi Hendrix, the newly discovered species was dissonant overtone, sonic bombast and feedback. Even though I was doing it before Hendrix, Hendrix was doing it in a more outrageous way. Plus the song craftsmanship of "Foxy Lady," "Fire," "Purple Haze"—are you kidding me? He did to the guitar what James Brown did to rhythm and blues, and what Little Richard did to honky-tonk. Thank God in heaven for those guys.

The Rolling Stones,
England's Newest Hit Makers

I would think because Les Paul had just electrified the guitar... a lot of those guys played non-electric instruments in the beginning. Howlin' Wolf just had a little acoustic guitar, you know, beating on it. And what the Stones brought to it was the same thing that I was bringing to it back home in Detroit, listening to the turntable, putting the needle on and learning those licks. But I heard Howlin' Wolf from the Stones before I heard it from Howlin' Wolf. It was they that woke me up to the black American influence.

The Kinks, *You Really Got Me*

The British guys figured it out before the American guys did. The black creators, the black founding fathers—that's who The Yardbirds and The Kinks and The Who emulated. And so I got it, immediately upon hearing it. As a guitar player, I just sat down with my little Fender Duo-sonic, and I would put the needle on this little, you know, shitty S.S. Kresge turntable–you know, that little girls had for sock hops (laughs).

Ted Nugent bares his musical soul, and more, performing in New York in 1980. PHOTO BY RICHARD E. AARON/REDFERNS

Lonnie Mack,
The Wham of That Memphis Man!
Certainly "Wham!" and "Suzie-Q" by Lonnie Mack. Holy God in heaven!

James Brown, *Live at the Apollo*
Every one of these records that I listed—I think I listed 11 or 12—every one of them, I'd say the same thing about. What James Brown's band, The Famous Flames, did, they really forced me to practice nonstop. I leaned over, putting the needle on the record, over and over, learning every note, trying to find the notes on the guitar neck, and I had a permanent welt on my chest from leaning over the guitar to listen to the little turntable, to learn all these licks.

Rolling Stones, *12×5*
They were addicted to Howlin', Muddy, Lightnin', Mose, Robert Johnson, Chuck and Bo, Motown and James Brown. They were all obsessed with the black influence. And they did it in such a way… those Stones albums, they did cover songs of all those heroes. And Jeff Beck too, and certainly, whether it was Jimmy Page or Eric Clapton, they were all obsessed with playing those black guitar licks, and so they brought that to us via the British invasion. Eric Clapton kind of Caucasian-ized it, even though he never lost the soulfulness. But it was more in tune. Even old Keith Richards and Brian Jones, in their occasional semi-stupor… somebody, you know, Andrew Loog Oldham, was demanding that they at least tune their damn instrument, because Howlin' and Muddy and Lightnin' did not (laughs).

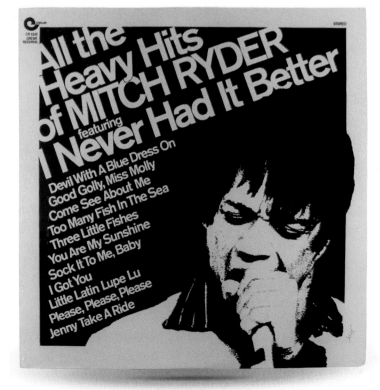

Mitch Ryder and the Detroit Wheels, *All the Heavy Hits*
My band, The Lourdes, won the battle of the bands in Detroit in 1963, against unbelievably killer rock 'n' roll bands with the kind of musical authority that ended up creating Mitch Ryder and the Detroit Wheels, The MC5, Bob Seger and Kid Rock. The original creators of this incredible music, the black gods, were already the most influential in Detroit because of Mitch Ryder. The competition to play tight, authoritative, powerful, soulful and really in the pocket was already established in Detroit before The Rolling Stones were even aware of it. And Jimmy McCarty—what a genius!

JOHN OATES
HALL & OATES

With echoes of doo-wop, Philly soul and Motown, John Oates and Daryl Hall created some of the catchiest tunes and biggest hits of the Pop era as Hall & Oates, the most successful duo in rock history.

Surpassing such dynamic pairs as the Everly Brothers and the Righteous Brothers, Hall & Oates has twenty-nine Top 40 hits. They are best known for their six massive No. 1 hits on the Billboard Hot 100: "Rich Girl," "Kiss on My List," "Private Eyes," "I Can't Go for That (No Can Do)," "Maneater," and "Out of Touch," as well as many others such as "She's Gone," "Sara Smile," and "You Make My Dreams."

In January 1985, Hall & Oates participated in the recording of "We Are the World," the star-studded charity single credited to USA for Africa. In May of that same year they helped reopen Harlem's legendary Apollo Theatre. The duo recruited their friends and former Temptations David Ruffin and Eddie Kendrick to join them on stage. The Temps medley they performed became a Top 20 single. Hall and Oates were inducted into the Rock and Roll Hall of Fame in 2014.

John Oates and Daryl Hall dominated the '80s airwaves with their catchy take on Philly soul. PHOTO BY ERICA ECHENBERG/REDFERNS

The Band,
The Band

A true classic album in every way—songs, mood, playing and singing. It sounded fresh and contemporary and at the same time sounded as though it came from a bygone era.

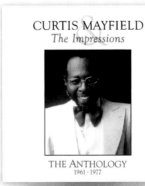

Curtis Mayfield and the Impressions, *The Anthology*

In the 1960s, Curtis was one of the very few R&B singers who played guitar and sang while he performed. That was unusual in those days, and I loved his playing and singing style. I also loved the Impressions' three-part harmony vocals. His social consciousness was also innovative and inspiring.

The Temptations,
The Temptations Live!

This record perfectly represents the original Temps lineup at its peak. The five-part harmony, the dance steps and the unique lead vocals of all the members are unsurpassed.

JON OLIVA
SAVATAGE/TRANS-SIBERIAN ORCHESTRA

Jon Oliva is a composer, multi-instrumentalist and singer best known for his work with the heavy metal band Savatage and the arena-rock juggernaut Trans-Siberian Orchestra. Savatage was originally formed as Avatar in 1978, changing its name in 1983. The band included guitarist Criss Oliva, Jon's younger brother, who was killed in a car accident in 1993. Since 1996, Jon Oliva has also been a music composer, musician and vocalist in Trans-Siberian Orchestra. The band's debut release, ***Christmas Eve and Other Stories***, became one of the best-selling Christmas albums of all time in the U.S., selling more than 3 million copies. Producer Paul O'Neill, who had worked with many of the rock's biggest acts, referred to Oliva in numerous interviews as the single greatest vocalist/musician he has ever worked with.

Savatage in 1990 (clockwise from upper left): Johnny Lee Middleton, Jon Oliva, Christopher Caffery, Criss Oliva, and Steve 'Doc' Wacholz.
PHOTO BY PAUL NATKIN/GETTY IMAGES

Black Sabbath, *Black Sabbath*
It was because of [guitarist] Tony Iommi, because he was left-handed and I'm left-handed. And that was the first concert I ever saw in my life. After that, that changed my life forever and ever and ever.

UFO, *Obsession*
It was an album that my brother Criss and I used to practice guitar to constantly. He played that album five times a day. I think we actually bought that album, like four times, because Criss wore it out. I always liked the songs on that. That was their best work by far. The song "Lookin' Out for No. 1" is a masterpiece. And there were good harmonies. I always loved that.

Scorpions, *Taken by Force*
Love that album. Uli Roth's guitar playing on that was phenomenal, and Klaus Meine's voice was phenomenal. And the song "The Sails of Charon" is still one of the best hard rock songs ever recorded or written.

GRAHAM PARKER
GRAHAM PARKER AND THE RUMOUR

Graham Parker's *Squeezing Out Sparks* is one of the great rock records of th post-punk era. PHOTO BY FRANS SCHELLEKENS/REDFERNS

 aybe you call England's Graham Parker a singer/songwriter or a pub rocker, but whatever the label, he's one of the treasures of that whole barely new wave scene of the late '70s, and a known influence on the likes of Elvis Costello and Bruce Springsteen to boot. Drawing heavily from Van Morrison and the Rolling Stones, Parker developed a sinewy fusion of driving rock and confessional folk-rock, highlighted by his indignant passion, biting sarcasm and bristling anger. With his packing band, the Rumour, Parker released *Squeezing Out Sparks*, in 1979. The album is generally regarded as Parker's best, combining pub rock, new wave and contempt that makes even his most conventional songs bristle with energy. Parker reunited with the Rumour in 2011 after being asked by longtime fan and filmmaker Judd Apatow, who made Parker a plot point in his film *This is 40*. After appearing in the movie, the group recorded an album of new material, *Three Chords Good*, which arrived in November 2012 around the time of the movie release.

PHOTO BY MARK SULLIVAN/GETTY IMAGES

The Rolling Stones, *The Rolling Stones*

I would've been around 12 or 13, so talking '63, I guess. My parents would've been the people who paid for it, and it was the Stones' first album. There was The Beatles and the Stones. That's why we all picked up guitars or drums at age 12, 13 instead of being a football player—you wanted to be a musician all of a sudden. And I never owned the Beatles album, because in those days you could buy one. We weren't poor but we were working class. So I chose the Stones. Something about that R&B, you know, you weren't sure where it was coming from. The thing about that first Stones album, it's an education in blues and R&B and then as we figured out where they got it.

I mean, I was aware of blues to a certain extent, and Chuck Berry. These kinds of things were popular in an underground way. Nevertheless all these acts that the Stones covered, whatever there was on that first album, those kind of people could come to England and play. In America, most of those people couldn't get arrested. They'd come to England and play and there's like 300 people watching them. So the first album definitely changed my life, but for Stones, just stick a pin on any album's names and I'm good, although second, I'd say **Sticky Fingers** is an album I've got to have.

Otis Redding, *Otis Blue/Otis Redding Sings Soul*

Then I heard Otis Redding. My friend, a cousin, was leaving, couldn't take records with him, he had too much stuff to take moving house and he said, "Here, wanna take this record?" It has Sam Cooke numbers on there, "Satisfaction" by the Stones, "Ole Man Trouble," Steve Cropper on guitar; that was incredibly influential.

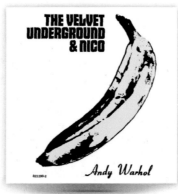

Four Tops, *Four Tops*

Going back again to that period of '64, '65, Four Tops' first album, the one with the hit, "Baby I Need Your Loving." Didn't sound like The Four Tops started to sound when they had all those hits. That album was orchestral and lush. That and the Otis Redding record brought me to tears. I thought these guys have got it, you know? This is the stuff. That influence starting coming back to me all those years later when I started writing songs seriously.

The Velvet Underground, *The Velvet Underground & Nico*

Parallel to getting into John Prine, I'd got the Velvet Underground with the banana cover, which came out much earlier. These two way different things were happening for me at the same time. Nobody I knew the Underground; they didn't sell any records in England. Their name was so obscure and it was this weird ass thing. David Bowie introduced me to that via his music.

Fleetwood Mac, *Fleetwood Mac*

Also known as Peter Green's Fleetwood Mac; the blues boom had happened really big. I was getting free records. My mom worked in an officer's mess, where the officers gathered, and she did some waitressing there they kept giving her records. But yes, that Fleetwood Mac, the first album, the one with the dog and the dustbin. But then after that blues explosion, I got more into the psychedelic stuff.

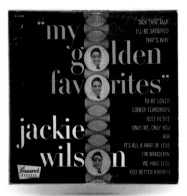

Santana, *Abraxas*

Things happened so fast with the change in styles and tastes. One minute I'm a short hair skinhead type dancing to soul music and then the next I've got long hair and I'm listening to white blues bands. And then I'm dropping acid like everybody else and smoking dope and listening to the trippier stuff like the Floyd. But that Santana album, *Abraxas*, let's put that in there. I just bought that again the other day. I don't listen to music much these days–not on my agenda–but there are some great tracks there that definitely have a few of those '60s and '70s tropes. Of course, they've got to suddenly go fast into rock. But that was influential and it was played every time I hung out with my friends when I was first in that scene.

Jack Bruce, *Songs for a Tailor*

I was into psychedelia, and my favorite album of that whole thing, although it wasn't exactly psychedelic, it was Jack Bruce **Songs for a Tailor**. Not psychedelic, but you know with that influence through the trippy lyrics. Peter Brown, the guy who wrote for Cream, his lyrics, I mean, that was just an acid trip set to music. With Jack Bruce's incredibly creative chord sequences and bass playing, that was really influential. And it helped my songwriting, I think, later on.

So there were all these scenes that were important to me, but oddly not pub rock. I never knew anything about it and nobody I knew knew anything about. And there was no punk until my career had hit, and there was no punk record that I would say, "That's what I want to listen to." Punk rock to me was something that you need to hear through a bad radio station. I tried out the Sex Pistols on a high-end stereo and I said, "This sounds awful." It's a great album but I want to hear it on the radio–slightly distorted. So yeah, I was more in the Santana and blues rock camp.

Van Morrison, *Astral Weeks*

Somewhere around here, **Astral Weeks** was in the mix. Incredibly influential, Van Morrison, ridiculous. It's like, this guy has been doing this all along and it doesn't get high in the charts. It's sort of obscure in a way, even though he had hits with Them. And I bought **Hard Nose the Highway** and **Saint Dominic's Preview** and I watched these things before my career started. They'd pop into the charts, get to about 30 or 20 and drop out of the English charts. So this was not exactly popular stuff. I mean, you can go **Tupelo Honey** too, all great. But I've got to say Astral Weeks–just one of those staggering albums.

PHOTO BY PAUL NATKIN/GETTY IMAGES

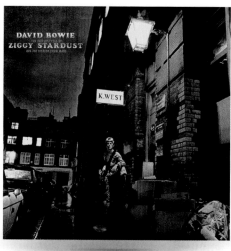

David Bowie, *The Rise and Fall of Ziggy Stardust and the Spiders from Mars*

What David did with Ziggy, I was sort of along those lines although it was four, five years before my career began. It was like, I know I'm on the right track. But I thought, I don't want to sing in an English accent; I don't think that's going to work for me. That's what he was doing, this arch English, and I was still in the soul and blues tradition that the Stones showed me. That's the way I wanted to sing.

John Prine, *Diamonds in the Rough*

I discovered quite a lot just before I got my record deal and they were all very eclectic. John Prine's second album, *Diamonds in the Rough*, it's like, this guy is really good. Loved that record to death.

Graham Parker performing in Santa Monica, California, in 1977. PHOTO BY FIN COSTELLO/REDFERNS

DAVE PIRNER
SOUL ASYLUM

Dave Pirner (center) and Soul Asylum earned a Grammy in 1994 for "Runaway Train." PHOTO BY JIM STEINFELDT/MICHAEL OCHS ARCHIVES/GETTY IMAGES

Throughout his career, Dave Pirner has consistently shown his musical adaptability. Prior to establishing himself as a swaggering front man known for emotive vocals and low-slung guitar, he taught himself drums and anchored the aptly-titled band Loud Fast Rules with future bandmates Karl Mueller and Dan Murphy. After Pirner switched to guitar and vocals, the trio changed its name to Soul Asylum in 1981 and became a rising star on Minneapolis' seminal punk scene. Another change in direction followed when the band's melodic instincts took over, bringing commercial success with the agitated yet accessible sound of songs like "Black Gold," "Misery" and "Runaway Train," which won a Grammy in 1994 for Best Rock Song. Although the group had become the poster boys for MTV, Pirner grew restless and eventually struck out on his own with the 2002 solo album *Faces & Names* and contributions to the films *Clerks* and *Backbeat*. Asked to list the ten albums that changed his life, Pirner gave us this list with the disclaimer that his Top Ten is really a Top 11, as his No. 1 album is always changing. Since you can't nail Jell-O to a tree (or an abstraction, either, for that matter), here are the ten albums he listed in our chat.

Miles Davis, *Kind of Blue*
I was raised a trumpet player and spent a lot of time listening to Maynard Ferguson, but then I discovered Miles, and he showed me the way. It's just beautiful music.

The Velvet Underground, Loaded
In my opinion, this band was one of the most pivotal American rock bands that ever existed–straightforward and powerful.

Various Artists, *Big Hits of Mid-America, Vol. 3*
This is an album that I got when I was still in high school. It made me realize that you don't have to be from Los Angeles or New York City to be a working musician. It's a great compilation of Minneapolis bands.

The Beatles, *The Beatles*
Number nine, number nine, number nine, number nine, number nine…

The Rolling Stones, *Sticky Fingers*
If you were to ask me tomorrow, I might pick a different Rolling Stones album, but if I'm picking my Top Ten, there has to be a Rolling Stones album in there, and this is just an amazing record.

The Stooges, *The Stooges*
When this record came out, it changed the rock 'n' roll paradigm. Bands like the Stooges and MC5 set a new standard, and I think people are still trying to figure out why.

Bob Dylan, *Blood on the Tracks*
Of all the Dylan albums, this is the album that speaks to me the most. If you want to write plays, you should probably know who Shakespeare is, and if you want to write songs, you should probably spend a little time listening to Bob Dylan.

Soul Asylum emerged from the Minneapolis punk scene that produced Husker Du, The Replacements and others. PHOTO BY JIM STEINFELDT/MICHAEL OCHS ARCHIVES/GETTY IMAGES

New York Dolls, *New York Dolls*

They were fearless, full of energy and rock 'n' roll madness in all the right ways. Set aside the lipstick, eye shadow and platform boots, and they just rocked out without a bunch of bullshit.

Stevie Wonder,
Songs in the Key of Life

Coming up, I was a big vinyl collector. I started collecting at eight or nine years old. When I got this album, it showed me something that I didn't know about yet, because I was just a dumb white boy from Minneapolis. This album opened my eyes. I think it's one of the most impressive musical works of the 20th century.

Meat Puppets, *Up on the Sun*

This is one of my favorite bands. I love the Meat Puppets, and I feel like we're kindred spirits. We're all friends, and like most musicians, we've traveled a lot of roads and we've shared highs and lows. I should probably pick their newest album, but I'm going to be sentimental.

SUZI QUATRO

Suzi Quatro gained notoriety in the U.S. playing Leather Tuscadero on "Happy Days." PHOTO BY MICHAEL MARKS/MICHAEL OCHS ARCHIVES/GETTY IMAGES

PHOTO BY ZAK KACZMAREK/WIREIMAGE

Although residing in London and Hamburg, Suzi Quatro came up the rock 'n' roll ranks in hometown Detroit. She was already a seasoned bass player, vocalist and song-writer by the time she hit the big time in the UK in the early to mid '70s. Hits like "Can the Can," "48 Crash" and "Devil Gate Drive" kept her and her rough boy band in the spotlight as Suzi took up residency in London. Quatro may be best known in the U.S. for her role as the bass-playing Leather Tus-cadero on the hit TV show, "Happy Days." Quatro returned in other cameo roles, earning widespread attention. While experiencing little musical success in the U.S., Quatro became a mainstay in mainland Europe, the UK and Australia, having sold over 50 million albums to date. She continues to write, record and tour, with her latest record being 2019's *No Control*, reflecting Quatro's trademark mix of styles, but heavy on up-tempo blues and R&B.

Bob Dylan, *Blonde on Blonde*
I was 14 when I got that. "Stuck Inside of Mobile with the Memphis Blues Again" just knocked me off my feet and I became a Bob Dylan fanatic. That was my first acquaintance with him. I missed a little bit of the original "Blowin' in the Wind" stuff but then once I was in, I was in, and I'd say he is the biggest influence on me lyric-wise of anybody.

Carole King, *Tapestry*
This album also got me through a very lonely period in my life before I had success when I was alone in London. A friend of mine brought it from Detroit on cassette and I played it non-stop.

Neil Young, *After the Gold Rush*
It's got some of the most beautiful songs I think he's ever written. Poignant. And it kind of helped me through my lonely days in London. That was important. I love Neil because he's one of those people who can't sing and sings wonderful—if that makes sense.

Dory Previn,
Mythical Kings and Iguanas
Okay, now here's a left field one. This was again before I made it. My mentor and record company boss—may he rest in peace also—Mickie Most, he gave me a copy of this album and I remember him saying, "This will change your life." He actually said, "This album will change your life." He was another Gemini like me. So we're very lyric people, you know? Same as Bob Dylan—we're words people. And it did indeed change my life. I can't explain it except to say that there isn't one uttered phrase or symbol that is wasted. She makes every single word count. What a brilliant album that is.

Tom Petty and the Heartbreakers, *Tom Petty and the Heartbreakers*
Tom Petty's first album. I saw them live in L.A. We were playing there too and it was just on the verge of them starting to become something. So you could say I saw them on the day before they made it. And they affected me because I thought that this was how a rock 'n' roll band should look and sound. I was a big fan from that day on. I actually recorded "Breakdown" and Tom Petty—bless him, may he rest in peace—he actually sent me a bouquet of flowers after coming to a show to say thank you for the plug every night. I played the album to death; it had a big effect on me.

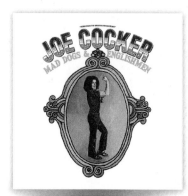

Joe Cocker,
Mad Dogs & Englishmen

Another favorite album, which I played off the wall–it's my favorite live album of all time. And it's the way I do my shows. I have a big nine-piece band. I break down to just piano or just bass and then I go up to full horns and it was that kind of thing. I love Joe Cocker.

Jackson Browne,
Running on Empty

Sorry about this, but these are my albums. Again, for the same reason, marvelously done live with even some recordings on the bus and it's got that fantastic song, "Rosie."

Janis Joplin, *Pearl*

She did her finest singing on this album and to me, she showed that she wasn't just a scream-er–she was a singer. I love the band that she had on that, The Full Tilt Boogie Band. I thought that was their finest moment.

Bob Seger & The Silver Bullet Band, *'Live' Bullet*

For something from home, Detroit, if anything it would be Bob Seger. Okay. And his first live album that he put out had all the great stuff. I played with him when I was in my first band. He was on the same shows as us and I was always impressed. And then I came to England and all of a sudden he was huge and it was great to see a friend from Detroit making it. I thought way, way back, when he came and he would do our shows with my first band, he'd come and play on the piano, and I'd think, wow. Then I'd think how weird this is and how good it was. So yeah, sometimes he'd just sit there and play the piano and sing his own songs.

Melissa Etheridge, *Melissa Etheridge*

She blew my mind. Again, she's very lyric-minded and I'm a lyric girl and I was a huge fan. And funny enough, I could see traces of me in her having no idea if this was a fact or not. And then in Australia I heard an interview on TV that she did and she indeed cited me, so it was well-spotted from me. No copy or anything, but I just saw an element.

Quatro with The Fonz, Henry Winkler, on an episode of "Happy Days" in 1977.

HENRY ROLLINS
BLACK FLAG

Henry Rollins was the angry face and force of the post-punk band Black Flag. PHOTO BY LINDSAY BRICE/MICHAEL OCHS ARCHIVES/GETTY IMAGES

Henry Rollins is best known as the fierce and raging lead vocalist for Black Flag, the acclaimed hardcore punk band from Los Angeles. Rollins was Black Flag's longest-serving frontman, leading the band through their greatest triumps and highest-profile era (1981-1986). Black Flag toured the country seemingly nonstop, becoming one of the most influential American post-punk bands. By extension, Rollins became something of an intellectual poster boy for America's underground rock press. Building upon his experiences with Black Flag, as well as his run as head shouter for the Rollins Band throughout the 1990s, Rollins went multimedia with publishing company 2.13.61. Author of a number of books, Rollins is also a well-known spoken word artist, with his well-attended shows featuring observations on politics, travel, pop (junk) culture and music (good and horrible), delivered with intensity and a fair bit of comedic self-deprecation.

PHOTO BY JASON LAVERIS/FILMMAGIC

Isaac Hayes, *Hot Buttered Soul*
My mother had this record. She let me have it so I could destroy it on my bad record player with my awful vinyl etiquette. I don't know why it hit me so hard, so immediately, but it did. I was in fifth grade and listened to it all the time. I was kind of surprised by that myself. Ike's version of "Walk On By" is amazing and "Hyperbolicsyllabicsesquedalymistic" is one of the coolest songs ever.

Miriam Makeba, *Miriam Makeba*
My mother bought this in 1967. She played it all the time and I liked it immediately. Ms. Makeba became one of my alt-moms. It wasn't a kid's record but I still liked it, which taught me that there's probably no such thing as a kid's record.

Various Artists,
Hair: The American Tribal Love-Rock Musical
I had this record in fourth or fifth grade. It was my mother's. I knew it was subversive and I probably shouldn't be listening to it and that's what made it irresistible to me. Some great songwriting and performances on this album.

Ted Nugent, *Ted Nugent*
I got this record when I was 15. I heard one of the older guys at school listening to it on a tape deck. I asked him who it was. He said, "Ted Nugent!" like I was the only one in the world who wouldn't know. I got this album and **Free for All** at the same time. I saw the **Gonzo** tour when it came through Maryland and it showed me how hard a band could kick an audience's ass.

The Stooges, *Fun House*
When I joined Black Flag in 1981, I was handed a couple of tapes and told that I needed to listen to these albums to understand the band I had just joined—and if I didn't like them, then I would have problems. They were **Fun House** and **Kick Out the Jams** by the MC5. I listened to both and got it immediately. After one listen, I realized that **Fun House** was the greatest rock album ever made and I would never do anything nearly as good. I was right on both counts.

The Velvet Underground,
White Light/White Heat
The first album is of course fantastic but it was the band's second album that really grabbed me. There was an intensity about it that I had never experienced before. It's as good as a record gets.

Jimi Hendrix Experience,
Are You Experienced

As a player, an innovator and young badass, Mr. Hendrix states his case rather well on this album. I identify heavily with the alienation in the lyrics. It's the first thing that I noticed about his songs.

The Doors, *Strange Days*

I had the Doors' first album when it came out, heisted from my mother, and liked it. As a young adult, I connected with **Strange Days** and it made me want to work harder on lyrics, knowing what could be achieved from having listened to **Strange Days** a lot.

The Birthday Party,
Prayers on Fire

As I've said many times, there are no bad records or songs by The Birthday Party. **Prayers on Fire** puts the band's nervy genius on full display in an almost schizophrenic, frenzied dash over the two sides. This album made me understand there were endless ways of going about things musically.

Rollins performing during Lollapalooza at Lakewood Amphitheater in Atlanta in 1987. PHOTO BY RICK DIAMOND/GETTY IMAGES

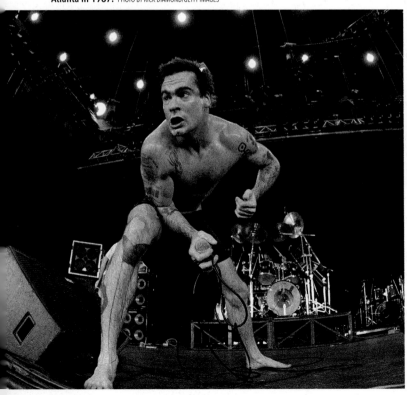

Black Sabbath, *Master of Reality*

Bill Ward and Geezer Butler are one of the greatest, if not undermentioned, rhythm sections in rock. This album not only has Tony Iommi capturing one of the greatest tones ever committed to tape, but Ward and Butler swinging as hard as they're crushing it. This is a perfectly balanced bit of playing. This is the record I evaluate other rhythm sections by.

Black Flag in 1983 (L-R): Dez Cadena, Henry Rollins, Greg Ginn, Chuck Dukowski and Bill Stevenson.
PHOTO BY ERICA ECHENBERG/REDFERNS

JORDAN RUDESS
DREAM THEATER

Dream Theater in 2014 (L-R): Mike Mangini, John Myung, Jordan Rudess, James LaBrie and John Petrucci   PHOTO BY CHRISTIE GOODWIN/REDFERNS

Keyboardist and composer Jordan Rudess has been a full-time member of prog gods Dream Theater since the recording of the band's 1999 album, *Metropolis Pt. 2: Scenes from a Memory*. He was also part of the progressive rock super group known as Liquid Tension Experiment and was once a member of The Dixie Dregs. Rudess has also collaborated with artists from David Bowie to Annie Haslam and Kip Winger. But his main gig, progressive metal titans Dream Theater, remains as popular as ever in the world of progressive rock, although it experienced some uncertainty in 2010 after the departure of superstar drummer Mike Portnoy, subsequently capably replaced by Mike Mangini. Four impressive albums later, Jordan and his Dream Theater cohorts are still wowing crowds worldwide with their post-Rush visions made epic.

230

Emerson Lake And Palmer, *Tarkus*

This album came into my life at a very important time. I was training to become a classical pianist at the Juilliard School in New York City, and a friend brought this over for me to listen to. I played this album over and over again, because for the first time in my life, I became aware of just how powerful a keyboard sound could be. Years later I recorded my own version of "Tarkus" for my solo album, The Road Home, and actually have the honor of getting a big thumbs-up from Keith Emerson himself!

Genesis, *Trick of the Tail*

Genesis represents what I call the glory rock side of prog rock and this album is the most glorious to me. There are a couple of elements in their sound that became huge influences in my own music, the first being the beautiful harmonic sense that Tony Banks has. An example of this is the kind of chordal movement in the song "Squonk," where the chords often change over a constant bass note. The other is that all-encompassing glory vibe that their music especially had on that album.

Gentle Giant, *Free Hand*

This album changed my world in the same way that Bach influenced me classically. I had never heard such glorious counterpoint in rock music before. That, mixed with their amazing sense of rhythm. All the ultra-cool meter changes, played by great instrumentalists, mixed together with some really cool keyboard playing, was a formula that I could not resist. After hearing Free Hand, I went back and listened to many of their albums and became a lifetime fan. There is never a time when I sit down to compose when the Gentle Giant influence is not with me.

Rudess performs in concert in Barcelona in 2017. PHOTO BY XAVI TORRENT/REDFERNS

Yes, *Close to the Edge*

When I think of Yes' music, I think of laser lights flying by my head and astral visions from another space and time. I've spent more time tripping out to Close to the Edge than almost every other album ever created. I'm a big Jon Anderson fan, and his voice always was my ticket out to a magical musical zone. I would stack this album up with some of the others on this list and keep it right next to my turntable, so it was never far from my reach. I guess it was the combination of all the amazing musicians, mixed with a touch of wizardry, that kinda blew my mind.

Rick Wakeman,
Six Wives of Henry the VIII

Rick Wakeman is one of my keyboard heroes. This album really turned me on to the sound of the Minimoog. **Six Wives** is a great mixture of classical and rock that I had never heard before. After spending time with this album, I posted pictures all over my bedroom wall of Minimoogs. I knew I had to have one! The album also was a keyboardist's dream because he had so much cool gear. Hearing the Moogs, Mellotrons, harpsichords and Hammonds on this incredible album made it so important in my life.

Tangerine Dream, Phaedra

When I got my Minimoog, I gravitated toward the otherworldly type sounds that I could create on it. **Phaedra** appealed to a similar place in my brain that no other classical music or rock music could get to. There is an organic quality they captured on that album that makes it stand up strongly to the test of time. Giving that album a spin would literally take me for a sonic cosmic ride. It was the first time I heard synthesizers and sequencers used to this incredible effect.

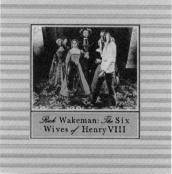

The Jimi Hendrix Experience,
Electric Ladyland

Jimi Hendrix taught me the meaning of cool, and whenever I play my instruments, I think of him. Nobody has ever been quite that cool, but it's important to try! I've never heard anyone else use the wah-wah effect on a guitar like that. **Electric Ladyland** was the Hendrix album that really affected me the most of any of his work. Jimi tapped into something mysterious and cosmic on this one, and I constantly go back to this source and drink from its waters.

King Crimson,
In the Court of the Crimson King

There was so much about this album that struck me and continues to stay with me through all the years, from the beautiful sound of Greg Lake's voice, through to the majesty of those chords on the title track. From the extremely gentle songs, like "I Talk to the Wind" to the madness of "21st Century Schizoid Man," this album is a total classic and influenced my musical path greatly.

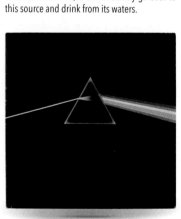

Aphex Twin, Come to Daddy

This opened up a new chapter in my life. When I heard this, I knew my sonic world was going to explode again! I think it was the "Bucephalus Bouncing Ball" track that blew my mind. It started me on a search to find out how that particular bouncing sound was made. It seems like so many of the new sonic tools that companies have developed all try to make possible what Aphex Twin did on that album. I believe that he really started the whole IDM movement!

Pink Floyd,
The Dark Side of the Moon

From beginning to end, this album is undeniably about as classic as an album can be. The smooth spaciness of the vocals, along with the universal quality to the words and music, all the way to the quirky and classic Floydian spoken words, all play a role in making this an album one that changed my life and influenced me so much. Never did the **Wizard of Oz** thing with it, though!

BUFFY SAINTE-MARIE

Buffy Sainte-Marie was named "Best New Artist" by *Billboard* in 1964 and a regular on "Sesame Street." PHOTO BY MICHAEL OCHS ARCHIVES/GETTY IMAGES

Buffy Sainte-Marie is a Canadian national treasure, whose astonishing width and breadth with respect to activism and education has helped First Nations worldwide. With 18 albums to her credit since her first record in 1964, Sainte-Marie came up in the folk and singer-songwriter ranks with the likes of Joan Baez, Bob Dylan and Joni Mitchell. In 1996, she founded the Cradleboard Teaching Project, financed with a grant from W.K. Kellogg Foundation and her own non-profit Nihewan Foundation for American Indian Education, which aims to present an accurate First Nations history as part of the school curriculum.

Named "Best New Artist" in 1964 by *Billboard*, Sainte-Marie is best known for the songs "Now That the Buffalo's Gone," "My Country 'Tis of Thy People You're Dying" (the theme song to the film *Soldier Blue*) and "Mister Can't You See," which was a Top 40 Hit in the U.S. Sainte-Marie is perhaps best known for her regular appearance on "Sesame Street," from 1976 to 1981. She joined the show on one condition: that education concerning Native American history and present day realities would be a regular part of her scripts. In a 1977 episode, she breastfed her son Cody, which is considered to be the first representation of breastfeeding ever aired on television.

St. Louis Symphony Orchestra,
Tchaikovsky, Swan Lake

When I was little I used to lie on the floor using the vacuum cleaner pipes as headphones—totally transported. I was engrossed in the drama and progression of orchestral colors and danceable rhythm changes. I figured out that music can reach the audience beyond the composer's own fascination.

Gil Evans and Miles Davis,
Sketches of Spain

What a magical combination these two artists were together. I found the album in my sophomore year of college, and still listen to it today. I love the use of flamenco elements among brilliant Miles improvisations, and particularly the tone of the ever-building and changing orchestra colors. It encompasses several "genres" and is a huge influence on me.

Edith Piaf,
Voices of the Sparrow

I discovered her through my U Mass housemother and I love her because she was unashamed of her passion, so that the emotion of the song dominated, overflowing into vibrato and a rare intensity that most pop singers avoid.

Carmen Amaya, *Paco Amaya & Jose Amaya, Carmen Amaya, Ano 1948-50*

Carmen Amaya is known for being the most wonderful flamenco dancer ever, but unknown to many people, she was the epitome of all things flamenco including singing. They say she sang from the soles of her feet. I get it and I feel it at every concert, and she's where that courage comes from.

The Beatles, *Sgt. Pepper's Lonely Hearts Club Band*

Although loved by the whole wide world, I love it most. For me it's the emotion, the fun, the drama, the stories, the harmonies, combination of instruments, the playfulness of the artists plus the cohesiveness added by George Martin that keeps it timeless. I remember I was in Cleveland for like a three-week engagement in the snow at a little coffeehouse and I heard **Sgt. Pepper** and didn't want to do anything else (laughs). I don't know what it is, but I can still listen to that album and it's still very beautiful. I mean obviously George Martin's use of the incredible songs that the Beatles provided was just the perfect combination. It doesn't happen like that very often.

Dr. John, *Gris-Gris*

This album is always on my playlist. I love every cut. It remains hip and original. I would make it required listening to any musician who seeks inspiration to break out of those boring "same-ol', same-ol'" chord progressions that keep you anchored to the small time. Give us something unique we can't get anywhere else. **Gris-Gris** is kind of like a magic potion from New Orleans. Dr. John, his real name is Mac Rebennack, but yeah, take your pick. It's a gumbo. Every track is just wonderful. It's a little bit like **Sgt. Pepper**, now that I think of it, in that every cut is great and somehow it just all flows together so that the entire album is an experience.

ZZ Top, *Chrome, Smoke & BBQ*
"I'm Bad, I'm Nationwide" is one of my favorite songs (I even wrote an Indigenous parody of the song). Despite complaints from my sisters who find ZZ Top's song "Legs" exploitive, their songs, like "Sharp Dressed Man" and "Cheap Sunglasses," usually make me laugh. Billy Gibbons is my favorite guitar player. You know, sometimes women will say, "How can you like them?" (laughs). And I say, "How can you not?" They're just fun to listen to. I love his voice. He has a very human voice; you know, Leonard Cohen used to say, "Ah, I have a very human voice." Billy Gibbons does too. Also just his style of guitar, which is that whole Mississippi Delta, Texas, New Orleans, you know, that whole kind of music. It's the same place that Jerry Lee Lewis came from. The guitar playing comes right out of the Delta blues from the '20s. I'm a big fan of Reverend Willie Johnson and just so many artists from that time, and it just kind of sunk into Billy Gibbons and he reflected that back to us (laughs).

Various Artists, *Romeo Must Die - The Album*
This film score album features Aaliyah and other hip-hop artists, such as Timbaland, Stanley Clarke, Chante Moore, Playa, BG from Cash Money and more. I loved the movie and the entire collection of songs. Together they tied hip-hop music into a cross-cultural love story involving Black and Chinese gangsters in San Francisco and made it work for movie theatre audiences. The story has Jet Li and Aaliyah playing the lead roles, and their hot connection gave perspective to the songs themselves.

The Incredible String Band, *The Hangman's Beautiful Daughter*
Okay, few listeners today know about these acid Druid hippies tripping out, playing toy and real instruments on songs about amoebas, water, minotaurs and the new moon. Trust me: there's nothing like this album anywhere. My favorite cut: "The Water Song." But the Incredible String Band, they were out there and unfortunately were so little known. And in the spirit of this album, I'm going to cheat a bit and add an 11th pick, the Bee Gees' **Saturday Night Fever Soundtrack***. I keep on loving it. It got me out of the house and dancing–still does.*

Various Artists,
Velvet Goldmine - Music from the Original Motion Picture
This film score includes music by Brian Eno, and Radiohead's Thom Yorke as part of Venus in Furs, and other great punk writers and musicians from the bands Roxy Music, T. Rex, Suede, The Stooges, Shudder to Think, Gumball, Sonic Youth and Mudhoney. I found out recently that Jimmy Webb considers me one of the influential pre-punks who inspired that bunch, and every candle on my cake lit up! I watch the movie again and again, and play the album a lot.

JOE SATRIANI

Hailed as one of the finest guitar players in the world, Joe Satriani's early influences represent the best of rock. PHOTO BY PETER PAKVIS/REDFERNS

J oe Satriani is one of the world's most commercially successful solo guitar performers, with six gold and platinum discs to his credit (including one more gold award in 2009 for the debut album by his band Chickenfoot), and sales in excess of ten million copies. Hailed by *Rolling Stone* as "The preeminent guitar virtuoso to emerge in the'80s," Satriani has toured with Mick Jagger and Deep Purple, and lent his talents to albums by Brian May of Queen and Alice Cooper and of course has co-founded Chickenfoot with ex-Van Halen members Sammy Hagar and Michael Anthony, and Red Hot Chili Pepper's Chad Smith. Satriani, a Long Island native, first picked up the guitar as a kid in 1970 on the day Jimi Hendrix died. Along with others on his list, Satriani says, "I've played all that music. I started out as a drummer wanting to be like Charlie Watts and Ringo Starr, and then moved onto guitar and I was always playing. Although Hendrix was my main influence, I was always playing Stones, Beatles, Zeppelin, lots of stuff in these high school bands I was in growing up."

Beatles, *1*

This is a good way to do it because I can't give you the whole catalog. Each record is so uniquely different that it's hard to pick one. This record, in general, is the best of what they did. Which is to combine music from around the world of all ages and somehow squeeze it down to something that was so timely for when they released it. It had all the great stuff, great vibe, sound, great performances and just fantastic writing and melodies, as well as economy of style, great use of harmony. Every record had a unique aspect with respect to how they used harmony and guitar chords. I mean it was rock 'n' roll. That's what their thing was; they grew out of the '40s and '50s. That was their basis. Very, very interesting. And growing up, it sounded exotic to me. The British are quite unique around the world. I mean we use the same language and yet it was so completely different. I've spent a lot of time all over the UK and Ireland, and they have produced so much great music. Their approach to communicating through music is just so unique.

The Rolling Stones, *Exile on Main St.*

Forward thinking, just like The Beatles. But the Stones had this thing about representing roots music and American blues music in a pure way. So their writing, on the one hand felt a little more Celtic, you know, to the American ear. And then when they would adopt an American style they would handle it very carefully, with kid gloves, and try to be as authentic as possible. *Exile on Main St.* is very unique in that way. As an example, "Casino Boogie" sounds like it could have come from 1920 or 1940, but you just don't know where it came from. And I love the sound of the album. It's very relaxed; nothing about it is methodical. It's both virtuoso and beautifully sloppy at the same time. Which is a hallmark of good rock music, that it's not too highbrow. It somehow retains this rough quality that you can enjoy with jeans and a T-shirt. They keep it real and kind of reflect what everyone is feeling.

David Bowie, *The Rise and Fall of Ziggy Stardust and the Spiders from Mars*

David Bowie is a perfect example of a musician you wouldn't want to corral. You can kind of count on him that he's going to sock you, and challenge what you think is cool or right, and at the same time give you something you can sing and dance to, party to. *Ziggy Stardust* hit me at exactly the right time, when I was a young kid playing Sabbath and Zeppelin and Hendrix in high school. When *Ziggy Stardust* came out, it was an obvious next step in opening the musical door to more influences for him. The British have the most unique way of bringing in the strangest musical influences. Whether it was "Rebel Rebel" or "Space Oddity," there was a campiness Bowie brought in that somehow enriched the music. And Mick Ronson was such a cool guitar player, a virtuoso but completely rough around the edges, playing just what was essential but always seemed to play the thing that hit you in the gut.

The Jimi Hendrix Experience, *Are You Experienced*

Are You Experienced had that sort of late '60s production where you could tell the producer really had a handle on what was going on right at that moment, tightening up the songs, grouping them together perfectly. And to me, that record had a very important song on it, which was "Third Stone from the Sun," which I'd call a science fiction and comedy-based instrumental. I remember it being so totally cathartic, even though I didn't know that word when I first heard it when I was 12 or 13 years old! It used to make me tremble and shake and I just couldn't understand why a little bit of music with feedback on a Stratocaster just sent me reeling. So that just had a huge influence on me. I remember thinking that this record stands up to the jazz and classical music that my parents are listening to, and I found it much more enriching than say the Motown or the British Invasion pop that my older siblings had been listening to. I saw the connection between what Jimi was doing and the American roots blues music that my brother had started listening to. It was like a glimpse of the future, because he was going far beyond what the guitar players of the '60s were doing. He just took a huge leap.

The Jimi Hendrix Experience,
Axis: Bold as Love

So different sonically from the debut, and his style of writing suddenly got groovier and smoother. Gone was the kind of hard-edged psychedelic sound and instead you had a song like "Up from the Skies," which was kind of jazzy. The album had very sexy rhythms and beautiful sounding guitars. And then the iconic "Little Wing" became the romantic anthem for me for every high school girl that I was falling in and out of love with! That album had such a strong imprint on my heart.

Satriani and Sammy Hagar perform with Chickenfoot onstage in Detroit in 2012.
PHOTO BY MICHAEL OCHS ARCHIVES/GETTY IMAGES

The Jimi Hendrix Experience, *Electric Ladyland*

I think this is the ultimate. I was getting more musically minded when that album came out, sort of wondering what I was going to do. This is when I realized that this guy is the supreme guitar player, and so diverse that he sounded like a million different guitar players on there at once. It went from complete visceral guitar playing to completely surreal. And the concept behind it, the science fiction, was bizarre and unthinkable, yet very futuristic and perceptive of where the world might go. Like when somebody came up with the concept of a cellphone, I'm sure everybody thought they were out of their minds. Or somehow getting to the moon. Those ideas seem totally far-fetched and a waste of time, but great minds get a hold of these things like a passion and they make them a reality. And of course it's a double record, and includes appearances from other musicians that were just fantastic at the time.

Led Zeppelin, *I*

When Zeppelin came on the scene, they brought a very different version of third generation electric blues playing. I guess of that group of guys, Jimmy Page was the last to actually put something together, because his local buddies, Jeff Beck and Eric Clapton, had quite a lot of success. Jimmy comes on the scene with a very different background and so he pulls together a bunch of players who had been in different bands, along with session player John Paul Jones who had been with him for years. But what they did was so unique. They really did suddenly wave this big flag and said "This is where it's going." But none of those guys were thinking that was the future; they just had fun and made the best music they could.

Great performances, good songs, just fantastic. Still, when I think of the songs, they're not as strong as those of the Beatles or the Stones or Hendrix. But something else was happening. They were creating a band vibe that I thought was new and unique. I had this feeling at the time that their other albums were going to crystallize their songwriting, and of course they did, sort of coming to a head with **Zeppelin IV**.

Black Sabbath, *Paranoid*

Once again, during those formative years when I was just learning how to play guitar, that was the sound of my high school days. We played a lot of Sabbath, if we could, in our funny little band. But Sabbath taught me the importance of creating a sound and a vibe that was unique, and Tony Iommi did that in the face of his tragic accident where he had some of his fingertips chopped off. Somehow he figured out a way to create an entire genre of music and a sound from this. When you're a 14-year-old kid and you hear that story, that a guitar player had his fingertips chopped off, it sounds like a horror film. I mean, the guy's a hero. And so just a few miles outside London, Sabbath sounded completely different. They talked different and they had a different attitude and they came up with this sound that nobody else had. But at the same time, Ozzy Osbourne was a Beatles freak. So it's very interesting how these things get tied together. And for us, being young and being exposed to these records, we gravitate toward them. And then later on we learned that there was a connection. As simple as Ozzy's melodies are, at least in his mind he's bouncing off what he thinks is the benchmark—Paul McCartney!

Queen, *A Night at the Opera*

I've been a fan of Queen forever, and certainly been blown away by Brian May's guitar playing. Again, completely different. These British guys, how do they wind up sounding so different? They have a way of playing as well. Instead of the American idea, which is stepping right to the edge of the cliff, playing with danger, crash and burn, the British always seemed to have one step in the safety zone, and this allowed them to create a very polished vibe to their sound. Some of the players get a little more dangerous, like Jeff Beck, but most of them have a way of not going all the way to 11. They go to like 9.9, and it remains satisfying and something that you never forget. Once Queen got together and started throwing ideas at each other in the studio, that's where the magic happened. And for us as fans, that's what we want. That's the greatest thing about any kind of a rock band versus a solo artist is the potential for that weird chemistry. Explosive new ideas get captured in the studio; some of the greatest records are like that.

Chickenfoot, *Chickenfoot*

I recently had to go back and really listen to our record, and I was like, "Who is that guy playing guitar?!" And oh my God, it just sounds completely crazy! It was one of the first times that I could hear the record the way the fans around the world heard it. The wild magic that was captured on those recordings was suddenly very obvious to me. You know, when you're in it and you're just doing it you never think of it that way. You see that, well, we could have written it 20 different ways—and I remember I played it 30 different ways. That's the curse of being in the middle of it—it's hard to hear it like a fan. But through all of it, we had to think on our feet. We did a lot of writing while we were just staring at each other. We'd just throw out ideas and then we'd record it. At the time we were thinking, "Oh if only we could rehearse this…" Then we could have played it better. But I think what we didn't see, what we were immune to, was the magic and the energy of being unfamiliar with it. It did work, and it may never work that way again. But I'm very happy that we had at least one record that was done with that kind of spirit.

RAT SCABIES
& BRIAN JAMES
THE DAMNED

The Damned outside CBGB in New York, 1977 (L-R): Rat Scabies, Dave Vanian, Brian James and Captain Sensible PHOTO BY ROBERTA BAYLEY/REDFERNS

n the blessed occasion of the release of ***Don't You Wish We Were Dead***, director Wes Orshoski's documentary on UK punk legends The Damned, we asked the band's original and classic era guitarist Brian James and drummer Rat Scabies to take a shot at a ***10 Albums***. They complied graciously, the theme turning out to be a survey of the pre-punk records that could create one of the seminal punk institutions. How seminal? Well, The Damned are often given credit for putting out the very first album of the UK punk scene, ***Damned Damned Damned***, issued on Stiff Records, February 18, 1977. What's more, the seething and speedy "New Rose" is considered the first UK punk single—The Damned had no problem with the charts, making the Top 40 in the UK fully nine times over their career. Additionally, The Damned were definitely the first of the punkers to mount a U.S. tour, one that took their brand of shock tactics to both coasts, mayhem inevitably ensuing. Noted Scabies on seeing the band's tale told on film, "Wes really just wanted to capture the personalities that made the band what it was, and I think he did that very well. The truth is, after nearly 40 years of a career, he could probably have made three movies and still not managed to capture the whole of the band's spirit (laughs)—it's a big story."

Ramones, *Ramones*

Rat Scabies: They had the first punk album that came out, and it was funny, because when it all started, we would look at photographs of the Ramones and Blondie and Television in **Punk** magazine, and none of them had an album out. So we used to have to guess what they sounded like. And then when the Ramones' album came out, and they actually sounded like the way they looked, they kind of went up a notch.

Brian James: Their visit to the UK was so important. I remember the first time I heard the Ramones was at journalist Nick Kent's place. He had been sent an advance copy of it. He had been over to New York and seen the Ramones, and maybe like, Blondie and stuff down at CBGBs. The only stuff we'd heard from New York had been the New York Dolls and the Patti Smith band. And the Patti Smith thing was good for like that couple of years earlier, but the Dolls had a sort of lovely trashiness about them. But the Ramones, was just like, wow, these guys are full-on. The album is relentless. And there was nothing like that before. The Ramones, they went for the jugular but in their own kind of poppy way. The Ramones inspired us to do "Help!," when we covered the Beatles song.

I would say that the Ramones influence on UK punk was like 80% because of the album, 20% because of them playing here. When the Ramones first came over here, they'd come over and they played a couple of days before our first gig. They played on the American Independence Day, a place called The Roundhouse, and the place was by no means full. The Ramones come on and they just tore the place apart. They were as good live as they sounded on the record. It was wonderful. And it really opened eyes. Straight after the show, we were talking to them, and it was a nice kind of communication going on. It was inspiring on a few levels–it really was.

Iggy and the Stooges, *Raw Power*

Brian James: Obviously, the other two albums were great–**Fun House** was fantastic and so was the original Stooges album. But when **Raw Power** came out, it was totally in-your-face. So if I had to pick between the three albums, I would pick that one. They had done one show at King's Cross, around the time that [Iggy] and James Williamson were recording **Raw Power**. I wasn't there, because I couldn't make it. I had a gig myself, which was a real shame, because I would've loved to have seen it.

Iggy didn't come over again live until he was touring **The Idiot**. Which was a vast sort of change he had done, in his David Bowie period. It was a big change from the rock 'n' roll that he played previous. I went to see him do that, and it was still Iggy dancing around and doing his thing, and the band were kind of good. But then the following year, he came back, and he was doing more of his back catalog, and he had the Sales brothers, and it was much more of a rock 'n' roll thing going on there. I was fortunate enough, like a year or two later, to be playing with Iggy meself. And that was a big turn-on.

Sandy Nelson, *Sandy Nelson Plays Teen Beat*

Rat Scabies: I think from my own point, you've got something like Sandy Nelson, **Teen Beat**. I started playing when I was 8 years old, and there wasn't really much around that I dug. When I was really young, jazz was the only kind of music that was on the radio, so I listened to a lot of jazz playing. The great thing about jazz is that every song has a drum solo, right? (laughs). So definitely Sandy Nelson, and also the Dave Clark Five were an influence.

Pink Fairies, *What a Bunch of Sweeties*

Brian James: That was another band that had come out that had like the English hippie thing but had a rock 'n' roll attitude. They were probably the first anarchic English band. You would go to the Isle of Wight Festival, you'd get told, oh, the Fairies were here, breaking down the fences and they're setting up a stage outside because they don't want to be part of the capitalist rubbish and all this stuff, and they're doing the alternative thing. But some of their music, I mean, particularly live, went on a bit, kind of veering on the hippie-dippy kind of side. But there was a lot of rock 'n' roll going on there, with a lot of attitude.

The Damned in New York, 1977 (L-R): Captain Sensible, Rat Scabies, Brian James and Dave Vanian PHOTO BY ROBERTA BAYLEY/REDFERNS

MC5, *Back in the USA*

Rat Scabies: With Brian, you'd be sitting there, and you'd be listening to Johnny Coltrane and then it would be the MC5. So he'd make a massive leap between jazz and kind of grungy rock. If grungy is the right word–it probably isn't. With the last MC5 album, they kind of learned to play, and that's when I went off them a bit. The Dolls I thought had a couple of cool tunes and **Fun House** and **The Stooges** are both massively influential, but I was more into the MC5.

The Rolling Stones,
Out of Our Heads

Brian James: If you're talking about inspirations from when you first start, then there would be the Stones, **Out of Our Heads**, and perhaps some Yardbirds; I'm from that original rock 'n' roll era.

John Coltrane,
My Favorite Things

Brian James: I've got to stick in a jazz album like **My Favorite Things**, where you've got the interplay. Really, what Rat does is jazz, but he would never admit it in a million years. But it is. It's totally off-the-wall, where you are feeding off another player, like me and him used to do, like Hendrix and Mitch Mitchell used to do, like Coltrane and Elvin Jones used to do. It's something that happens very rarely between players, and he totally inspires me.

The Who, *My Generation*

Rat Scabies: Definitely The Who's first album but also **Live at Leeds**. The Who turned up, and later on, Mitch Mitchell and Ginger Baker, and people took the drums out of just being a metronome and played them in more of an orchestral way, I suppose. When [Keith] Moon played, I was hearing a lot more drums, and that's all I wanted. I didn't want to just have a light snare drum playing. I wanted somebody that had those sexy tom-toms pounding away.

Robert Johnson, *King of the Delta Blues Singers*

Brian James: I was influenced by blues guys. It's a tough one, because with albums, how do you encapsulate Robert Johnson or Howlin' Wolf, all these incredible, great people? They were the original punks; there's no two ways about it. Attitude coming out of their fingernails, out of their ears, out of everywhere.

John Mayall and the Bluesbreakers, *A Hard Road*

Brian James: I'd include this album John did with Peter Green or even the original Fleetwood Mac album, with Peter Green. Since I first started listening to music in the time of like early '60s, through to the punk thing, that's a lot of albums, a lot of changes and a lot of interesting things going on. Particularly up until the very early '70s, and then it just went blah, terrible. But before that, there was a lot of action, a lot of attitude and a lot of beautiful playing, particularly jazz and blues playing.

The Damned rockin' The Roundhouse in London, 1977. PHOTO BY ERICA ECHENBERG/REDFERNS

BILLY SHEEHAN
DAVID LEE ROTH

Billy Sheehan, voted one of rock's best bass players, performs with Mr. Big in Chicago in 1989. PHOTO BY PAUL NATKIN/GETTY IMAGES

When you've earned the nickname of "the Eddie Van Halen of the bass" and made a living playing in David Lee Roth's solo band, it's probably not much of a surprise that at least one classic lineup Van Halen album makes the list of ten albums that changed your life (spoiler alert: a lot of these feature prominent bass players). Billy Sheehan's first full-time band, Talas, was a popular Buffalo, New York, group. Sheehan experienced his first taste of rock stardom playing on Roth's hit album, **Eat 'Em and Smile,** and the follow-up **Skyscraper**. Sheehan also found success with Mr. Big, work with G3 and a plethora of supergroups and solo creations. Sheehan has won the "Best Rock Bass Player" readers' poll from Guitar Player magazine five times for his "lead bass" playing style.

244

PHOTO BY C BRANDON/REDFERNS

The Yardbirds, *Having a Rave Up with the Yardbirds*
Bassist Paul Samwell-Smith was breaking new ground. The guitar players weren't bad either.

The Mothers of Invention, *Freak Out!*
I know every single thing on this record by heart, having listened to it about 2,000 times. Changed my outlook on life as well as music.

The Jimi Hendrix Experience, *Are You Experienced*
This record changed everything for me. The entire world looked different after I heard it. Jimi was the first concert I ever attended as well. The coolest human being ever. Period.

Vanilla Fudge, *Vanilla Fudge*
Playing songs I was already familiar with, their re-arrangement/interpretation chops were second to none, showing unlimited possibilities for musical creativity. Tim Bogert is my biggest bass influence, combining Motown sensibilities with psychedelic overtones. Awesome!

The Beatles, *Sgt. Pepper's Lonely Hearts Club Band*
Probably the single most important record of all time, in my humble opinion. I learned it backwards and forwards. I still play along with it. Paul McCartney's bass is absolutely incredible.

Montrose, *Montrose*
Ronnie Montrose with Sammy Hagar. A perfect rock record. I think I've played every song on it in a club band at one point or another.

King Crimson, *Red*
This version of King Crimson, though not the original, had a vibe to it that touched me very much. John Wetton's voice is spectacular, his bass tone I've blatantly and shamelessly imitated, and [Robert] Fripp and [Bill] Bruford made this record one of my all-time favorites. I went on a trip once with only this record to listen to. Brilliant. I was a huge fan of King Crimson and as a matter of fact, I actually got to meet Robert Fripp when we played in Japan one time. He came to one of our Mr. Big shows and sat by the side of the stage for the whole show. He hung out afterward, told me all the stories about making "21st Century Schizoid Man" and *In the Court of the Crimson King*. We got along great; it was amazing. And as I was playing on stage, with Robert Fripp standing 20 feet away from me, I realized how much of what I was playing I had gotten from him or King Crimson. It was pretty interesting.

 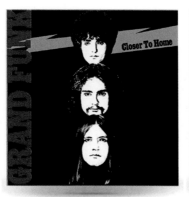 

Van Halen,
Van Halen
This record changed the course of musical–and other?–history. Absolutely incredible on all fronts.

Grand Funk Railroad,
Closer to Home
Awesome bluesy, soulful vocals over a relentless bass and drum monster groove. I still love every second of this record and know the whole thing by heart.

Frank Sinatra, *Live at the Sands with the Count Basie Orchestra*
This is heavy metal! The metal happens to be brass, though. Frank is utterly perfect on this—a snapshot of a time and a place in music that we may never see again. It's almost too good.

Sam Kinison, Sheehan and Poison's C.C. DeVille and Bobby Dall at 1988 MTV New Year's Eve Party taping. PHOTO BY JEFF KRAVITZ/FILMMAGIC, INC

NEAL SMITH
ALICE COOPER GROUP

The Alice Cooper group, here in 1972, was inducted into the Rock and Roll Hall of Fame in 2011. MICHAEL PUTLAND/GETTY IMAGES

ock and Roll Hall of Fame inductee Neal Smith is the tall, blond, glam-clad drummer for the original Alice Cooper group, with Smith playing on every album from the *Pretties for You* debut in 1969 through the last, 1973's *Muscle of Love*. His playing on "Billion Dollar Babies" essentially serves as the song's riff, helping propel the album to platinum status in the U.S., the band's fourth album in a row to achieve that certification. Post-Cooper, Neal famously became a top realtor in Connecticut, but he's also created solo material with his Killsmith concept records and long-gestated *Platinum God* album. As well, Smith has guested on Alice's last two records, *Welcome 2 My Nightmare* and *Paranormal*, and participated in a celebrated reunion of the original band, for tour dates in the UK, traditionally one of the band's best markets.

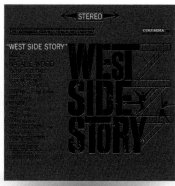

Sandy Nelson,
Let There Be Drums

In the early '60s, Sandy Nelson had a hit with "Let There Be Drums" as a single and I bought that album. There was one song on there called "The Birth of the Beat," I believe, and it was a big solo that started off with dinosaurs screaming and yelling and jungle sounds and primitive toms. And then you heard a drum beat and it just evolved from there. So he brought the idea of playing drums like a lead instrument, as did Gene Krupa. But I bought that album and appreciated that and also the fact that he was doing things that were a little bit out of the ordinary to almost shine a light on the drums.

Shotts & Dykehead Caledonia Pipe Band, *World Champions! Pipe and Drums*

When I lived in Ohio and I started playing snare drum, one of the first people I was hugely inspired by—because I played snare drum for two years before I ever had a set of drums and probably started like nine or ten years old—was Alex Duthart, who was a pipe band drummer from Scotland who was the world champion for many years back in the '50s and '60s. I still have one of his albums. They were the tightest, most precision drummers on the planet. They still to this day have the championships every spring. And that's a bucket list thing for me to do, is go be part of that. The drum corps were phenomenal, but he did a solo with the tightest single-stroke roll I've ever heard in my life. It's just unbelievable. So that made me really want to show my ability to work with rudiments, once I was in the Alice Cooper band.

Leonard Bernstein,
West Side Story: The Original Sound Track Recording

By this time, when I was still in Akron, Ohio, there was an amateur theater called the Weather Vane Community Theatre. And I played The Threepenny Opera and The Fantasticks; I played the drums in the band for those. It was just really drums and piano in this little showcase for an amateur playhouse. So I was exposed to that music. And of course I was a greaser back in those days. So when *West Side Story* came out, I remember playing the album, stealing a cigarette from my mom's purse while she was at work and then I would smoke it, comb my hair, put my collar up and be one of the characters from *West Side Story*. So that's one reason that on the *School's Out* album, we have "Grand Finale," because of "Jet Song" from West Side Story. So that was an album that not only myself but, you know, Alice and Glen [Buxton] and Dennis [Dunaway] and Michael [Bruce] were also very much into and inspired the vibe of the *School's Out* album.

Fabian, *Hold That Tiger!*

My first album that I ever bought of a rock singer was Fabian, which probably a lot of people laugh at. But, you know, I like drums, I like guitars and I like singers and I've done them all in my lifetime with my solo careers as well. But Fabian was cool for the simple reason he wasn't Elvis—he was different than Elvis. And on his album cover, *Hold That Tiger!*, he had not... I mean, it was cool to wear an ID bracelet, but he had two ID bracelets on, and on the same wrist, and I thought that was really cool. So he wasn't a great singer, but his image was great and so I started really realizing the importance of image at that point.

The Beach Boys,
Surfer Girl

My first real rock band was The Beach Boys. I'd moved from Akron to Phoenix. Phoenix was a huge test ground for all new music. So not only did we get the music from the British Invasion but also all the music coming from California. And the **Surfer Girl** album was just an unbelievable life-change for me. I was a greaser. I had my hair combed back, looked dark, and then when I came out here I washed my hair and I never put a drop of grease in it since 1963. And Dennis Wilson, of course, the drummer of The Beach Boys… I saw them at the fairgrounds here in Phoenix in 1963 or '64 and they played with The Kingsmen who had "Louie Louie" as a hit; The Kingsmen opened for them. And the Beach Boys show was amazing. Their vocals were fantastic.

Rolling Stones,
England's Newest Hit Makers

My next big band was when we got nailed by the British Invasion and that was cool. I liked The Beatles, I liked a lot of the bands, but the Rolling Stones were my number one when I got the first album, **England's Newest Hit Makers**. That really changed my life. And then I saw them at the Phoenix Coliseum on their first American tour. And by that time I said, okay, that's what I want to do. I mean, the kids were going crazy, girls were screaming. And Brian Jones was the reason in that band. Brian Jones was the coolest guy I ever saw in my life on stage. He just sat there with this teardrop guitar and his long blond hair; it was blond, The Beatles were dark hair. I had blond hair and his hair was longer than The Beatles' hair. And I said, you know what? If Brian Jones can have hair that long, I can have hair an awful lot longer than that. So that Stones first album was huge.

The Who,
My Generation

When I first heard the song "My Generation," I was riding in the car with my band The Laser Beats, here in Phoenix, my high school rock band. There were six members in the band and I was the drummer. And we were driving around in our bass player Roger Eich's car. He had a Fairlane convertible and all of a sudden "My Generation" comes on the radio and we were all laughing so hard. We'd just never heard anything so crazy as that in our lives and we almost crashed the car because we were laughing so hard. And how amazing and cool that The Who were on the AM radio in the car. So not only was the guitar great with Pete Townshend, and the singing with Roger Daltrey, but of course Keith Moon became a big influence to me at that point.

Cream, *Disraeli Gears*

This record was amazing from the standpoint of… I wasn't a big Clapton fan, but I was a huge Ginger Baker fan. And in 1968 we went to see them, at the Shrine Auditorium. That was after my hunting accident where Alice almost shot me. Well, he did shoot me and I had a cast on my leg. And our roadie, who jumped ship from Pink Floyd and joined us in Santa Monica where we lived, he knew all the roadies from all the English bands. We were dirt-poor then when we were still the fledgling Alice Cooper group; we'd just changed our name from The Nazz. And so he got us in the back door to see Cream without paying, the whole band, and we met them backstage. And then the second show, they just went up and they jammed on "Spoonful." And because I had a cast on my leg, they put a chair behind Clapton's amp right next to Ginger Baker's drums. So not only did **Disraeli Gears** blow me away as an album and Ginger Baker's drumming, but I was also right on stage with him about five feet away and watched the whole set—pretty amazing.

The Jimi Hendrix Experience, *Axis: Bold as Love*

My biggest influence guitar playing was Jimi Hendrix, and more so on **Axis: Bold as Love**, although **Are You Experienced** was amazing and got me into the band. I was always thinking that that rock god guitar player was going to come along. I thought it was Jeff Beck and Jeff Beck is still my second favorite guitar player of all time, but Jimi's my first. And we got to meet him and hang out with him four or five times as the Alice Cooper band. Eddie Kramer produced the amazing albums and on stage they were also amazing. And like The Who, they had what I call the triple crown of rock 'n' roll: you write great, you're a master of your instrument and you put on an amazing show on stage. Those three elements can make you a superstar. And Jimi had them all.

Various Artists, *Stanley Kubrick's A Clockwork Orange*

The movie was amazing, and that, plus **West Side Story**, led to the whole vibe of our School's Out album. Glen was really the bad boy of rock 'n' roll, always had a cigarette in one hand and a beer can or a beer bottle or a whiskey bottle in his other hand. But we wanted that; we took that image. When you look at the album cover for **School's Out**, and you open the desk and see the picture inside, I actually have the derby hat on similar to what Alex wore. And the album, I still have it; it's back at my home in Connecticut. And it just really captures the vibe of the movie. It's like a time capsule of the movie and it was considered very futuristic-sounding music at the time.

Neal Smith with Alice Cooper group during the Rock and Roll Hall of Fame induction ceremony. PHOTO BY KEVIN KANE/WIREIMAGE

MARK STEIN
VANILLA FUDGE

The psych-driven Vanilla Fudge (from left): Carmine Appice, Vince Martell, Mark Stein and Tim Bogert   PHOTO BY GAB ARCHIVE/REDFERNS

Vanilla Fudge is known for taking hit songs from other artists and skilfully (and successfully) injecting a loud and extended psych-driven rock trip to each one. The band's cover of the Supremes' "You Keep Me Hangin' On," for instance, reached the Top 10 in the U.S. in 1967. The band's last album, 2015's *Spirit of '67*, their first in eight years, furthers the example of the band's talent of reshaping popular songs—this time by covering tracks that were culturally pivotal in 1967. The album includes covers of "I heard It Through the Grapevine," "I Can See for Miles" and "The Tracks of My Tears." With all that in mind, it's easy to draw the conclusion that vocalist/organist Mark Stein knows his fair share of quality music.

PHOTO BY MARK HORTON/GETTY IMAGES

The Incredible Jimmy Smith,
Organ Grinder Swing
There were lots of cool albums by this Hammond B-3 legend, but **Organ Grinder Swing** was one I listened to a lot. Smith was amazing, to me, the greatest innovator of soul, jazz and funk. With lightning-speed licks, the coolest passing tones and chord progressions were created by the one and only. Single-handedly, Jimmy Smith opened the door for the great Hammond sound in progressive music, with Kenny Burrell on guitar and Grady Tate on drums rounding out this killer swing/jazz trio.

Miklos Rozsa,
Ben-Hur
Never was there music that had more grandeur, mood and dynamics. It really set my soul on fire and I believe influenced me in my arrangement concepts for Vanilla Fudge early on. Rozsa truly was a brilliant composer and got every ounce out of the symphony orchestra he conducted.

Various Artists,
Goldfinger Original Motion Picture Sound Track
Another score filled with great melodies and dynamics. John Barry's arrangements are mesmerizing, as he had the ability to take the audience through a journey in this classic James Bond thriller, leaving you breathless. Again, another influential piece of music that influenced me—just listen to the Vanilla Fudge's version of "Eleanor Rigby" on our very first album.

The Beatles, *Revolver*
This album, one of my favorite Beatles albums, is filled with great songs and the production is clean and crispy. "Taxman," "Eleanor Rigby," "Good Day Sunshine"… the way the lads from Liverpool used their voices was totally innovative. "Here, There and Everywhere"—just a terrific record.

Toto, *IV*
This was a super-talented group of L.A. studio players who came together to record a brilliant piece of work during the early 1980s. The sounds they created were ground-breaking on songs like "Africa" and "Rosanna." The vocal arrangements and production gave you chills. Kudos to David Paich, Bobby Kimball, Steve and Jeff Porcaro (RIP) and Steve Lukather. A classic!

Jeff Beck, *Blow by Blow*
One of rock's greatest guitarists took the world by storm with this all-instrumental album. One of the truly great "kick back and listen" records from the mid-'70s. Art at its finest.

The Moody Blues,
Days of Future Passed
One of the great early concept albums, filled with beautiful songs like "Nights in White Satin." The London Festival Orchestra, conducted by Peter Knight, took you on a journey that was unforgettable. Anytime you want to disappear for a while into a different sphere, check this one out. The Moodys still tour today.

Led Zeppelin, *II*
"Whole Lotta Love" blew away the airways when this single was released from the LP. This is the one that brought them into the beginning of superstardom, and they never looked back. "What Is and What Should Never Be" is another great song from that effort. Hard to believe they opened for Vanilla Fudge on their first tour in America in 1968!

The Mahavishnu Orchestra,
Birds of Fire
This album was a trendsetter that brought jazz/fusion rock into prominence. This band housed some of the great players of the time, 1973, namely John McLaughlin on guitar, Billy Cobham on drums, Jan Hammer on keys, Moog and synths, Jerry Goodman on violin and Rick Laird on bass. These guys introduced mind-blowing energy and technique to their instruments. *Birds of Fire* was a powerful influence that led to a whole new level of musicianship.

Mark Stein (left) and Vanilla Fudge. Photo by Estate Of Keith Morris/Redferns

The Jimi Hendrix Experience,
Electric Ladyland
This one is special to me because back in 1968, while on tour with Vanilla Fudge, we opened for Hendrix for many shows, and one enchanted evening Jimi actually played me "And the Gods Made Love" and a few other cuts from this, his first double album, before it was released. Certainly a pivotal moment in rock history. "Crosstown Traffic" was a huge AM radio hit, and "All Along the Watchtower" and "Voodoo Chile" were huge FM radio mainstays. Hendrix himself produced this album.

DEREK ST. HOLMES
TED NUGENT

Derek St. Holmes hit it big with the classic Ted Nugent band lineup, singing and playing on the band's biggest albums. PHOTO BY LYLE A. WAISMAN/GETTY IMAGES

D erek St. Holmes rose to fame as rhythm guitarist and co-lead singer in the classic Ted Nugent band lineup, having sung on the likes of "Live It Up," "Dog Eat Dog," "Hey Baby" (his own song, and a hit for the band), plus Ted's epic smash "Stranglehold." During this era, he struck gold and platinum with *Ted Nugent*, *Free for All*, *Cat Scratch Fever* and *Double Live Gonzo,* reporting sporadically back at the Ted survivalist camp over the ensuing decade for both recording and touring duties. St. Holmes has also issued solo albums, records with St. Paradise and Whitford St. Holmes (that's Brad Whitford, from Aerosmith), and even did some work with UFO legend Michael Schenker.

PHOTO BY R. DIAMOND/WIREIMAGE

B.B. King,
Rock Me Baby

My dad bought me that album. It was the first time that I had heard a guy play the blues like that. B.B. was so polished, and it really got my attention.

Chuck Berry,
Mr. Rock 'n' Roll

I was blown away with the way he was playing rock 'n' roll. I thought it was coolest thing in the world and it made me want to play guitar.

The Beatles,
Meet The Beatles!

I watched "The Ed Sullivan Show" like so many other people, and I was totally immersed in what was happening. It was a changing point in my life. I was a big John Lennon fan. Paul was great, but John was the revolutionary, and I liked that.

The Rolling Stones,
The Rolling Stones

When The Beatles got too pop for me, then I slipped into the Rolling Stones. Every Friday my dad would come home with a record for me. I remember the day he brought the Stones home and hearing that music for the first time.

Marvin Gaye,
What's Going On

I'm from Detroit, and I learned how to sing by sitting in the back of the car and trying to impress my older sister. This album was really a big deal for me, and I really learned a lot about singing from Marvin Gaye.

The Jimi Hendrix Experience,
Are You Experienced

This album was very important to me, because I had never heard anything like it. When I first heard Jimi Hendrix, I was like, "Are you kidding me?!" I remember trying to use feedback on my amp in my bedroom and figuring out the beginning to "Foxy Lady." Round about this time, hearing "I'm So Glad" made a big impression on me too. Cream and Hendrix sort of went together.

Ted Nugent, *Ted Nugent*

I was a big fan of the song "Journey to the Center of the Mind." I was thrilled when I found out I was going to get to sing and play with Ted Nugent on his first solo album. It changed my life forever.

"I was in a three-piece band called Scott. Don't ask me where we came up with that name. We would open up shows for Ted. I would go out there and just slam it and try to steal all of the glory. The guys were going, "We have got to get that kid in our band." Ted would never bite on it. I don't think his ego would let him. In a weak moment, they talked him into it. I was packed up and headed to California. I was literally leaving—I had a U-Haul truck packed up with a car dolly behind it.

I walked into the apartment to unplug the phone and it rang. Ted Nugent's agent was on the other line. This is after I had gone up to Ted and had dinner and hung around four or five times. Ted was never chummy enough to invite me in. The sixth time, however, they invited me up for an audition. I told them, "Sorry fellas, I have been up there and he is not interested." They said, "No, I think this time he is interested." I told them I was leaving for California as I had a job and everything waiting for me. They asked me to come over for a couple of hours. I put him on hold and I went out to ask my wife. She asked me where they were and I told them Jackson. She said, "Go over there and do it. I will go over to my mother's house and wait for you." I went up there and we played for 20 minutes and Ted goes, "How many Marshalls do you want?" He didn't say I was in the band or anything like that. I told him, "I will take two." Those two Marshalls are still in his garage.

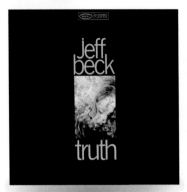

Jeff Beck, *Truth*

Rod Stewart would not even stand out front when he started touring with Jeff Beck. It took him a while to get comfortable enough to do that, which I find amazing, because he has such as strong voice.

Derek St. Holmes and Keith St. John of Montrose in 2016. PHOTO BY SCOTT DUDELSON/GETTY IMAGES

Led Zeppelin, *I*

I remember clear as day hearing "Communication Breakdown" for the first time. I knew I had to go see that band live. And I did, and so here's a story. We see Led Zeppelin in Detroit, on a Friday night. And they rocked it; they were great. This is 1970, 1971 maybe. And then we said, hey, they're playing in Toronto the next day, let's jump on the train, go up, from Detroit, we'll see the show. So we get up there, we get over to Maple Leaf Gardens and it's sold-out. Can't get in. So we say, well, let's make it 'round back and we'll at least sit on the curb and watch them come in. At least we'll get a chance to see them.

We go 'round back, we sit down on the curb, like three little monkeys, me and the two guys I was with. Lo and behold, here comes two limos, they come rolling up, they come to the backstage door, and it's not opening. It's not sliding up and letting them in. So they got out, and this guy gets out of the car and lights a cigarette and it's John Bonham. And he looks at us and he walks over and he goes, "Man, you've come to see the show?" "Yeah, well, we did, but we can't get in. But we saw you last night in Detroit." And he goes, "Oh man, that's great." Just then the big rolling door starts to go up and those guys start to get back in the cars. He looks at the three of us and goes, "Go on, man—run on in." And he got us in the show. Can you believe it? That's the kind of stuff you remember. But that first record, I remember thinking, John had the biggest drum groove known to mankind. And playing as loud as he plays, when you stand next to a drummer playing loud, it makes you play loud. And then if the whole band is playing loud, you bring it to a level of intensity that is hard to match. It's hard to beat. I know that's what he did for Led Zeppelin, and I think that's what he did for many, many drummers in the rock industry, because they just went, well, he's such a powerhouse, we have to be like that.

MC5, *Kick Out the Jams*

I remember seeing these guys when they played at our high school. I was sitting cross-legged in front of the stage on the gymnasium floor and it was heavy as hell. It was life-changing. You can hear them a bit in our song, "Light My Way." It's kind of "Kick out the jams, mother…" you know. That's where I kind of got the idea for the lyric. And a couple of those guys come from the downriver Detroit area where I come from, and I was always a big fan of theirs, and I've since been able to speak with Wayne Kramer a couple of times now, because we're both from sort of the same neighborhood. And there was some talk about getting together with them and going out as a second guitar player in MC5 a couple years ago. But that's kind of fallen to the wayside now. But any chance I had to work with those guys, I would be there in a heartbeat. Because I come from the same tradition, the same vibe.

BENMONT TENCH

TOM PETTY AND THE HEARTBREAKERS

Tom Petty and The Heartbreakers, 1977 (L-R): Mike Campbell, Stan Lynch, Benmont Tench, Tom Petty and Ron Blair.

enmont Tench is the keyboardist and a founding member of Tom Petty and The Heartbreakers. Not only does Tench go all the way back to 1976 and the beginning of this cherished American roots rock institution with Tom Petty, but the two—along with Mike Campbell—first came together in the early Seventies as Mudcrutch in their hometown of Gainesville, Florida. Inducted into the Rock and Roll Hall of Fame in 2002, Tom Petty and the Heartbreakers were a celebrated success for years, with no less than the band's first ten albums scoring gold or platinum or multiplatinum designations. Durable, resourceful, hard-working, likeable and unpretentious, Tom Petty and the Heartbreakers rank among the most capable and classic rock bands of the last quarter century. Tench has also written hits for other artists, recorded in supergroups and maintains a solo career.

Robert Johnson, *King of the Delta Blues Singers*

This is volume one. It's essential; it's Robert Johnson. They didn't have any of the crazy digital noise reduction stuff yet, so while there's certainly value in that, I tend to prefer this. I got this record when I was in boarding school.

The Rolling Stones, *England's Newest Hit Makers*

This is the American mono, not a reprocessed album, by the Rolling Stones. Again, this is not a damn reissue–this is a real record. This is the way they put it out in the day. Enough said.

Wilson Pickett, *Greatest Hits*

It's a two-record set on Atlantic. I bought this when I was barely 20 and it was the only record on my turntable for a really, really, really long time. It's one of the ways I learned to play the piano.

Director Peter Bogdanovich (center) joins the band for the opening of the 2007 film *Runnin' Down a Dream*. PHOTO BY CHARLEY GALLAY/GETTY IMAGES

The Everly Brothers, *Greatest Hits Vol. 1*

This is on Barnaby. I picked volume one just for the heck of it, but there's three volumes that I have and they've got everything from "Poor Jenny" to "Bye Bye Love" to "Maybe Tomorrow" and "Hey Doll Baby" and more obscure stuff like that. This is a great set, and I believe it's the pre-Warner Bros. recordings. These really great records. If you can seek this out, do it!

Louis Armstrong, *Satchmo's Greatest 1947-1965, Vol. 42*

It's a French pressing on RCA Victor and it's volume 42 of a series called Black and White. And of course it's mono. The selection of songs on it is just fantastic. It's stuff from the '40s and '50s. If it's Louis, it's going to be special anyway, but this is such an excellent compilation.

Elvis Presley, *Elvis' Golden Records*

This is mono. None of what I'm picking is reissues; these are real records. You never know when you get the vinyl reissues if they were done from a digital source. It's mono; it's not reprocessed for stereo. This record was hard to find. I got it at Second Hand Rose in New York, which is one of my favorite record stores I've ever been to in my life. Good Lord. It's Elvis' *Golden Records*. What more do you need? (laughs).

Bob Dylan, *John Wesley Harding*

It's the first Bob Dylan album I ever bought apart from a greatest hits. Again, none of these are reissues; these came from when I was a teenager or when I was in my early 20s or else they were brought in used record shops recently. It's Bob Dylan. And it's my favorite Bob Dylan record. So how can you leave that out?

The Byrds, *Greatest Hits*

Gene at Second Hand Rose turned me onto this album, because it's mono. Now the stereo version of this is actually great, but if you get it in mono, you find that it sounded like it sounded on the radio back in 1965, '66, which is a really powerful thing. But I'm not some kind of "back to mono" fanatic; I am a back to vinyl fanatic.

Daddy Cool, *Daddy Who?*

It's apparently out on CD, but it's never gonna sound like it sounds on the vinyl. They're an Australian country rock roots doo-wop band. This American record came out in 1971, and it was one of the first records I bonded with Tom Petty and Mike Campbell over. All three of us discovered that we loved this record.

The Beatles, *Something New*

Just to prove I'm not a purist, a Japanese pressing of the American version of the Beatles' **Something New** album, which was Capitol's version of the **A Hard Day's Night** soundtrack. It's got most of the songs on the British **A Hard Day's Night** album, but it doesn't have the song "A Hard Day's Night" (laughs). I'm sure it's some kind of second-generation tape, and it was remastered by Capitol, but I love the way this record sounds.

Tom Petty and the Heartbreakers in 1977 during the *Damn the Torpedoes* tour. PHOTO BY AARON RAPOPORT/CORBIS VIA GETTY IMAGES

DEVIN TOWNSEND
STRAPPING YOUNG LAD

Devin Townsend, a metal thrasher with Cheap Trick sensibilities. PHOTO BY KEVIN NIXON/METAL HAMMER MAGAZINE/FUTURE PUBLISHING VIA GETTY IMAGES

Typically weird for his impressive career path, Devin Townsend first came to some semblance of rock fame as lead vocalist on Steve Vai's *Sex & Religion* album from 1993, issued under the band name Vai. But then it came time for Townsend to do the inevitable, which is strike out on his own, as a solo artist of sorts, as the leader of a band called Strapping Young Lad, or perhaps serving as the Strapping Young Lad himself. Hugely respected in the metal industry, Strapping was a seductive cross between thrash, industrial and, well, Cheap Trick, through Townsend's use of melody as well as the singing similarity to Robin Zander at full roar. Since then, in addition to producing, Townsend has built a massive catalog and similarly voluminous and dedicated cult following, with all manner of band projects such as Ocean Machine, Casualties of Cool, Devin Townsend Band, Devin Townsend Project, Punky Brewster and simply Devin Townsend.

Trevor Jones, *The Dark Crystal: The Original Soundtrack*

Formatively there was the soundtrack of *The Dark Crystal*. First rock 'n' roll in my life would have been Moody Blues or Hendrix, but when I was a kid, before I started playing guitar, I did puppet shows. When I first saw the movie, *The Dark Crystal*, I was probably eight years old. I don't know what it was about it, but it changed my life. The story, the music, and the fact that [Muppets creator] Jim Henson had made this immense world to play in creatively, was a big deal. And I started fetishizing over the idea of making puppets. The toy stores then had little furry puppets you could buy, and one that I bought was a shark, and I named him Snorkel, because that was what was on the tag. I would set up a table in the front yard, and I would bring out my stereo with extension cords, and play whatever I was listening to at that age. Around ten years old, it was Eurythmics and Styx and Taco, and I would have the puppets lip-synch to the music for other confused kids in the neighborhood.

Led Zeppelin, *III*

Pink Floyd and Led Zeppelin were both a huge thing but that caused a complication. My connections with Jimmy Page put me into an alternate tuning, almost at the same time as I started playing guitar. The notes that typically apply when you're talking to different guitar players—this fret on the E string is an A, etc.—didn't apply to me, because I was in an open tuning. So I just never bothered to learn guitar music other than tablature.

I didn't use open tuning exclusively. But I heard the song "Friends" off of *Led Zeppelin III*—*III* and *Presence* were really influential to me. I really resonated with the whole tone vibe that Jimmy Page was doing in "Friends" and I wanted to learn how to do it. So of course I tried to learn it in standard and it was very difficult. And then somebody clued me into the fact that that song was in open C, and when I put my guitar into that, I realized that I could sing a lot more efficiently, given that I didn't have to finger the guitar in the standard way. And also because of my love for the suspended chords that I'd experienced through honor choir, and because of opera, a standard power chord in open C tuning is a suspended chord, so everything became Midian.

W.A.S.P., *W.A.S.P.*

W.A.S.P. were a big deal because they were the darker, bad-ass version of Mötley Crüe. And I really liked Blackie Lawless' voice. In fact, I hear that guy's influence when I play the records I would later make with Strapping Young Lad. And oddly, my favorite W.A.S.P. record is the first one, which is produced by Mike Varney, who I would later be in contact with. The whole guitar hero thing that he had done with Shrapnel Records was of huge importance to me when I was in my teens. But similar to the way I felt about Metallica, it wasn't the production of that sort of music that was my reasons for liking it. I didn't listen to those records for the sound quality per se.

Judas Priest, *Unleashed in the East*

Much more than W.A.S.P., it was Judas Priest that got me intrigued, and more so from a performance point of view, specifically K.K. Downing. He was a huge hero to me because his style was wild and off-the-chain, almost like Hendrix, although I never listened to Hendrix—it never interested me in the slightest. The aspect about K.K. that I thought was great was that he was blues-based, and that the notes that he chose to hang on, or put echo on, were atonal. I particularly loved his solo in "Sinner" because it had tons of echo on it and it was out of tune but purposely so. His sound was so wild and so free

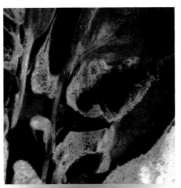

from patterns and structures, which was completely compelling to me.

Although **Defenders of the Faith** was one of the better sounding productions at the time, it was **Unleashed in the East** that affected me the most. There's a note K.K. hits on "Victim of Changes" that he holds and then it feeds back. You know, any 15- or 16-year-old metalhead playing that today would probably just hear some dated classic rock thing, but at the time, it was immersive. It implied something to me that perhaps wasn't there. It was out of tune, it had a lot of echo on it and it was completely intentional—I loved it.

Enya, *Watermark*

I loved Enya. That was a huge record for me. It was such a profoundly beautiful record to me because even though it was dark—it had minor chords—t was more so this sort of tumultuous sounding, uber-produced Celtic thing. Plus I was really attracted to the image of Enya. I had no idea what she looked like, but it was the thought of this really romantic woman. And so my relationship to women was much more based in romance. It's also because of Enya that I wound up including so many female vocalists on my albums later on. I was 15 or 16 when I heard **Watermark** and I was in awe of it. It was upstairs in my parents' house, probably around the same time as Def Leppard and **No Rest for the Wicked** by Ozzy, several of those records, which were all so macho. There's a power to metal that I totally relate to, of course, but then I heard "Orinoco Flow" on the radio, this ethereal pop with a female vocal, and it was just so well produced.

Def Leppard, *Hysteria*

It was because of Def Leppard that I aspired to production. There would be times I wasn't interested in a band because the production wasn't slick. So my technical acumen came into play based off of my opinion that nothing sounded as good as **Hysteria**. Regardless of whether or not the songs were great—which they were; they were cool songs, for sure—the sound of that record was immersive in the same way that that first Metallica concert was immersive for me. It put me into a place where I saw music as an intensely rich experience. But **Hysteria** was a record where everything had a purpose—it was modern and yet dense. I've never been a true audiophile debating the merits of vinyl versus MP3 or anything like that, but I certainly like immersive experiences. And on my little Sony Walkman that I was prancing around with, Def Leppard just sounded better than anything else.

PHOTO BY KEVIN NIXON/TOTAL GUITAR MAGAZINE VIA GETTY IMAGES

Godflesh, *Streetcleaner*

Godflesh was an awakening for me, as it was for many, many people in the metal world. We all liked Queensryche and other progressive metal, the really sort of middle class or safe heavy metal stuff. But Godflesh was where the separation came between a lot of these musicians and myself. It was immersive in a way that painted such a vivid picture for me. At first, it was more of a curiosity because production-wise it was so limited, but after a while it could really paint a picture. It was primal and dissonant and soon I was gravitating towards the wider Earache scene like Meathook Seed and Napalm Death, as well as Nine Inch Nails and Einsturzende Neubauten—that's where the separation came. I could no longer play with the people I was learning with back home in Surrey, BC.

Grotus, *Slow Motion Apocalypse*

Weirdly, another epiphany was this little San Francisco band called Grotus. I'd seen Mr. Bungle play in Vancouver, 1991 or so, and they had this independent band that they had taken out on tour with them—I don't even remember seeing Mr. Bungle. I'm just like, that is it. That's what I want to do. And then I was like that kid that followed his favorite band around. "You can stay at my house when you come to town," and all this shit. The singer, Lars, has now got this thing he does in San Francisco where he tunes vocals for Christina Aguilera and stuff. And I sent him an email, saying, "Hey man, my name is Devin, and I ended up using a Grotus lyric in one of the Strapping songs, and I don't know if you remember, but I used to follow you around." And he's like, "Oh, we remember you, dude. You're that f---ing weird kid."

Steve Vai, *Passion and Warfare*

When I was in my teen years I was absolutely enraptured with new age music and I don't know how that happened. Spacey flutes and synths and anything you would hear in meta-physical and self-help bookstores, I had a massive collection of that type of music. When I'd first heard **Passion and Warfare**, that was exactly what I was hoping that someone would write about, because of this obscure interest I had at 14 or 15. Steve was kind of the first guy to incorporate those elements. So I remember being very drawn to him as a result of that. More so than his music, it was that kind of spiritual connection. Everything that I do in my life and in my music and in my world is based on a sort of spiritual quest. Which is frustrating, of course, because there's no guidebook. So Steve was certainly an inspiration right off the bat.

Fear Factory, *Soul of a New Machine*

My love of Godflesh was what led me to Fear Factory, who I soon saw, opening up for Sepultura and Clutch, at The Commodore in Vancouver. That changed everything. That was the moment where all of a sudden I was like, yeah, now I have to do that. If you look at Fear Factory being Mötley Crüe, I wanted to be the W.A.S.P. version of that. I'd heard Fear Factory and I thought, wow, I could try doing that, blast beats and roaring vocals, so I tried that as an experiment. Much of the heavy, pivotal material, including "In the Rainy Season" and "SYL," was written in the UK in that spirit as I bided my time with The Wildhearts in Birmingham, plus when we were on tour in Europe with Suicidal Tendencies.

MARK TREMONTI
CREED

Creed, with Scott Stapp and Mark Tremonti, scored a massive hit with the song "With Arms Wide Open." PHOTO BY VICTOR SPINELLI/WIREIMAGE

Y ou can't recall Creed without also remembering the distinctive guitar sound of Mark Tremonti, co-leader of that band with vocalist Scott Stapp. Creed were beyond huge at the turn of the millennium. On the strength of the hit song "With Arms Wide Open," Creed's second album, *Human Clay*, sold an astounding 11 million copies in the U.S. Tremonti and Stapp won a Grammy Award for "Best Rock Song" as the writers of "With Arms Wide Open," a tune that hit No. 1 on *Billboard Hot 100* in 2000. Since those halcyon days, Mark has brought his guitar skills to a more purely metallic guitar-centric act called Alter Bridge. As can be heard on the band's recent album *The Last Hero*, Alter Bridge is a band built with class, style and professionalism. Besides Tremonti at the axe position, the band also happens to be blessed with the vocal talents of Myles Kennedy from Slash's band, which give Alter Bridge something of a Queensrÿche vibe. Needless to say, Tremonti is influenced by all things heavy and metallic.

Metallica, *Master of Puppets*

Biggest game-changer for me. When I was a kid, I was just like everyone else my age. I was just a casual music fan. But then I heard **Master of Puppets** one night because my brother Dan was playing it and I kept on hearing a song about a sanatorium that I really liked. He let me borrow the album and it just blew my mind. And from that moment on I was just a robot and a zombie that needed more and more metal. It changed my life.

Celtic Frost, *Morbid Tales/Emperor's Return*

It was originally released as two separate albums but I bought it paired together. A friend of mine at school had handed me **Into the Pandemonium** by Celtic Frost and from there I just got deeper and deeper into the catalogue. I'm not a dark person but I like to find dark, moody stuff. It didn't get any darker or moodier or heavier than that. The guitar playing wasn't the most technically difficult but it was just the best chord progressions and the best moods.

Metallica, *Ride the Lightning*

One of my favorite songs ever by them is "The Call of Ktulu"—it had a big effect on my guitar playing because I learned that by ear and kind of learned how to use my fingers, and since then I have a finger style that I've used since I learned that song.

Slayer, *Reign in Blood*

One of the most brutal, best guitar riff records ever written. That was another one I can thank my brother Dan for—he had that record. When I was a kid growing up in Detroit, I wanted to find the most dangerous, scariest, heaviest stuff, and I heard "Angel of Death" and it was like, what in the world is this?! I was just sucked in (laughs). I think it's my favorite guitar riff album of all time.

Megadeth, *Peace Sells... But Who's Buying?*

The guitar playing is tremendous and the lyrics are great. Megadeth was just another one of those dangerous thrash bands with a lot of talent. A lot of anger there—you can hear their anger. So when you're a kid and you want to release some of that anger, you hear this record and it's perfect.

Bad Brains, *Rock for Light*

I went through a period where I got into punk a little bit. I think Bad Brains and Black Flag were my two favorite punk bands, but Bad Brains, they just had something about them that blew me away. The way H.R. sang with that cool rhythm and intensity, everything about it was intense. They were badass back in the day.

Creed (from left) Scott Phillips, Scott Stapp and Mark Tremonti.
PHOTO BY HULTON ARCHIVE/GETTY IMAGES

MARK TREMONTI // **CREED**

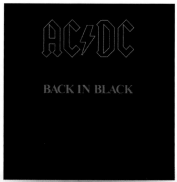

Death Angel, *The Ultra-Violence*
They've always been one of my favorite thrash bands. The album blew me away and they're still coming up with great stuff.

Bob Marley, *Legend*
Can't be all metal and punk and thrash, you know? **Legend** is my one album to have on an island for the rest of my life. That's the one album I would pick. It's a feel-good record. It's also a very deep and powerful record. Tremendous lyrics, melodies and everything. Every time I hear it, it just makes me feel good.

AC/DC, *Back in Black*
When they came out with that record ... what a comeback. I know how it is to have to start over and those guys coming back strong with a new singer, they came out and knocked it out of the park. Incredible record.

Mercyful Fate, *Melissa*
I'm a massive King Diamond fan. As an adult it's hard to turn your buddies on to King Diamond because it's such a niche thing, but I think King Diamond's a genius–all those guys are. I think if you had an orchestra play the melodies and music to their stuff, it's got such good moods to it. You might have a song that's four minutes long but then there's this little 30-second part in there that's absolutely perfect.

Mark Tremonti loves all thing heavy and metallic.
PHOTO BY SCOTT LEGATO/GETTY IMAGES

JOHN WAITE
THE BABYS/BAD ENGLISH/SOLO

During the 1970s and 1980s, John Waite was a fixture of album-oriented rock radio stations, both as a solo artist and as the lead singer of the Babys and Bad English. Waite's voice was instantly recognizable in power ballads and driving arena rock. Waite had hits as a solo artist ("Missing You"), with the Babys ("Isn't It Time") and Bad English ("When I See You Smile"). Waite's solo album **No Brakes** (1984) became a Top 10 hit on the strength of the No. 1 single "Missing You," a tune that became one of the best-remembered songs of the early MTV era. **AllMusic** reviewer Stephen Thomas Erlewine called "Missing You" a "minor miracle—a flawlessly written, classicist pop song, delivered with a stylish, MTV-ready flair. It deservedly became not just a number one hit, but one of those records that everybody knows, capturing a time yet transcending it to become part of the very fabric of pop culture."

"Songs, and songwriting keeps me inspired, moving forward," says Waite of his art. "I tend to scribble down notes, lyrics or just random thoughts on pieces of paper, backs of cigarette packs, sometimes on my shirt cuff. Rock 'n' roll is closest thing I've got to a spiritual power. It's been the higher voice in my life and it's never let me down."

John Waite's unmistakable voice fronted The Babys (here in 1979) and Bad English, while serving him well in his solo career. PHOTO BY MAUREEN DONALDSON/GETTY IMAGES

Humble Pie,
Smokin'
The first time I heard "C'mon Everybody," the hair on the back of my neck stood up. I turned pro that Sunday and bought my first amp on Monday.

The Shadows,
The Shadows to the Fore
Me and my brother Joe pooled our money and went into town on the bus to get it. "Apache" was my first inkling of sex in music.

The Beatles, *Please Please Me,*
With the Beatles
I got both albums as my main Christmas present. My room was on the corner of the house and had no heating. I could see my breath! I stayed in there all day. I couldn't leave.

The Jimi Hendrix Experience,
Are You Experienced
"Hey Joe" had seriously got me. And then came the album. I lived through it. It was art, sex and guitars. It profoundly influenced me.

John Mayall, *Bluesbreakers with*
Eric Clapton
As a kid, I'd liked Big Bill Broonzy a lot. This was like the blues coming around a second time. I wore it out. A young, raw Eric going for it with a vengeance. The songs are all spectacular. I still play it and get off.

Bob Dylan, *Blood on the Tracks*
His best, and that's saying something. Every six months or so, I dig it out and play it for days. It reminds me of the writings of Jorge Luis Borges. A masterpiece.

Rolling Stones, *Sticky Fingers*
The first time I became aware of "room sound" in production. The songs were vivid London hip life. Drugs, sex and America on the horizon. F**king great!

Marty Robbins, *Gunfighter Ballads and Trail Songs*

I used to leave school at the age of seven and run into town before my bus would come so I could spend an extra minute or two just staring at the album in the window of Kenneth Gardeners shop. It was the first one. Love at first sight. Day-Glo red cover with a cowboy going for his six-gun. Wow! America. Stories of the West. Alison Krauss found a copy, had it framed and gave it to me for Christmas.

John Mayall, *Blues Breakers with Eric Clapton*

As a kid, I'd liked Big Bill Broonzy a lot. This was like the blues coming around a second time. I wore it out. A young, raw Eric going for it with a vengeance. The songs are all spectacular. I still play it and get off.

Fairport Convention, *Liege and Lief*

Sandy Denny and Richard Thompson in the same band! The most beautiful album I'd ever heard. I saw them play live at Lancaster University. I love folk as much as country, if not more. I adored this record, and I've had to buy it several times. It gets worn out or stolen.

John Waite performing in Atlanta while with The Babys in 1979.
PHOTO BY TOM HILL/WIREIMAGE

JAMES WILLIAMSON
THE STOOGES

The Stooges in 1973: (front) Iggy Pop and Scott Asheton; (back) Scott Thurston, Ron Asheton and James Williamson.

Guitarist James Williamson came of age as a member of the proto-punk rock band the Stooges, particularly for his work on the incendiary 1973 classic, ***Raw Power***. Fronted by the legendary Iggy Pop, the Stooges were inducted into the Rock and Roll Hall of Fame in 2010. Williamson joined the Stooges in 1971 at a time the band was struggling with drugs and disinterest. With the addition of Williamson and the guidance of David Bowie, the Stooges unleashed ***Raw Power***, one of the most untamed and powerful releases in rock history. The album started with "Search and Destroy," a song many consider a punk-rock manifesto. Williamson played guitar and produced the fifth and final Stooges' album, ***Ready to Die***, plus he's the producer of one of Iggy's most underrated solo albums ***New Values***, from 1979. Finally, perhaps his second most high-profile record was ***Kill City***, issued as a duo with Iggy Pop in 1977. This "10 Albums" from Williamson was a particular challenge to compile since Williamson is famously and curiously known for paying little attention to outside music once he joined the Stooges.

The Beatles, *Rubber Soul*
The songwriting was amazing. The Beatles were moving away from kind of a sweet, poppy band to a more introspective band, and all that stuff came across. And I think that the sound of the record was pretty incredible too. Per se, I'm not really a dyed-in-the-wool Beatles guy, but I'd have to say that was a very impactful album.

Bob Dylan, *Highway 61 Revisited*
Certainly many albums by Bob Dylan had a huge impact on me. So right off the bat, I would take ***Highway 61***, and then I would pick ***Blonde on Blonde***. And he continued to inspire me in the '70s.

Jimi Hendrix Experience,
Are You Experienced
I mean, that was enormous and has to be noted. You know, I'm not even sure what heavy metal means but ... Jimi certainly raised the bar on what a guitar player could be and what it means. If you're gonna call somebody the best guitar player, I think it's him. All these guys like Eric Clapton and so forth... he was a fine guitar player, but they completely got smoked when Jimi Hendrix came around. Jimi was a really, really talented guy that had his own thing.

The Paul Butterfield Blues Band,
The Paul Butterfield Blues Band
They were just enormous. Paul Butterfield, especially that band in that time, was one of the first sort of interracial blues bands that came up, where they actually hit. You knew those guys were down and dirty, and they knew how to play the blues. And so for white, middle America kids, that was more accessible than say a real blues player, even a real Chicago blues player. Because we didn't really know that many of them. But they sort of introduced us to all that stuff.

The Rolling Stones, *Aftermath*
Again, the Stones were evolving into a better writing unit, and so [Keith] Richards and [Mick] Jagger are actually writing better songs and I think they were more cohesive as a band. So it was an evolution for them and for me as well.

PHOTO BY BRIAN RASIC/GETTY IMAGES

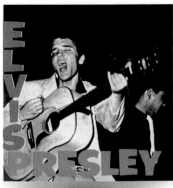

The Who, *My Generation*

I can't name off albums without naming The Who, *My Generation* in particular. But all that stuff was enormously impactful.

Yardbirds, *Having a Rave Up with the Yardbirds*

"Train Kept a-Rollin'" and all those numbers were huge in my period of sort of growing up. Jeff Beck's lineup of the band was pretty smoking hot. I am very largely a rhythm guitar player although I guess I play a lot of everything. That's kind of why I play with one guitar in the band, because I don't leave a lot of air for people in my writing or in my playing. So, yeah, I always like a good beat and a good syncopated rhythm and so on, but Jeff Beck is much more than a rhythm guitar player (laughs).

Elvis Presley, *Elvis Presley*

My very first records were singles, and they were actually Elvis Presley. My sister brought home "Hound Dog" and "Love Me Tender" and all those singles. I watched him on *Ed Sullivan* just like the next person at that time and was totally impressed. Probably if I had to name a single influence on why I bought my first guitar, he was it, even though I couldn't play it.

Williamson with The Stooges at Bimbo's Club in San Francisco, 1974. PHOTO BY RICHARD MCCAFFREY/MICHAEL OCHS ARCHIVE/GETTY IMAGES

The Rationals, *The Rationals*
Locally, I was never a big MC5 guy, and I actually was in a band with Scott Richardson from SRC. But The Rationals I thought were a tremendously good band. But they just never made it to the national stage.

Little Stevie Wonder,
The Jazz Soul of Little Stevie
The Motown influence, at the time I moved to Detroit, was enormous. I'm talking about an environment where I could go—and I did go—to the state fair, and have Little Stevie Wonder playing on a stage about two feet high with four guys on each corner, you know, so he wouldn't fall off, and playing "Fingertips" right there for free (laughs). So this was entirely different environment. So that one, plus The Temptations and Martha & the Vandellas. When I moved to Detroit, you couldn't turn on the radio without hearing them.

Iggy Pop, Williamson and Patti Smith backstage at the Whiskey a Go Go, West Hollywood, 1974. PHOTO BY MICHAEL OCHS ARCHIVES/GETTY IMAGES

NANCY WILSON
HEART

Heart during a music video shoot circa 1982 with Ann and Nancy Wilson center stage. PHOTO BY RICHARD CREAMER/MICHAEL OCHS ARCHIVES/GETTY IMAGES

Nancy Wilson gained fame as the lead guitarist of the classic rock band, Heart. With Nancy and her mega-vocalist sister Ann Wilson at the helm, Heart quickly ascended the rock 'n' roll hierarchy, entering the Rock and Roll Hall of Fame in 2013. With nine platinum and multiplatinum albums since 1975's *Dreamboat Annie* debut, Heart are one of the rare acts whose late-era music is some of the band's most vital and bravely creative across a distinguished catalogue.

After a few name changes, bassist Steve Fossen started Heart with brothers Roger and Mike Fisher at the start of the 1970s. But it wasn't until Ann and Nancy joined the band that Heart really took off. Over a three-decade stretch, Heart had 28 singles make the *Billboard Hot 100*, including two No. 1 hits—"These Dreams" and "Alone"—as well as such classics as "Crazy on You," "Magic Man," "Barracuda," "Straight On," "What About Love" and "All I Wanna Do Is Make Love To You."

Wilson's formative years were spent in the music epicenter of Seattle.
PHOTO BY GARY MILLER/FILMMAGIC

The Beatles, *Sgt. Pepper's Lonely Hearts Club Band*

Sgt. Pepper descended like a Technicolor epic on an otherwise black-and-white world. Impossibly beautiful and maybe the pure distilled essence of the magic spell The Beatles cast over the whole world. In every nook and cranny of this masterpiece the songs are stories we all know. Songs speaking the language that our mind-expanding brains were ready to receive.

The Beatles, *Revolver*

The first time I dropped the needle on **Revolver** it was like being let in through a secret backstage door where the recording session was going on. The sound of this record was smashed into the grooves so deep it felt physically mind-altering. You could feel the air move. You could feel their collective consciousness leaning toward new heights of greatness.

Steely Dan, *Gaucho*

There are rock bands and then there's Steely Dan. With a heavy Jersey accent and the highly skilled jazz-rock inventions of their songs, they created a new genre all their own. **Gaucho** is the album that depicts the blending of their East Coast studio cat swagger with West Coast scene and hubris. Needing no video footage, these songs are elaborately visual.

The Beatles, *Abbey Road*

This album's a blessing and a saving grace that bridged the generation gap in my family. There actually was a joint passed around my family dinner table as we all listened to **Abbey Road** together. It was certainly an odd feeling to be high with your mom and dad though. I would have normally been feeling rather guilty. But The Beatles had created an open, loving atmosphere.

Robert Plant and Alison Krauss, *Raising Sand*

When **Raising Sand** was released it was like a call to join forces with a new breed of beautiful. Located at the corner of "high lonesome" roots and American/English rock, these haunting classics in the hands of Robert Plant's and Alison Krauss' voices create an intimate personal portrait of America. Such a brave, unexpected concept to pair these songs with those two incredible singers.

Pink Floyd, *Wish You Were Here*

I remember hearing Pink Floyd's follow-up to **The Dark Side of the Moon** for the first time in a hotel room in Montreal. They'd announced on the TV/radio that the album would be unveiled in its entirety that night, at that time, and we were in position to absorb it thoroughly. This was the church of Floyd and the calling for our lives to come out into the light from that point forward.

Crosby, Stills, Nash & Young, *Déjà Vu*

This album contains the Holy Grail sound of the singer-songwriter hippie counterculture in late '60s California. Steeped in the folky harmonies from the previous era, this blend of rock jams with hard-hitting acoustics and poetry made a new cultural imprint full of depth and meaning. As a guitar player and songwriter, CSNY was a huge part of my growth.

Led Zeppelin, *Houses of the Holy*

The summer I graduated from high school was the summer of ***Houses of the Holy***. This album conjures up the exotic, misty magic of Old English lore blended with the riffs and beats of deep south American blues. Led Zeppelin is a big weather system moving over hill and dale. They shift and turn together like a school of fish through some deep, magical current.

Joni Mitchell, *Hejira*

Among Joni Mitchell's masterful albums, this one is my all-time favorite. This is such a peak moment in Joni's many poetic confessional works. She paints rich interior landscapes blended with the sweeping travelogue of her wanderlust. These songs are wonderful paintings much like her own paintings.

Elton John, *Tumbleweed Connection*

The songwriting of Elton John and Bernie Taupin has given us so many incredible anthems and this album was a watershed moment in the musical world they created together. In my junior year of high school, under the covers with the Seattle rain falling outside, the headphones were my ride through this cinematic wonderland. The American West translated back through a poetic English lens.

Pairing rock sensibilities with two-part harmonies, Ann and Nancy Wilson catapulted Heart to stardom.

MICHAEL WILTON
QUEENSRŸCHE

Queensrÿche in 1983 (L-R): Eddie Jackson, Michael Wilton, Geoff Tate, Scott Rockenfield and Chris Degarmo. PHOTO BY PAUL NATKIN/GETTY IMAGES

G uitarists Michael Wilton and Chris DeGarmo formed Queensrÿche in 1981 in the Seattle suburb of Bellevue, Washington. The duo recruited high school friends Geoff Tate (vocals) and bassist Eddie Jackson (bass), as well as drummer Scott Rockenfield. Exploding out of the Northwest with a sound that married Rush to Iron Maiden and Judas Priest, Queensrÿche created a buzz with their seminal self-titled EP and then rose quickly through the cerebral metal ranks during a decade in which metal ruled. 1988's *Operation: Mindcrime*, featuring the Grammy-nominated hit "I Don't Believe in Love, was named by *Rolling Stone* to their list of "The 100 Greatest Metal Albums of All Time."

The Jimi Hendrix Experience,
Are You Experienced
First to come to mind, in my formative years, this is what I was listening to. Jimi blew my mind.

Al Di Meola, *Land of the Midnight Sun*
But tied with **Elegant Gypsy**. A different style of music but with very efficient guitar playing.

UFO, *Force It*
Big Michael Schenker fan. What I loved about Schenker was that he was fluid, very melodic, very European and had a very interesting tone. But great control with the pick and great phrasing.

Michael Wilton and Geoff Tate rock Detroit in 1983. PHOTO BY PAUL NATKIN/GETTY IMAGES

Yes, *Close to the Edge*
I listened to a lot of Yes, but this was a big one for me. I loved the progressive feel. Steve Howe had a bit of a jazzy touch, but he had his own unique way of playing and was just a virtuoso. He's one of the players that played more clean, rather than distorted, and I really respected that. And the songwriting, the progressive nature of it, with different time signatures and interesting chord changes, I loved it all.

Scorpions, *Lovedrive*
A good one for songwriting and just good rock guitar. Lovedrive made a big splash in the United States. Michael Schenker played on it as well, so maybe that has a lot to do with the magic that is in the recording. There's a German tightness on the album that is just squeaky, squeaky tight—Rudolf Schenker, you know, just super tight, latex tight. The guy was just a machine.

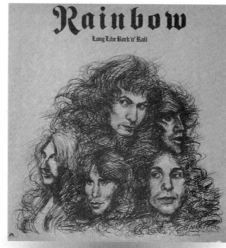

Rainbow, *Long Live Rock 'n' Roll*

Another old school but very influential one was Ritchie Blackmore. He had more of a cleaner Strat tone, very unique to his playing, and some really great songwriting and great live playing. Back then, in our teens, we were listening to the British bands—that's what the cool kids were listening to. And we definitely listened to that, as well as the heavier bands in the U.S. I mean, it was that or listening to Top 40 on radio. We would go to Easy Street Records and buy all these albums that were imported. And we thought we were so cool, because we were playing,

The Mahavishnu Orchestra, *The Inner Mounting Flame*

John MacLaughlan stretched the boundaries of guitar player for me. That was, to me, just true progressive playing, but jazzy and individual and aggressive all at the same time. Somehow they shined a light on all their microscope parts and how well they were intertwined together. That record's something I recommend for any guitar player to listen to.

you know, Accept and Iron Maiden and Rainbow. And so that music played a huge influence on me. Everybody as a musician—guitar player, drummer, bass player—wanted to play that type of music, because it was way more interesting than Top 40. But "Kill the King," that was every young guitar player's dream, to play the guitar parts of that song.

Led Zeppelin, *Houses of the Holy*

And really any album by Led Zeppelin, because I was a Jimmy Page nut! Oh my gosh, I loved everything about them. It was magical at the time, being a young kid. Jimmy's writing, phrasing, everything just had a sparkle to it. He just commandeered the guitar and steered it in all the right, great directions. But *Houses of the Holy*, I just liked the atmosphere of that album and it was a big part of my childhood, growing up. Hearing the song "Over the Hills and Far Away" on the radio, that's when I got interested in that... I believe it's a Martin guitar, that acoustic he plays during the intro to that song. That blew my mind and afterwards I was forever trying to get that acoustic guitar sound.

Van Halen, *Van Halen*

I was going to high school and I heard it in people's cars (laughs), blasting out; you know, "Running with the Devil," with the car horns, and then "Eruption." You don't need to say anymore. It just took off. The whole Eddie Van Halen thing took everybody's attention away from the British bands, and suddenly everybody wanted to play like Eddie Van Halen. But you just go your own route. Sure, you wear all your influences on your sleeve, but you don't copy them directly, I just try to liquefy them all to the point where it becomes your personality as a musician and as a player.

Judas Priest, *Killing Machine*

The title of this album was changed to **Hell Bent for Leather** in the U.S. I love the drum sound on it. It's just ferocious. The tom-tom sound is just so powerful. And the dual guitar team are amazing. K.K. [Downing] and Glenn [Tipton] opened up my playing with respect to dual guitar leads and teaching me that aspect of how harmonies can work within the song structure.

JAMES "JY" YOUNG
STYX

James "JY" Young (left) and Tommy Shaw with Styx at The Spectrum in Philadelphia in 1981. PHOTO BY WARING ABBOTT/GETTY IMAGES

Prog rock? Classic rock? Pomp rock? A ballad band? Whatever label you choose to slap on Styx, rest assured that top-quality music is a given. Styx is one of the '70s-era acts most demonstrative of the axiom "If you build it, they will come." Styx decided long ago that it wanted to maintain the showmanship and larger-than-life quality of the shows it began back in the 1970s. So to this day, the band loves it, the fans love it, the venues are packed, and everybody goes home happy. And it's quite the legacy they are bringing: Styx had an astonishing run that should not be forgotten: fully five albums in a row from 1977 to 1981 that went platinum, with four of those scoring multi-platinum, flanked on each end by a few more golds. Along the way, Styx had such hit singles and classic rock radio standards as "Come Sail Away," "Renegade," "Blue Collar Man," "Fooling Yourself," and the power ballad "Babe." So what albums helped shape James "JY" Young—co-guitarist in the band with Tommy Shaw—into the crowd-pleasing musician he is today?

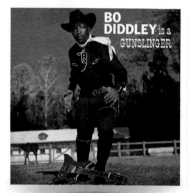

Bo Diddley,
Bo Diddley Is a Gunslinger

First LP I ever bought. I don't even know if I had heard the music before I bought it. It just embodied, I guess from a pop culture standpoint, the idea that there was this guy with a crazy guitar. I had two older sisters who listened to some rock music, and we had some singles–Jerry Lee Lewis and Elvis and stuff like that. But Bo Diddley, for me, was some guy who would put on this Western outfit and sing about kind of Wild West stuff. And to an 11-year-old mind, that was just it: Wild West, firearms and rock 'n' roll guitar.

The Who, *My Generation*

I played music starting at the age of 5. I started out on piano and then went to a band instrument and then inherited my older sister's clarinet from eighth grade through high school. I picked up the guitar about age 14 and I made great strides. I went through a few guitar teachers who said, "I can't really teach you anything; you're already beyond what I can help you with." But there was this jazz guitarist who would come over, with a mop head of hair. He was a jazz guitarist, but he would get hired a lot because he had that British look. So he was kind of riding on the coattails of the British Invasion because he played guitar. But he brought up The Who as a negative example, saying, "These are just crazy guys that turn their guitars up to ten, turn their amps up to ten and it gets feedback, and they break their guitars and equipment up," and what have you. And it was like a negative example of what a pure musician wouldn't do. But for me, that was like, "Man, when they comin' to town?"

The Jimi Hendrix Experience,
Are You Experienced

I saw Jimi live five times and he's just above it all, as far as I'm concerned.

What's a rock god do on his day off? Driveway hoops, of course. Young playing basketball at home in 1981.
PHOTO BY WARING ABBOTT/GETTY IMAGES

286

Deep Purple,
Shades of Deep Purple
This is the album that had "Hush" on it. I started on keyboards at age 5, and Jon Lord's keyboard solos on that record were just… I wanted to play in a band with somebody who could play organ like that.

Jeff Beck, *Truth*
Another guitarist who influenced me was Jeff Beck, with the Jeff Beck Group. I just think their version of "I Ain't Superstitious," with Rod Stewart on vocal, is just a classic, one of the greats. I saw that band play live with Ronnie Wood on bass and it was badass. And I mean, I love a bunch of the Yardbirds' things.

The Mahavishnu Orchestra,
The Inner Mounting Flame
Brilliant rock instrumentation. Used to play this crazy fusion thing. I really loved it.

Jethro Tull, *Aqualung*
I just thought Ian Anderson as a vocalist, lyricist and front man was just supremely intelligent, supremely sarcastic, supremely sort of irreverent. I'd seen Jethro Tull play live for the first time, actually at a rock festival that happened in LA, a month before Woodstock. It was set in Devonshire Downs, although I don't remember what it was called. He was just so charismatic from the stage. *Aqualung* was, I think, the ultimate album of his, sort of capturing the whole thing. Plus, it sounded like it was a quantum leap in terms of recording quality.

Aerosmith, *Toys in the Attic*
Aerosmith was a band I definitely looked up to, that I thought had really gotten out ahead of us. And I really dug the toughness of the guitar/bass nature of their sound. And the true irony was that they were sort of going through their first meltdown when our *Grand Illusion* album was peaking on the charts, and we were put on as an opening act on a tour with them in the Northeast. And we were loaded for bear. The guys from Extreme, who are from the Boston area, I mean, they said they went to that show, and Styx just came along and killed everybody, in their opening 60-minute set, whereas Aerosmith came out and they were fighting on stage and all drugged-out. We kind of stole the night pretty much every night back then.

Van Halen, *Van Halen*
That, to me, was clearly the first time I heard a guy [Eddie Van Halen] who could do those kinds of things on electric guitar. An incredible rock attitude. "Runnin' with the Devil"–I can still picture myself in England in '78, listening to that on a tiny little radio.

Cream, *Wheels of Fire*

I met Eric Clapton at the Crossroads in Chicago, and I told him that I took his guitar solo in "Cross-roads" from that live performance on that LP, slowed it down to half speed—because they had spoken word records that were played on 16—so all the notes in his solo would be an octave down. They would be half speed and an octave down, but they would be going slow enough so that I could sing them, memorize them by ear, and then I would think of them on the guitar, an octave up, you know, where I would normally play, just to kind of figure out how he figured it. So I told him that solo is what stepped my game up, because I learned that note for note. And he goes, "I made some mistakes in there." And I go, "I didn't notice it."

James "JY" Young and Styx shined bright on the strength of bombastic rockers and power ballads. PHOTO BY WARING ABBOTT/GETTY IMAGES